Annual Review of
Jazz Studies 3

Annual Review of Jazz Studies 3

Editors

Dan Morgenstern, Charles Nanry, and David A. Cayer

Assistant Editor

Edward Berger

Transaction Books

New Brunswick (U.S.A.) and Oxford (U.K.)

Published in the United States by Transaction, Inc., New Brunswick, New
Jersey.

© 1985 by Rutgers—The State University of New Jersey
  (Rutgers Institute of Jazz Studies, Newark, New Jersey 07102).

ISSN 0731-0641
ISBN 0-87855-965-5 (paper)
Printed in the United States of America

Contents

Preface

This third volume of the *Annual Review of Jazz Studies*, the successor to the *Journal of Jazz Studies*, again demonstrates the ever-widening range of scholarly approaches to this unique art form. In addition to such well-established subfields as discography and bio-discography, with subjects as diverse as Joe Sullivan, Mildred Bailey, and Ted Curson, this volume includes oral history (Slam Stewart); four other essays examining varied historical, cultural, and social aspects of the music; and five musical analyses spanning the art form from Jelly Roll Morton through the bebop era to contemporary musicians. The aspects of jazz illuminated in this volume reflect the technological history of our century, with articles analyzing controversial early photographs of the Buddy Bolden Band, exploring the impact of recording technology on the first jazz record reviews, and utilizing computer technology to analyze jazz melody.

In the twelve years of the combined publication history of *JJS* and *ARJS*, the editors have witnessed a gradual but significant broadening of the base of jazz studies. Not only has the range of disciplines and methodologies expanded, but the gradual acceptance of jazz as a field acceptable in traditional academic environments has augmented the ranks of jazz scholars seeking avenues of publication. The nonacademic scholars and critics who have advanced jazz studies—often on an avocational basis—for so many years are still mainstays of the field, but their efforts are increasingly supplemented by jazz scholars in the academic community. The promise for the future is extraordinarily rich.

Once again, the editors express appreciation to the scholars in the field, whatever their base of operations, and to the many individuals and institutions whose support has sustained *ARJS*.

The Forms and Orchestration
of Five Jelly Roll Morton Piano Solos

Jeffrey Jeckovich

Jelly Roll Morton's piano solo and ensemble recordings of "Grandpa's Spells," "Kansas City Stomp," "The Pearls," "Jelly Roll Blues," and "London Blues" ("Shoe Shiner's Drag" in the Red Hot Peppers version) exhibit Morton making an important transition from the formal procedures of ragtime music to those of jazz. This is achieved through his initial use of archetypical multithematic rags, to the use of monothematic chorus-by-chorus[1] strophic forms. These recordings also display a move from incidental improvisation to considerable improvised variations, with the subsequent addition of solo choruses in later arrangements of a composition. (These pieces are the only Red Hot Peppers titles that were originally Morton piano solos.)

On the basis of established discographical data and the formal constructions of these pieces, the solo piano versions fall into two groups: (1) those built on 16-measure, rag-like strains and recorded in 1923: "Grandpa's Spells," "Kansas City Stomp," and "The Pearls"; and (2) those built on 12-measure, blues choruses and recorded in 1924: "Jelly Roll Blues" and "London Blues."

Morton utilized both linear rag and rounded rag forms.[2] The solo piano arrangements of "Grandpa's Spells" and "Kansas City Stomp" both have essentially the same rounded-rag form: INTRO—A—A'—B—B'—A''—C—C'—INTRO'—A'''—CODA; with C—C' in the subdominant, and A'' and the coda returning to the tonic. (In "Kansas City Stomp," the introduction is not repeated before A'''.) In "The Pearls," the form is a linear-rag, concluding in the subdominant: INTRO—A—B—A'—BRIDGE—C—C'—CODA. A unique feature of this piece is that the subdominant C-sections, which are preceded by a modulatory bridge, are 32 measures long, double the length of the other strains in this composition and those in "Grandpa's Spells" and "Kansas City Stomp."

Group 2 (1924) of the piano solos ("Jelly Roll Blues" and "London Blues") uses the 12-measure blues as the sole formal unit. The construction of "Jelly Roll Blues" is: INTRO—A—A'—B—B'—C—BRIDGE—D—D'—D''—D''' and, in "London Blues," it is: INTRO—A—B—B'—C—C'—BRIDGE—D—D'—D''—D'''—CODA. The four D-sections in these two pieces are set off from the rest of the composition by the use of a

Jeffrey Jeckovich received a Bachelor of Fine Arts in Music Performance from the State University of New York at Buffalo and is a graduate student in music theory at that university. He is a member of the piano faculty at Music School of Niagara, Niagara Falls, New York, and frequently performs in popular styles.

contrasting textural division or nondivision of the strophe, and, in "Jelly Roll Blues," the modulatory bridge acts as an introduction to the D-choruses which end the piece in the subdominant. (There is no modulation in "London Blues"; i.e., every chorus is a blues in B-flat.) In "Jelly Roll Blues" and "London Blues" each 12-measure blues chorus in A—A'—B—B'—C and C' is divided into two smaller, dissimilar parts, unequal in length: first, a four-measure phrase (sparse and break-like in "Jelly Roll Blues"), then one of eight, different in texture or dynamics or both. In the D-choruses of "London Blues," the internal division of the strophe is reversed (eight measures, then four), with the eight-measure phrase improvised each time in a different register in addition to a textural change, and the concluding four-measure phrase composed and always the same. There is no textural division of the D-sections in "Jelly Roll Blues," but each presentation is improvised at a different, usually louder dynamic level (*mf, p, f* and *ff,* respectively), and additional contrast is achieved by the bridge modulation. Because of length and a wealth of improvisation the bridge and concluding subdominant D-sections in "Jelly Roll Blues" can be heard as a smaller monothematic piece within the whole. This technique of melodic embellishment, dynamic levels, and modulation to the subdominant was previously used to a lesser degree in the C—C' part of "The Pearls," (*f,* then *ff*). But, there is more similarity between the initial C-strain and its return in "The Pearls," than similarity among each D-strophe of "Jelly Roll Blues" and "London Blues." The technique (melodic embellishment, dynamics, and modulation) and also hinted at in "Grandpa's Spells" and "Kansas City Stomp," where each return of the A-strain is louder and additionally embellished, and by modulation to the subdominant in section C. Charts 1-3 illustrate three of these solos schematically.

Chart 1. "Grandpa's Spells," Morton Solo (July 18, 1923)

SECTION	INTRO.	A	A'	B	B'	A"	C	C'	INTRO.'	A'"	CODA
TOTAL NUMBER OF MEASURES	4	16	16	16	16	16	16	16	4	16	4
KEY AREAS	C: I ———————————————————						IV——		I ———————		

Chart 2. "The Pearls," Morton Solo (July 18, 1923)

SECTION	INTRO.	A	B	A'	BRIDGE	C	C'	CODA
TOTAL NUMBER OF MEASURES	4	16	16	16	4	32	32	4
KEY AREAS	G: I —————————————				~~~~	IV ———————		

Chart 3. "Jelly Roll Blues," Morton Solo (June 9, 1924)

SECTION	INTRO.	A	A'	B	B'	C	BRIDGE	D	D'	D"	D'"
TOTAL NUMBER OF MEASURES	4	12	12	12	12	12	4	12	12	12	12
INTERNAL DIVISION	-	4-8	4-8	4-8	4-8	4-8	-	-	-	-	-
KEY AREAS	B♭: I —————————————————————						~~~~	IV—————			

Red Hot Peppers Versions

Most of the Red Hot Peppers recordings of these compositions also display this extension of the final improvisational section and conclusion in the subdominant, even in the pieces originally constructed on a rounded-rag form ending in the tonic ("Grandpa's Spells" and "Kansas City Stomp"). In the band version of "Grandpa's Spells," the important formal alteration is the elimination of the introduction repeat and final A''' section of the piano solo, and addition of two improvised C-sections: INTRO—A—A'—B—B'—A''—C—C'—C''—C'''—CODA (the coda is shortened from four to two measures). This change to a linear-type rag eliminates the modulation from the subdominant back to the tonic that occurred in the solo version, i.e., the Red Hot Peppers version of "Grandpa's Spells" ends in the subdominant. On the first available take of this number, Morton retains two simple, but ingenious, parts that beautifully enhanced the solo version: the piano figuration in the second half of each A-presentation, and the left hand clusters in section C, which are given to the bass drum in the Red Hot Peppers version. He omits the former in the second and only other surviving Red Hot Peppers take of "Grandpa's Spells."

In "Original Jelly Roll Blues," there also seems to be an urge to arrive quickly at the areas where the improvised solos take place.[3] The A and B sections are not repeated as they are in the solo version but are made up for in overall length of the piece by the addition of two D-strophes, similar to what was done with section C, in the ensemble recording of "Grandpa's Spells." Thus, the construction of the Red Hot Peppers "Original Jelly Roll Blues" is: INTRO—A—B—C—BRIDGE—D—D'—D''—D'''—D''''.

Morton backs away from these formal and improvisational advances on the Red Hot Peppers record of "The Pearls," which is identical in form to the piano solo, recorded almost four years earlier[4]: INTRO—A—B—A'—BRIDGE—C—C'—CODA. This recording is "nostalgic" in having few improvised solos accompanied by the rhythm section alone, the only solo being taken by the alto saxophone in A'. (The cornet leads the B-section, but its part is obviously composed, since it is very similar to the respective part of the solo version.) Thus, "The Pearls" is more New Orleans-like in texture and conception than the other Red Hot Peppers pieces discussed. And, at the same time, the recording paradoxically anticipates later jazz textural preferences by having the most extended homophonic passages of all the ensemble titles discussed and also contains a curious mixture of New Orleans-like counterpoint texture, homophony, and breaks in section C.

The improvised solo surfaced in full force a year later when the Red Hot Peppers recorded "Kansas City Stomp." As in "Grandpa's Spells," the final A''' of the solo is eliminated and another improvised C-section is added, ending the piece in the subdominant. Also, the two consecutive appearances of section A after the introduction in the solo version are reduced to a single presentation, and a third A-section occurs before C. Thus, the Red Hot Peppers version of "Kansas City Stomp" has the form: INTRO—A—B—B'—A'—A''—C—C'—C''—CODA (the coda which was two measures long in the solo is here lengthened to six measures). An inspired feature of Morton's orchestration is the instrumentation of the measure-long motif, presented an octave lower in each measure of the introduction, successively given to the clarinet, trumpet, trombone, and tuba, with each playing the figure in the register in which it originally appeared in the piano solo. This is an excellent case-in-point of Morton's statement that he treated his piano solo work as an extension of the jazz band: "No jazz piano player can really play good jazz unless they try to give an imitation of a band, that is, by providing a basis of riffs."[5] He probably "heard" this orchestration in the original solo piano context, and chose to preserve it when the opportunity for an ensemble recording was presented. Charts 4-8 illustrate the structure of four Red Hot Peppers performances and the solo source of "Kansas City Stomp."

Chart 4. "Grandpa's Spells," Jelly Roll Morton and His Red Hot Peppers (December 16, 1926)

SECTION	INTRO.	A	A'	B	B'	A"	C	C'	C"	C'''	CODA
TOTAL NUMBER OF MEASURES	4	16	16	16	16	16	16	16	16	16	2
ORCHESTRAL DISTRIBUTION AND LENGTH IN MEASURES	FULL ENSEMBLE (HOMOPHONIC)	GUITAR 4 / FULL ENS. 4 / GUITAR 4 / FULL ENS. 4	CORNET 4 / FULL ENS. 4 / CORNET 4 / FULL ENS. 4	FULL ENSEMBLE	CLARINET	TROMBONE 2 / BASS 2 / FULL ENS. 4 / TROMBONE 2 / BASS 2 / FULL ENS. 4	CORNET	CLARINET	PIANO 8 / CLARINET 8	FULL ENSEMBLE	GUITAR
KEY AREAS	C: I						IV				

Chart 5. "Original Jelly Roll Blues," Jelly Roll Morton and His Red Hot Peppers (December 16, 1926) (*indicates stop-time sections)

SECTION	INTRO.	A	A	B	BRIDGE	C	D	D'	D"	D'''	D''''
TOTAL NUMBER OF MEASURES	4	12	12	8	4	12	12	12	12	12	12
ORCHESTRAL DISTRIBUTION AND LENGTH IN MEASURES	PIANO 3 / FULL ENS. 1 (HOMOPHONIC)	GUITAR 2 / CORNET 1 / TROMBONE 1 / FULL ENS. 8	*CLARINET 4 / FULL ENS. 8	FULL ENS. 8	FULL ENS. 4	*PIANO 4 / FULL ENS. 8	CORNET / CLARINET 8	*CLARINET 6 / FULL ENS. 6	CORNET 6 / FULL ENS. 6	*PIANO 6 / FULL ENS. 6	FULL ENSEMBLE
KEY AREAS	Bb: I							IV			

Chart 6. "The Pearls," Jelly Roll Morton and His Red Hot Peppers (June 10, 1927)

SECTION	INTRO.	A	B	A'	BRIDGE	C	C'	CODA
TOTAL NUMBER OF MEASURES	4	16	16	16	4	32	32	4
ORCHESTRAL DISTRIBUTION AND LENGTH IN MEASURES	FULL ENSEMBLE	CORNET	FULL ENSEMBLE (HOMOPHONIC)	ALTO SAXOPHONE	FULL ENSEMBLE (HOMOPHONIC) (CLARINET OBLIGATTO)	FULL ENSEMBLE (HOMOPHONIC & POLYPHONIC)	FULL ENSEMBLE (HOMOPHONIC & POLYPHONIC)	TUBA 2 / CLARINET 1 / FULL ENS. 1
KEY AREAS	G: I					IV		

Chart 7. "Kansas City Stomp," Morton Solo (July 18, 1923)

SECTION	INTRO.	A	A'	B	B'	A''	C	C'	A'''	CODA
TOTAL NUMBER OF MEASURES	4	16	16	16	16	16	16	16	16	2
KEY AREAS	Eb: I ————————						IV ————		I ————	

Chart 8. "Kansas City Stomp," Jelly Roll Morton and His Red Hot Peppers (June 11, 1928)

SECTION	INTRO.	A	B	B'	A'	A''	C	C'	C''	CODA
TOTAL NUMBER OF MEASURES	4	16	16	16	16	16	16	16	16	6
ORCHESTRAL DISTRIBUTION AND LENGTH IN MEASURES	CLARINET 1 TRUMPET 1 TROMBONE 1 TUBA 1	FULL ENSEMBLE	CLARINET 14 FULL ENS. 2	PIANO 14 FULL ENS. 2	FULL ENSEMBLE	BANJO	FULL 4 (HOMOPHONIC) TRUMPET 4 FULL 4 (HOMOPHONIC) TRUMPET 4	(SAME AS C)	FULL ENSEMBLE (CLARINET OBLIGATTO) (LAST MEASURE HOMOPHONIC)	FULL ENS. 1 (HOMOPHONIC) CLARINET 2 FULL ENS. 1 (HOMOPHONIC) DRUMS 2
KEY AREAS	Eb: I ————————						IV ————			

Unless stated otherwise all full ensemble passages are polyphonic

(Unless otherwise stated, all full ensemble passages are polyphonic.)

Chart 9. "London Blues," New Orleans Rhythm Kings (July 18, 1923)

SECTION	INTRO.	A	B	B'	C	C'	D	D'	CODA
TOTAL NUMBER OF MEASURES	4	12	12	12	12	12	12	12	2
ORCHESTRAL DISTRIBUTION AND LENGTH IN MEASURES	FULL ENS. 4 (HOMOPHONIC) CLARINET 4 4x	FULL ENSEMBLE	FULL ENSEMBLE (HOMOPHONIC 4) (POLYPHONIC 8)	BANJO 4 FULL ENS. 8	FULL ENS. 1 (HOMOPHONIC) CLARINET 1 FULL ENS. 1 (HOMOPHONIC) TROMBONE 1 FULL ENS. 8	(SAME AS C)	CLARINET 8 (STOP TIME) FULL ENS. 4	PIANO 8 (HOMOPHONIC ACCOMPANIMENT) FULL ENS. 4	FULL ENSEMBLE (HOMOPHONIC)

Chart 10. "London Blues," Morton Solo (April or May 1924)

SECTION	INTRO.	A	B	B'	C	C'	D	D'	D"	D'''	CODA
TOTAL NUMBER OF MEASURES	4	12	12	12	12	12	12	12	12	12	2
INTERNAL DIVISION	-	-	4-8	4-8	4-8	4-8	8-4	8-4	8-4	8-4	-

Chart 11. "Shoe Shiner's Drag," Jelly Roll Morton and His Red Hot Peppers (June 11, 1928)

SECTION	INTRO.	A	B	C	D	D'	D"	D'''	D''''	CODA
TOTAL NUMBER OF MEASURES	4	12	12	12	12	12	12	12	12	2
ORCHESTRAL DISTRIBUTION AND LENGTH IN MEASURES	FULL ENS. 1 (HOMOPHONIC) CLARINET 1 FULL ENS. 1 (HOMOPHONIC) TROMBONE 1	FULL ENSEMBLE	PIANO 4 FULL ENS. 8 ← Similar 4 mm. →	FULL ENS. 1 (HOMOPHONIC) CLARINET 1 FULL ENS. 1 (HOMOPHONIC) TROMBONE 1 FULL ENS. 8	CLARINET 8 FULL ENS. 4	PIANO 8 FULL ENS. 4	TRUMPET 10 FULL ENS. 2	FULL ENSEMBLE	TROMBONE 8 FULL ENS. 4	FULL ENSEMBLE (HOMOPHONIC)

(Unless otherwise stated, all full ensemble passages are polyphonic.)

Versions of "London Blues"

The various arrangements of "London Blues" also display Morton's preference for addition of improvised solo choruses in later recordings of a piece (see Charts 9-11 for full schematic analyses). Morton's 1923 recording of this composition with the New Orleans Rhythm Kings contains two improvised D-section choruses, while the piano solo recorded in 1924 contains four, and the 1928 Red Hot Peppers version, five. In the first D-strophe of the New Orleans Rhythm Kings recording, a stop-time clarinet solo is followed by four measures of ensemble work, and in the second D-section an eight-measure piano solo precedes four measures by the ensemble. This is similar to the subdivision procedure followed in those sections of the solo version, where Morton improvised for eight measures and followed it each time with the same composed material. In the Red Hot Peppers version of "London Blues" ("Shoe Shiner's Drag"), the repeats of sections B and C are skipped over to accommodate additional improvised choruses. In the five D-sections of "Shoe Shiner's Drag," the clarinet, piano, trumpet, and trombone each take a solo for eight measures (the trumpet solo is ten measures long), followed by a four-measure statement by the band. Again, the aforementioned subdivision procedure is used. Also, the introduction is altered in "Shoe Shiner's Drag": in the New Orleans Rhythm Kings and piano solo versions of "London Blues" the introduction is related to the harmonies which begin the B-section, but the introduction of "Shoe Shiner's Drag" is very similar to the first four measures of section C. Since this is the only ensemble recording in which the original piano solo introduction is altered, it might account for the title change.

These solo and ensemble recordings do not prove or disprove Morton's claim to be the "inventor" of jazz, but they definitely display him as an "innovator" in early jazz and popular music, in general. The earlier piano solos ("Grandpa's Spells," "Kansas City Stomp," and "The Pearls") utilize rag structures while the later solo pieces ("Jelly Roll Blues" and "London Blues") are based on the 12-measure blues. And, in general, ensemble arrangements of the compositions exhibit a chronologically increasing emphasis on soloing, while, at the same time, simplifying the formal structure. Soon after these recordings, other composers and arrangers began to emphasize the soloist, as Morton had done. In time, ensemble performances exhibited a distinct preference for monothematic/chorus-by-chorus structures, often focusing the interest of a piece on the solos.

The recordings of these five Morton pieces present crucial formal and improvisational transitions from ragtime. Moreover, they are fine examples of an early compositional approach to the successful merger of form and individual display in jazz.

Discography and Personnel

Jelly Roll Morton's piano solos; matrix numbers, first issues, and recording dates:
    "Grandpa's Spells" (matrix 11544; Gennett 5218)
    "Kansas City Stomp" (matrix 11545; Gennett 5218)
    "The Pearls" (matrix 11547; Gennett 5323)
        July 18, 1923—Richmond, Indiana
    "Jelly Roll Blues" (matrix 11911-A; Gennett 5552)
        June 9, 1924—Richmond, Indiana

"London Blues" (matrix 535; Rialto, no number)
    April or May, 1924—Chicago

Jelly Roll Morton and his Red Hot Peppers; matrix numbers, first issues, and recording dates:
    "Grandpa's Spells" (matrix 37255-2, 37255-3; Victor 20431)
    "Original Jelly Roll Blues" (matrix 37256-1, 37256-2; Victor 20405)
        December 16, 1926—Chicago

    Jelly Roll Morton, piano; Omer Simeon, clarinet; George Mitchell, cornet; Kid Ory, trombone; Johnny St. Cyr, guitar, banjo; John Lindsay, bass; Andrew Hilaire, drums.

    "The Pearls" (matrix 38662-2, 38662-3; Victor 20948)
        June 10, 1927—Chicago

    Jelly Roll Morton, piano; Johnny Dodds, clarinet; George Mitchell, trumpet; Stomp Evans, alto saxophone; George Bryant, trombone; Bud Scott, banjo; Quinn Wilson, tuba; Baby Dodds, drums.

    "Kansas City Stomp" (matrix 45620-3; Victor 38010)
    "Shoe Shiner's Drag" (matrix 45621-3; Victor 21658)
        June 11, 1928—New York City

    Jelly Roll Morton, piano; Omer Simeon, clarinet; Ward Pinkett, trumpet; Geechy Fields, trombone; Lee Blair, banjo; Bill Benford, tuba; Tommy Benford, drums.

New Orleans Rhythm Kings; matrix number, first issue, and recording date:
    "London Blues" (matrix 11550; Gennett 5221)
        July 18, 1923—Richmond, Indiana

    Paul Mares, trumpet; George Brunis, trombone; Leon Rappolo, clarinet; Glen Scoville, saxophone; Jelly Roll Morton, piano; Lou Black, banjo; Steve Brown, bass; Ben Pollack, drums.

Notes

1. Monothematic/chorus-by-chorus structure—a formal procedure favored in the big band era in which an initial thematic statement is followed by a string of improvisational choruses.

2. "A linear rag consists of the presentation of up to four new strains within the bisectional rag structure, one following another and its corresponding repetitions. . . . In contrast, in a rounded rag the first section of the rag is followed by one or two new strains and the return-quote of either its first or second section."

    An example of a linear rag is:
        Scott Joplin's "Maple Leaf Rag":
        A—A—B—B—A—C—C—D—D
        I ——————————— IV —— I —

Examples of rounded rag are:
    Scott Joplin and Scott Hayden's "Felicity Rag":
    INTRO—A—A—B—B—C—C—BRIDGE—A—A
    I ———————————— IV —   I ——

    Scott Joplin's "The Chrysanthemum":
    INTRO—A—A— B—B— A—C—C—D—D—C
    I ——————— V —— I - IV ——————

William J. Schafer and Johannes Riedel, *The Art of Ragtime* (Baton Rouge: Louisiana State University Press, 1973), p. 59.

3. While this essay was being prepared, the question of similarity of solos on successive takes of the same title in the Red Hot Peppers recordings was raised. As far as the author is concerned, whether or not the solos were "improvised" is irrelevant. Even if a given player recorded a "worked-out" passage, it is still an *improvised-sounding* solo by a single musician. The important point in the light of the essay is that they are solo choruses, i.e., Morton chose to feature himself or another instrumentalist in a given place. What the musician did with this allotted time was at his discretion. See Alan Lomax, *Mister Jelly Roll* (New York: Grosset and Dunlap, 1950), pp. 194-196.

4. Morton does change the formal structure of "The Pearls" in a 1938 solo version to: A—A′—B— B′—A″—BRIDGE—C—C′—C″ (no coda), that is, adding another strain of each theme (A′, B′, C″) and eliminating the coda.

5. Lomax, *Mister Jelly Roll,* p. 62.

Notes for a Bio-Discography of Joe Sullivan

Part IV: 1947-1971

Norman P. Gentieu

This is the fourth and final article in a series drawn from Norman P. Gentieu's book-length study of Joe Sullivan's life and recording history. "Part I: Chicago, 1906-1928" appeared in the Journal of Jazz Studies, *vol. 4, no. 2 (Spring/Summer 1977), pp. 33-42; "Part II: New York and Los Angeles, 1928-1937" in the* Annual Review of Jazz Studies 1 *(1982), pp. 128-145; "Part III: 1937-1947" in the* Annual Review of Jazz Studies 2 *(1983), pp. 81-108.*

—The Editors

From the fall of 1947 until the early 1960s, Joe Sullivan's career consisted largely of short-lived engagements and sporadic recording sessions that had him shuttling back and forth between the East and West Coasts. He finally settled down—though that expression may be applied only loosely to Sullivan—in San Francisco in the 1950s and remained there for the rest of his life, leaving only for a few special occasions. Although he gradually disappeared from the memory of the general public, he was, paradoxically, to record some of his most creative improvisations in the years of his greatest frustrations and ultimate decline.

Norman P. Gentieu has written on jazz since the 1930s, when his first articles appeared in *Metronome*. He has blended his musical interests with a career in science writing about topics in chemistry and metallurgy. His recent research includes a study of the Paul Whiteman Orchestra of 1926-1929. This final article in Mr. Gentieu's series on Joe Sullivan is dedicated to the memory of Robert Miller, jazz collector and founder of the Hot Platter Club of Central Jersey, which commissioned and supported this series of articles as a memorial to William G. Cleland, a dedicated Sullivan collector.

The Itinerant Sullivan

A glance at Sullivan's documented engagements from 1947 to 1951 indicates the nomadic nature of his career in that period:

October 1948. He is reported as stirring up quite a breeze at Mercur's Music Bar in Pittsburgh.[1]

May 1949. "For the first time since 1940, he says, Joe Sullivan is working a steady Chicago job." This residency at Jazz Limited brought Joe back with his old friend, Muggsy Spanier. The rest of the band included the club's owner, Bill Reinhardt, clarinet; Munn Ware, trombone; and Wally Gordon, drums. Although the ensemble work did not impress *Down Beat's* reporter, he praised the solos, including Joe's: "Besides, like someone said, don't worry about that beat. Muggsy and Joe will straighten it out. They're a rhythm section in themselves."[2]

March 1950. At a jazz concert at New York's Barbizon-Plaza concert hall,[3] Sullivan stars, despite a bad wrist, "sailing through the program in rare form," according to John S. Wilson's review. This excellent concert was fortunately preserved on records (as noted in the appended discography). Joining Joe were veteran musicians Wild Bill Davison, Bobby Hackett, Edmond Hall, George Wettling, and Vic Dickenson. Wilson wrote:

> Although Davison and Hackett got top billing, the star of the evening was Joe Sullivan. . . . His rhythm numbers had that bright, vibrant, compelling gaiety that is rarely heard from even the best of pianists, while his slower pieces were gems of relaxed mood playing. He was at the top of his form in a solo on "Coquette," which practically rocked the house down."[4]

August 1950. Ralph Gleason reports on "the battle of Bush Street" in San Francisco, with Club Hangover and the Say When both claiming imminent appearances by Sullivan.[5]

August 1950. In New York, "in one week recently . . . you had a choice of hearing Art Tatum at Cafe Society, Erroll Garner at Birdland, Joe Bushkin at the Park Sheraton, Joe Sullivan at the Hickory Log, both George Shearing and Earl Hines on top of the Turf, . . . Ralph Sutton at Condon's, Billy Kyle at La Commedia, and Cy Walter at the Drake Room."[6]

August 1950. Just two weeks later, the same source reports Sullivan as having appeared at the Club Hangover in San Francisco.[7]

October 1950. Sullivan is the pianist at the Music Box in Los Angeles.[8]

December 1950. He appears at the Hi-Hat Club in Boston.[9]

May 1951. Sullivan plays at a jazz concert sponsored by the Southern California Hot Jazz Society to raise money for a marker for Jelly Roll Morton's grave in a cemetery near Los Angeles. The report of this concert has discographical significance: "Incidentally, recordings taped at that concert, where Joe Sullivan, Zutty Singleton, and others donated their services, have bobbed up for sale as commercial platters at some local disc dispensaries."[10]

The Fertile Fifties

For jazz veteran Joe Sullivan, the 1950s proved to be one of his most productive periods, although changing stylistic preferences relegated him to comparatively low ratings in such measurements of popularity as the annual *Down Beat* polls. Thus, in 1951, the poll winner among pianists was Oscar Peterson with 726 votes, while Sullivan received a scant 27. The questionable value of such tallies over the longer history of jazz is made apparent by other 1951 results, which gave Art Tatum a mere 153 votes, only a few more than the 138 garnered by Stan Kenton, hardly a comparable keyboard artist.[11]

From March 11, 1950—the Barbizon-Plaza session discussed above—to March 2, 1951, the Sullivan discography demonstrates both Sullivan's continuing productivity and his importance to the continuing vitality of traditional jazz. In those 12 months, he recorded 30 tunes on five dates with such veteran colleagues as Davison, Dickenson, Hall, Hackett, Sidney Bechet, Jimmy Archey, Red Allen, Buster Bailey, and Eddie Condon.

In October 1951, a news item announced that "Joe Sullivan cut eight sides here [San Francisco] in August with Smoky Stover on drums and Dave Lario on bass . . . . Joe intends to peddle them to a major label."[12] In fact, the rhythm section appears on only three of these sides, and the provenance of the four additional solo selections eventually issued on LP remains an unsolved discographical mystery. The twelve selections, issued about two years after the session on the Riverside label and later reissued with a different album title and jacket design, rank among Sullivan's best performances and give the listener the opportunity to hear an extended recital of his solo piano.

This rhythm section of Stover and Lario was well accustomed to working with Sullivan; they played in the ensemble at Club Hangover. An example of such an ensemble was the special variety show presented to the inmates of San Quentin prison on April 8, 1951, by "The Hangover Sextette" of Sullivan, Stover, Lario, Marty Marsala on trumpet, Albert Nicholas on clarinet, and Julian Laine on trombone.[13]

Still highly mobile, "Joe Sullivan took off for New York early in November and was replaced on piano at the Hangover by Lee Countryman from L.A."[14] However, on December 13, Sullivan returned to California to join Louis Armstrong's sextet, replacing Earl Hines, who returned to New York to direct his own new group.[15] (Wally Rose took over Joe's spot at the Hangover instead of Countryman.)[16]

Joe's association with Armstrong lasted but a brief time, for by May 1952 a news item on an all-star dixieland band touring the country mentioned Sullivan, Pec Wee Russell, George Brunis, and Ruby Braff.[17] But the months with Armstrong seem to have been productive. Armstrong was quoted as saying, "We have Joe Sullivan, now. Pops [i.e., Sullivan] plays fine piano."[18] And the pianist's crowd appeal, in San Francisco at least, must have been an asset, for Ralph Gleason reported that "Louis Armstrong's week at the Hangover was nothing short of sensational. There were lines outside the club every night three feet deep and half a block long. Hundreds were turned away."[19]

Sullivan Records Eight Unpublished Waller Tunes

A six-month recording hiatus followed the August 1951 session, but Sullivan was busy in early 1952 with several small group dates issued under the name of the Stuyvesant Casino Orchestra (or trio) and including Russell, Hot Lips Page, Lou McGarrity, George Wettling, Bob Wilber, Bud Freeman, and Jimmy McPartland. These recordings, issued by "Amalgamated," are very rare.

In the spring of 1952, Jimmy and Marian McPartland listened to Wild Bill Davison's recording of "On the Alamo" in one of Leonard Feather's blindfold tests. Marian's laconic comment was: "I'd say the piano was Joe Sullivan. Heavy."[20]

An extremely important project, produced by George Avakian for Epic in June and

September 1952, was the recording by Sullivan of eight unpublished compositions of Fats Waller. George Hoefer—a Sullivan enthusiast who once stated that "Joe Sullivan's famed 'Gin Mill Blues' . . . is one of the great classics of blues piano"[21]—devoted his entire *Down Beat* column of March 1954 to these performances "worth obtaining not only for Waller fans, but also for the legion who like Sullivan."[22] Avakian's rationale for choosing Sullivan is significant:

> I selected Joe Sullivan, not only because of his great respect and understanding of Fats and his music, but also because Joe is one of the most inventive and stylistically individual of Waller's contemporaries. I felt that I could be sure of sympathetic and completely authentic interpretations of the music without undue imitation of Fats' own style. The results justified this faith: Joe, as I hoped and expected, frequently plays half or a whole chorus as Fats himself might have played it, but more often there is only an echo or flavoring of the Waller style, with Joe's own personality coming through just as strongly as the music which Fats wrote. There are sections which are much more Sullivan than Waller, in fact—which is as it should be in this kind of jazz piano, regardless of whose compositions are being played.[23]

Home base for Sullivan in the latter part of 1953 was the Club Hangover, as documented in *Down Beat* items:

July 1953. "Joe Sullivan returns to the Hangover club July 23 as leader of the house band, with a lineup consisting of Lee Collins, trumpet; Bert Johnson, trombone; Pud Brown, tenor sax and clarinet; Smoky Stover, drums; and Dave Lario, bass."[24]

August 1953. "Joe Sullivan's band at the Hangover club which opened July 24 featured Pud Brown, tenor, Dale Jones, trombone, Lee Collins, trumpet, and Dave Lario, bass. Ralph Sutton continued as intermission piano."[25] Two Sullivan solos recorded at this time exist and are the only 1953 entries in his discography.

September 1953. "Ralph Sutton was replaced at the Hangover (when he left for Europe) by Don Ewell playing his first date in town. . . . Joe Sullivan was switched from the piano slot in the band to solo work. . . . "[26]

September 1953. "Joe Sullivan was relieved of his intermission chores by New York gal pianist Ginger Laird."[27]

October 1953. "Joe Sullivan staying over in town [San Francisco] and planning to put in his card. . . . "[28]

The trend indicated by these items was reflected by the *Down Beat* Poll for 1953, in which Sullivan's name did not even appear. As a commentary on the faddish tastes at least some of the magazine's readers, one may note that the egregious Liberace received 62 votes in the same poll.[29]

Alcohol and Emotion

At an unspecified date in 1954, Sullivan made his only recording date of the year for Jazztone, with such stalwarts as George Wettling, Jack Lesberg, Miff Mole, Max Kaminsky, and Pee Wee Russell. One of his piano solos, "Stuyvesant Blues," has been transcribed and analyzed for its influences on the development of jazz piano style.[30] According to one jazz historian, the producers of this session introduced a case of whiskey with predictable and unfortunate results: "anger and a valiant struggle to maintain musical equilibrium. . . . These must have been harrowing moments for Wettling and Lesberg, for the pain and fury of Sullivan's performance fairly leap from the grooves to this day."[31] The ethanolic anger manifested on this occasion no doubt indicate a deep-seated discontent which was to become exacerbated as changing tastes, including the advent of rock, eroded the musical opportunities for Sullivan and his peers.

A letter, written the same year to Sullivan's sister, alludes to the demons which were eventually to destroy Joe. His fate paralleled that of Bix Beiderbecke, whose decline Sullivan had unhappily witnessed at least once at close hand.

> Yet, his weakness—which you seem to be so well aware of—is a very real one. And although he has controlled it at one time or another, something personal happens—and he's off again. Goodness knows with that great talent of his (and in my judgment, he is the world's greatest jazz pianist) we think at times that Joe would be strong enough to overcome the crave to drown his misshappen dreams, and imagined disappointments. . . . He's being reasonable now; living a fairly normal life at his hotel . . . and besides doing a few jobs a week here, has just signed for an indefinite stay in Columbus, Ohio.[32]

This engagement was recalled by a longtime admirer:

> I first heard Joe in 1953 or 1954 when he appeared periodically in Columbus, Ohio. I saw him first at a club called "The Grandview Inn." My recollection is that he was appearing with George Wettling and Ruby Braff. Again (with possibly faulty recollection), I believe "The Grandview Inn" burned to the ground twice . . . each time following an appearance by Joe!
>
> He also appeared in Columbus during this period at a club called "Lou Posey's Frolics" located on North High Street. He appeared there as a single and at another time played solo piano between sets by the "Saints and Sinners Jazz Band." The only member of that band I'm sure of is trombonist Jimmy Archey (another of my favorites).
>
> I was attracted to Joe's playing, mostly by the force and dedication. He came to our table . . . he drank doubles. We listened. He was clearly alcoholic and quite emotional. My impression was that he was confounded by the passing of the 1930s and stubbornly refused to venture into the 1940s.[33]

Nevertheless, Sullivan was back in New York by early October and remained active there for the rest of the year in the company of various veteran jazzmen at such clubs as the Heat Wave, the Metropole, and the Stuyvesant Casino. "Though the Heat Wave unzipped to strippers, Muggsy Spanier and Joe Sullivan had contracts. Result: Muggsy worked his out by backing the strippers, while Joe played intermission. . . ."[34] In reviewing the opening of "this new Dixieland haven," George Hoefer commented that "Joe Sullivan at the piano plays his usual fine barrelhouse solos and, of course, is unable to avoid the many requests for 'Little Rock Getaway.' " Others at the Heat Wave included Bob Wilber on clarinet and tenor sax, Henry Goodwin on trumpet, Jimmy Archey on trombone, and George Wettling on drums, the latter commended for fronting "affably with a newly acquired talent for making the introductions and announcing the tunes."[35]

By the end of October, Joe had moved to an uptown club noted for its long, narrow platform behind the bar, from which the musicians played, and for its generally misanthropic bartenders:

> Jimmy McPartland is again heading one of the regular bands at the Metropole. Red Allen has the other. Newly added to the Metropole's roster are the Conrad Janis band and Tony

Parenti's trio with Joe Sullivan and Zutty Singleton. Also heading a trio there is Bud Freeman.[36]

Towards the end of 1954, Bob Maltz put on a celebration of George Wettling's birthday, with a Dixie Jamboree at the Stuyvesant Casino in New York City. During the festivities, Jimmy Rushing led a group of musicians in a jam session that lasted almost an hour. The ensemble consisted of Joe Sullivan, piano; George Wettling, drums; Walter Page, bass; Jonah Jones, trumpet; George Stevenson, trombone; Jimmy Rushing, vocals and conducting. Pops Foster was there and danced a lively New Orleans jig on the stand.[37]

June 1955 found Sullivan back again at Club Hangover in San Francisco, playing intermission piano between sets by Teddy Buckner's band.[38] During this engagement, on six dates between June and September, Sullivan recorded as many solos of standards.

TV Recalls Sullivan's Struggle with Tuberculosis

Although Sullivan's current popularity was limited (the *Down Beat* Poll for 1954 again ignored him, while Liberace fell to 46 votes), a dramatic episode of his life—his triumph over tuberculosis in 1936-38 and the support he received from other jazz musicians—was the subject of a coast-to-coast "Live From Hollywood" television show on August 4, 1955. Written by Bob Crosby and Gil Roden, Crosby's manager, and sponsored by the Chrysler Corporation, the one-hour show featured Crosby and several former members of his Bob Cats portraying themselves in a melodrama recounting Sullivan's nearly fatal struggle with tuberculosis and his eventual triumph.[39]

A *Down Beat* review credited the show as being more factual than any previous television biography and coming "closer to catching an authentic dance band atmosphere than any similar attempt in films, radio, or TV." The authenticity of the presentation, which centered on the 1937 tribute to Sullivan by the Crosby band, was of course modified by the requirements of casting and dramatization, as noted by the reviewer:

> The role of Gil Rodin, who did not appear, was played by actor Bob Sweeney. Drummer Ray Bauduc, on tour with Jack Teagarden, was unavailable; his role was enacted by drummer Jack Sperling, who like [Eddie] Miller and some of the others, is now a regular on Bob Crosby's afternoon TV series.
>
> Another important real-life character who did not appear was Bob Zurke, who took Sullivan's place during his illness. Zurke died here some years ago after a long engagement at Hollywood's Hangover night club. The excellent portrayal of the talented but eccentric Zurke by actor Donald Buka was one of the highlights of the production. The piano music for the Sullivan role, well acted by John Fosythe, was played by Ray Sherman; the pianist for the Zurke role was Paul Smith. Scatman Crothers was effective in a brief appearance as a blues-singer and friend of Sullivan.[40]

The article commented favorably on the current state of Sullivan's health and gave a somewhat overly glowing assessment of his current success as a nightclub pianist. It was accurate, at least, in placing him in San Francisco as of the date of the telecast.

"Tone Poems in Jazz"

It is clear that Sullivan's uncompromising attitude towards jazz as an art form was one element in Bob Crosby's motivation to recall events almost two decades past, for Crosby was quoted at length in the liner notes to an extremely important LP recorded by Sullivan sometime in mid-1955. Crosby's words emphasize that Sullivan's artistic stance was much like Bix Beiderbecke's—whatever else you did with your own life, you treated the music with full respect. It is worth quoting Crosby at some length:

> This is the kind of dedicated musician Joe Sullivan is. . . . One time back around 1937 our band was playing a dance at the Nicollet Hotel up in Minneapolis. At one point, our drummer ran into a little trouble—his drumhead broke and he was trying to get by as best he could. After a few minutes of this, Joe Sullivan shrugged, covered his piano keys and walked off the stand. I went right after him. "I'm sorry, Bob," Joe told me. "I can't play. The music isn't *right* that way." "But it was an unavoidable accident and it'll be fixed up," I tried to explain. Joe just puffed away on his cigarette. "When the drum's ready to be played *right,*" Joe insisted, "that's when I'll be back on the stand." And that's exactly what he did.

> With Sullivan the music was either right or it wasn't worth bothering with. You have to admire him for being such a stickler for the right thing, for perfection. It must have been his classical training and it was the nature of the man himself. I'll tell you something else about Joe Sullivan. In our band, Joe was a tremendous driving force. He was never ever just a piano player—he was like Bix; every time he touched the keys, he wanted to tell a story, musically. He wanted to play tone poems in jazz, and every time he played, he sought out a jazz pattern, not just sounds. He wanted meaning in his music. With our band, Joe Sullivan was great. In my book, Joe Sullivan is still great.[41]

This mid-1955 LP contains some of Sullivan's most notable "tone poems in jazz." Recorded for the Down Home label under the supervision of Norman Granz, it is, in my opinion, one of his best efforts in the recording studio—perhaps the best—and, unfortunately, out-of-print as of late 1983. It was Sullivan's last commerical recording as a soloist at the peak of his power and form, a monument to his musicianship and integrity, and a summation and concentration of a lifetime as a jazz pianist. It seems to have been made under ideal conditions, far from the distractions of the nightclub environment which was now Joe's fate. Three selections are Waller tunes—"Black and Blue," "Ain't Misbehavin'," and "Keepin' Out of Mischief Now"). Four others are his own compositions—"Just Strolling," "Bush Above Powell" (a reference to the location of the Club Hangover), "Frolicking Fido," and "In the Middle of a Kiss." The last tune is a poignantly lyrical ballad with melodic and harmonic attractions which grow with repeated hearings. With the exception of an up-tempo "I've [sic] Found a New Baby," all the solos are played in medium or medium-slow tempos, with plenty of time for improvisation and for Sullivan to draw upon the jazz tradition in order to honor other great pianists with quotations or passages suggestive of their styles. "Go Back Where You Stayed Last Night," an extended exercise in such creative electicism, provides an excellent example of Sullivan's "instant composing," jazz pianism of impeccable and enduring excitement.

Chicago Revisited

During the middle months of 1955, Sullivan continued at the Club Hangover as intermission pianist opposite various bands. Several recordings of solos were made between sets by the Teddy Buckner band, probably deriving from air checks of broadcasts from the club. By September, Sullivan was opposite Earl Hines's band, which included Darnell Howard on clarinent and Jimmy Archey on trombone.[42] During much of 1956, he alternated with other solists at the Hangover, being replaced by Meade Lux Lewis in April,[43] returning by June,[44] and being replaced in turn by Lionel Reason, formerly with Kid Ory, sometime in the early fall.[45]

Except for the local audiences in the San Francisco area, Joe Sullivan was largely invisible between 1955 and 1961. On October 30, 1961, the National Broadcasting Company, under the sponsorship of Dupont, taped "Chicago and All That Jazz!", a show designed to give the television audience a glimpse of jazz history through the performance of some surviving pioneers. Two fine veteran bands performed, and one of them—reincarnating the McKenzie-Condon Chicagoans—made a record of the music played on the telecast.

This group included Sullivan, Eddie Condon, Bud Freeman, Bob Haggart, Gene Krupa, Jimmy McPartland, Pee Wee Russell, and Jack Teagarden. Frank Teschemacher was dead, Jim Lannigan had retired, and there had been no trombonist on the original Chicagoans date, but the replacements and the addition proved compatible with the spirit of the 1927 ensemble.

The occasion led to some conflicting notices. Whitney Balliett took a dim view of the Verve recording by "exhausted musicians":

> . . . Pee Wee Russell, who recently escaped from his Dixieland bondage, sounds exactly like a recaptured slave, McPartland quavers, Freeman baubles. And Sullivan, Bob Haggart, and Krupa resemble nervous cattle.[46]

On the other hand, John W. Norris, reviewing the telecast rather than the disk, wrote:

> . . . the most important part of the show, to me, was the excellent music played by both bands. [The other group had Red Allen, trumpet; Buster Bailey, clarinet; Kid Ory, trombone; Lil Armstrong, piano; Johnny St. Cyr, banjo; Milt Hinton, bass; and Zutty Singleton, drums.] Everyone rose to the occasion to give of their best. These musicians must have got a lift out of playing together again and, too, a slight sense of rivalry may have keyed them up a little more.[47]

It seems unlikely that the Condon group would have lost its spirit in a recording session which so quickly followed the television taping, and the record indicates that the old Chicago brio was still in evidence in the Condon group. Sullivan's solo on "China Boy" is particularly noteworthy.

Joe Sullivan's Twilight Years

"Chicago and All That Jazz" was the last commercial recording Sullivan was to make in his lifetime. Other records would be issued, but all of them posthumously. For most of his last decade, Joe lived not far from the Club Hangover—without a piano. In 1961, he played for a short time with Muggsy Spanier and then led his own group at the On the Levee Club. This gig lasted only a few weeks but produced music of sterling quality:

> Drawing on the best young local talent he could get, the pianist built a roaring, stomping Dixielandish sextet. Featuring clarinetist Vince Cattolica and trombonist Bob Mielke, the group played at an almost unbelievably intense level on every set, yet never sacrificed its integrity or sense of musical discovery. Sullivan spurred his men with so much enthusiasm at the keyboard that he frequently went home with bleeding fingers.[48]

A recording of 23 numbers by this band was made on at the club on September 2, 1961, some or all of which may someday be issued on LP.[49]

A letter Sullivan wrote in the spring of 1962 offers a glimpse of his private life and a recollection of the 1961 television show and recording:

> Night club business is real slow. I may come East, try my darnest [sic] to look you up.
>
> After rehearsing for 'Dupont's Show of the Week' we recorded two (2) nights in a row till the wee hours in the A.M. I went without sleep for over 38 hours. . . . I am fat and sassy now. Enjoying life but now my friend Dr. Rogers would like me to cut down. I weigh 220 and he's worried, like me to cut down to 190.[50]

The letter was signed "Big Joe and Little Jo." Little Jo was his new wife, Josephine, a professional pianist, who for a few years brought a measure of happiness and content into Joe's disorganized and often purposeless later life. Her death from cancer late in the decade deprived Sullivan of his companion and stabilizer, and he seemed finally to have lost the will to live.

Yet this final decade produced some flurries of activity and creativity, for Sullivan retained his dedication to the piano almost to the end. The year 1963, for example, was unusually active. He recorded the sound track for a documentary film about blind children, appeared in two National Educational Television programs, played in the Sixth Annual Monterey Jazz Festival, and began playing on Monday nights at the Trident, a posh restaurant and club across San Francisco Bay in Sausalito. Also in that year, Gerry Mulligan's big band recorded his "Little Rock Getaway" in a version that pleased Sullivan.

The experience of improvising a score for the film documentary may well have drawn upon Sullivan's experience of improvising accompaniments for silent films in the 1920s. One of the film's producers described the event as follows:

> The blind children's camp film was made in my department, then Radio-Television-Film at (then) San Francisco State College. It was sponsored by the Lighthouse for the Blind who perhaps still distribute it. Titled "Who's Enchanted?" Directed by David Coffing. Recorded March, 1963. We just asked Joe to improvise against the visuals and later mixed his music with commentary. There was a nice Baby Grand Steinway which he loved to play, so the pleasure was shared.[51]

Sullivan's own account of this offbeat engagement reveals much about his generous nature and his professional perfectionism:

> Six or seven years back I was asked to do the very same thing [Joe had had a dream about scoring at a theatre a picture he'd never seen before] for "Lighthouse for the Blind." I got permission from the union here in S.F. local 6 as I refused to accept any money for such a worthy cause and it was a challenge that I accepted. They picked us up around 11 P.M. drove to Berkeley the only studio they could get. I had instructed Momma Jo my sweet wife to put a pint of Jim Beam in her bag tho' she said there goes one good purse! and away we go. I watched it once then sat down at the piano, a Steinway thank God and briefly it went like this. There were blind children ages around six to fifteen. From the time they got up, breakfast, a little school work, outside playing, crossing a bridge with no one to guide them, exercising, dinner, prayers, then to bed. It doesn't sound much like my background, all improvised had to fit each mood, gay, thoughtful, sad, laughing, etc.

I even had a chance to put in about 72 bars of blues that was like nothing I'd ever played before in my lifetime. Jo and I watched it after it had been put together. Everybody was pleased. Jo who was an excellent classical pianist in her own right was thrilled. Me? Like everything I've done I always see where I could have done better. . . . I sure wish Jo were alive now, maybe I'd feel different now.[52]

At the Monterey Festival, Sullivan was received enthusiastically in the company of such performers as Jack and Charlie Teagarden, Pee Wee Russell, and Gerry Mulligan. Nine sides were recorded privately, and several of them have appeared on LP.

Ralph Gleason has commented on the two 1963 television appearances:

"A 30-minute video tape exists of him all alone playing the piano and talking about his early days, about music, and about other pianists. I did it for Educational Television, as part of 26 half-hour jazz shows, in the early 60s. Joe just came to the studio and we let him ramble for the full programme.

"Earlier, Joe had played with Muggsy Spanier in a programme we did for Educational Television with a bottle of whisky in his inside coat pocket which he sipped from with a straw, thinking no one had noticed! On both programmes he was delightful: a co-operative, intelligent and skillful performer who really had the ability to communicate through his music even by way of the TV screen.[53]

Soon after the Monterey appearances, Sullivan began his series of Monday night performances at the Trident in Sausalito, where he enjoyed a fine, well-tuned piano and an audience far more attentive than is customary in clubs. He was inspired to expand his repertory:

As if he had been waiting 40 years for the opportunity, the pianist played pieces seldom heard from him before, reshaping each into a gem of newly improvised musical thought and form. He took no easy ways out; always there was the probing, the searching for new means of expressing old feelings.[54]

Among his explorations of new material were such ballads as "One Morning in May," "I Didn't Know What Time It Was," "Alone Together," and "What Is There To Say?" The pianist had told Ralph Gleason during the Jazz Casual show that he now found playing such pieces more rewarding than the fast numbers usually requested by club customers. Like so many other jazz performers, Sullivan bitterly resented affronts to his musician-ship. In an interview with a Scottish journalist, he loosed a broadside on the subject of piano bars:

Is my name Joe Schmuck that I should play in these lousy places? Should I take that kind of job where you end up as accompanist to a succession of drunks? No. No. I'm still Joe Sullivan. I'm still a jazz piano player, whether they want to remember me or not in this lousy city. I don't take jobs like that and I don't take jobs for cut rate either. Lots of guys do when things get tough. But I don't. And I don't lower my musical standards either. I'd starve right here in my apartment before I did that. That would be the end of everything. . . . O.K., I can't kid you. Things are bad but they'll never be so bad that I play rubbish in one of these piano bars. Hell, what's this country coming to anyhow. There's this woman making records now and appearing on the Ed Sullivan Show because she *cannot* sing in tune. Yet good musicians don't get breaks like that.[55]

Last Performances

In 1964, Sullivan made a brief appearance at the Newport Jazz Festival. Stricken and hospitalized with an unspecified illness on his arrival, he rallied to play a set that *Down Beat* called "brief but moving."[56]

What is apparently Sullivan's last recording was made on the last day of that year, a New Year's Eve performance at San Francisco's Apostleship of the Sea, the Catholic Rescue Mission for Homeless Seamen. Richard Hadlock, leader and soprano saxophonist, taped the job, as he had so many earlier Sullivan dates, and Bob Osibin played drums. His colleagues found they had a tiger by the tail, and Hadlock's commentary is a valuable analysis of the pianist's approach to jazz ensemble playing:

> It was an educational evening for me. I learned a lot about his remarkable sense of time as I struggled to play my soprano saxophone over constantly shifting cadences, startling accents and unexpected syncopation. I discovered, too, why he often had problems with drummers. To play well with Sullivan one had to be very sure of oneself, and very sure of just where the pulse lay. (The same sort of pressure affects rhythm players who work with Earl Hines, if you try to follow him, you are lost.) Yet Sullivan was a superb accompanist, always prodding, complementing and feeding the soloist new ideas.[57]

By now Sullivan's long professional career was virtually ended. But occasionally the convivial and communicative artist would surface, and long months or years away from the piano would be forgotten in an access of raw desire to play. On these occasions, random audiences would hear superb jazz. His nephew, Daniel O'Sullivan, tells about one such impromptu session:

> It was the New Orleans Room (a cocktail lounge and piano room) in the Fairmont Hotel in San Francisco, and I would guess that the time would have been about 1965 to '67, when Joe had, to all intents and purposes, given up playing piano professionally, and was content just to spend his remaining days in his apartment. In this particular case, I prevailed on Joe to come up to our hospitality suite which at that time we had engaged in the Fairmont for a convention that was going on, and Joe decided to do so, and he did come up and visit us.
>
> After spending a couple of hours in the suite, we had received permission from the manager of the hotel to go down to the New Orleans Room because the pianist that day had a day off; it was a Sunday afternoon and Joe decided he'd play a few numbers for us. And at the time, Bill Hunsinger, who was a colleague of mine and an admirer of Joe's, and I and Joe were the only three that were there and a few people at the bar; and after Joe had begun to play the room in the next half hour practically filled up with people who realized that they were listening to not a run-of-the-mill pianist but a man of tremendous professional ability and talent. On that particular day, Joe played perhaps for an hour and a half to an hour and forty-five minutes. And it was my opinion at the time that although he said he had done little or no playing for several years, I just felt that Joe was still the great piano player that he had been in the forties and fifties; and I thought he sounded as good as or better that I had ever heard him sound. He himself seemed to be pleased with his performance that day.
>
> . . . In the evening Joe was in a great mood, was happy and relaxed and asked us if we would join him in a little saloon downtown that had a black female pianist whom Joe admired. Said he'd like to go down and have a drink with her and listen to her play. Which

we did, and shortly after entering this particular bistro—and I don't remember the name of it, nor do I remember the name of the black pianist—Joe was introduced by this little gal and she prevailed on him in the next twenty minutes or so to sit down at the piano, which he did and, to my utter amazement, played "Little Rock Getaway," as somebody requested it, and played it very well.[58]

Excerpts from Sullivan's correspondence in the last year of his life show him languishing, as man and as artist, in involuntary "retirement" and solitude:

. . . I hit 64 last week! Ten years ago if anybody hinted that I'd live beyond 60 I'd've shouted them down. Keep up the good work on the piano. I'm sorry to say that I have'nt [sic] touched the keyboard in over two years. I talked to Jess Stacy [by telephone] in Los Angeles while I was down there visiting my son. He also has retired from the music business. Jess is feeling fine, a damn fine musician.[59]

I retired over two years ago. All of a sudden my dear wife died. Almost 10 days later, Muggsy, then Wettling, Pee Wee, Pops Foster, Edmond Hall. Too many more to mention. No incentive, haven't touched the keyboard in years.[60]

I wonder if Dykes [Joes's nephew] is coming to S.F. this year? It won't do him any good to put in a piano when he and his partner reserve their suite at the Fairmont. I haven't played the piano in more years than I care to remember. Sure, I dream about me playing in orchestras and by myself. Even think about how it could maybe be a wonderful feeling again like when I was active and Jo, bless her, would say "Dear, I sometimes feel you love the piano more than you do me." She was never jealous. Always said God gave me a wonderful gift and that I was the best jazz pianist in the country.[61]

A Last Appearance—For Five-Year-Olds

Joe Sullivan's last public appearance took place in a kindergarten class. A West Coast jazz pianist, who was a friend and devotee of Joe's, has described that unlikely event:

I did hear Joe and I listened to records with him, but he was despondent in his last years, played little, drank heavily and lived on royalties. I do have one experience with Joe which was memorable . . . .

Richard Hadlock, who was teaching kindergarten at the time (1970), had pushed to get Joe out of his hotel room to do something, anything to keep his spirit alive and to play in a relaxed setting. And so Joe agreed to play for Richard's kindergarten class and I was to transport him there. The trip from San Fran. to Berkeley was not long, but long enough for Joe to be apprehensive about how he would sound (even in front of five year old children). He was gentle and courteous, ever the artist who wanted his music to be right—not just entertainment, but the art of jazz piano. He grew bitter when he said "Our parents (generous in including me as a piano player) spent money on lessons for us so that we could play well. And we studied hard. Well, look at that guy lifting a box. What skill does that take? But he probably makes more money." I could see that the *business* side of music, his drinking, his belief in his art, and the loneliness of his last years seemed to be too much for him.

What made something a success puzzled him too. He said "I don't know why everybody remembers 'Little Rock Getaway.' I wrote others too." And that reminded him of "Onyx Bringdown." He said "I don't know why I called it 'Bringdown.' I was feeling *good* when I wrote it."

At Richard's school his quiet manner caught the children's attention, and he sat at the piano and announced "I Got It Bad and That Ain't Good." One of them corrected his "mistake" but he said "ain't" was just a way of talking. He played several pieces, as ever, full of dynamic surprise and expressed eloquently over the full range of the piano. His power, his stomping power was diminished, but his artistry was complete.

On the way home he turned to me and said "Was it any good or did I stink up the joint?" I tried to reassure him. I mention all of this because it was the last time Joe ever played and I was moved deeply.[62]

Joe Sullivan died on Wednesday, October 13, 1971, in the San Francisco General Hospital. His death seems a merciful termination of an inexorable process that had wasted his substance for the last decade, a period of frustration, disappointment, and personal sorrow at the loss of his wife and so many fellow artists. As so often happens in the fickle realm of the arts, belated recognition is now being accorded; among other commemorations, the time-Life *Giants of Jazz* series has devoted a three-record album to Sullivan (Time-Life STL J-27). And in England—where, in some important ways, appreciation is better managed—the poet Roy Fisher in 1978 published a book of poems called *The Thing About Joe Sullivan,* which is also the title of his poem about the pianist, whom (on the verso facing the title page) he honors with the simple accolade of "musician."[63]

The Thing About Joe Sullivan

The pianist Joe Sullivan,
jamming sound against idea

hard as it can go
florid and dangerous

slams at the beat, or hovers,
drumming, along its spikes;

in his time almost the only
one of them to ignore

the chance of easing down,
walking it leisurely,

he'll strut, with gambling shapes,
underpinning by James P.,

amble, and stride over
gulfs of his own leaving, perilously

toppling octaves down to where
the chords grow fat again

and ride hard-edged, most lucidly
voiced, and in good inversions even when

the piano seems at risk of being
hammered the next second into scrap.

For all that, he won't swing
like all the others;

disregards mere continuity,
the snakecharming business,

the 'masturbator's rhythm'
under the long variations:

Sullivan can gut a sequence
in one chorus—

—approach, development, climax, discard—
and sound magnanimous.

The mannerism of intensity
often with him seems true,

too much to be said, the mood
pressing in right at the start, then

running among stock forms
that could play themselves

and moving there with such
quickness of intellect

that shapes flaw and fuse,
altering without much sign,

concentration
so wrapped up in thoroughness

it can sound bluff, bustling,
just big-handed stuff—

belied by what drives him in
to make rigid, display,

shout and abscond, rather
than just let it come, let it go—

And that thing is his mood:
a feeling violent and ordinary

that runs in among standard forms so
wrapped up in clarity

that fingers following his
through figures that sound obvious

find corners everywhere,
marks of invention, wakefulness;

the rapid and perverse
tracks that ordinary feelings

make when they get driven
hard enough against time.

—Roy Fisher

Reprinted from *Poems 1955-1980* by
Roy Fisher (1980) by permission of
Oxford University Press.

Coda

This series of articles on Joe Sullivan's life and music has been concerned primarily with his career and the commercial recordings he made for such labels as Victor, Columbia, Okeh, and Decca. It is intended to be an introduction to Sullivan's art—a stepping-stone, the author hopes, to some eventual exhaustive bio-discography.

The discography which has accompanied these articles includes not only the 78 rpm and LP disks which contain most of his recorded legacy but also air check, transcription, privately recorded, and posthumously issued material, but in this hazy area no claim is made that the subject has been exhausted. In fact, the author expects additional listings in such categories to surface occasionally and welcomes both addenda and corrections.

If these "notes for a bio-discography" have helped to bring Joe Sullivan the recognition he merits as a jazz immortal and to illuminate his total dedication to the art of jazz piano improvisation,[64] my efforts will have been amply rewarded.

EXPLICATION OF RECORD LISTINGS
(FEBRUARY 19, 1949–DECEMBER 31, 1964)

Name of recording group/place/date

Personnel (The conventional sequence of naming players—brass, reeds, rhythm—has been abandoned to list Sullivan and his rhythm section first, a logical modification in view of the primary emphasis of this article.)

Matrix and take / title / original label and number / LP (if known)

(Original label and number is generally limited to the record which was first issued commercially, although a few exceptions have been made. With this information, readers will be able to use Rust, Jepsen, and other discographies to investigate record issues in depth.)

JOE SULLIVAN   **NEW YORK, FEBRUARY 19, 1949**

No matrix number	Gin Mill Blues	Amalgamated (unnumbered)[65]

Note: This is a recording of a radio broadcast of a jazz festival, unidentified. Joe talks on the record.

JOE SULLIVAN AND THE ALL-STARS   **NEW YORK, MARCH 11, 1950**

p-Joe Sullivan, d-George Wettling; c-Wild Bill Davison, tb-Vic Dickenson; cl-Edmond Hall.

No matrix number	Jazz Me Blues	Voice of America VOA No. 71	LP: Shoestring SS-114
	Memphis Blues	Voice of America VOA No. 71	LP: Shoestring SS-114
	That Da-Da Strain	Voice of America VOA No. 71	LP: Shoestring SS-114
	Save It Pretty Mama	Voice of America VOA No. 72	LP: Shoestring SS-114

	Basin Street Blues	Voice of America VOA No. 73	LP: Shoestring SS-114
	Royal Garden Blues	Voice of America VOA No. 73	LP: Shoestring SS-114
	High Society	Voice of America VOA No. 74	LP: Shoestring SS-114
	Sister Kate	Voice of America VOA No. 74	LP: Shoestring SS-114
	Tin Roof Blues	Voice of America VOA No.73	LP: Shoestring SS-114

p-Joe Sullivan, d-George Wettling; c-Bobby Hackett.

No matrix number	Coquette	Voice of America VOA No. 72	LP: Shoestring SS-114
	Body and Soul	Voice of America VOA No. 73	LP: Shoestring SS-104
	I Cover the Waterfront	Voice of America VOA No. 74	LP: Shoestring SS-104

p-Joe Sullivan, d-George Wettling; c-Bobby Hackett; cl-Edmond Hall.

No matrix number	On the Sunny Side of the Street and Sweet Lorraine	Voice of America VOA No. 72	LP: Shoestring SS-114

SIDNEY BECHET BLUE NOTE JAZZMEN   NEW YORK, APRIL 19, 1950

p-Joe Sullivan, d-Slick Jones, b-Pops Foster; c-Wild Bill Davison, tb-Jimmy Archey;
ss-Sidney Bechet.

BN 376	Copenhagen	Blue Note 572	LP: Blue Note BLP 7001, BLP 1203
BN 377	China Boy	Blue Note 573	LP: Blue Note BLP 7001, BLP 1203
BN 378	I Ain't Gonna Give Nobody None of My Jelly Roll		LP: Blue Note BLP 7014, BLP 1204
BN 379	Runnin' Wild		LP: Blue Note BLP 7014, BLP 1204
BN 380	Mandy		LP: Blue Note BLP 7014, BLP 1204
BN 381	Shim-Me-Sha-Wabble	Blue Note 572	LP: Blue Note BLP 7001, BLP 1203

JOE SULLIVAN   NEW YORK (?), c. SUMMER 1950

No matrix number	Honeysuckle Rose	Voice of America VOA No. J-20	LP: Shoestring SS-114

<u>Note</u>: With Eddie Phyfe, drums and band at coda, with, perhaps, "Big Chief" Russell
Moore, trombone and Omer Simeon, clarinet.

WNYC MUSIC FESTIVAL (12th ANNUAL)   **NEW YORK, FEBRUARY 17, 1951**

p-Joe Sullivan, d-Arthur Herbert; t-Red Allen, tb-Sandy Williams; cl-Buster Bailey.
Vocals-Red Allen et al.

No matrix number	Royal Garden Blues	Amalgamated
No matrix number	When the Saints Go Marching In	Amalgamated

WNYC MUSIC FESTIVAL (12th ANNUAL)   **NEW YORK, FEBRUARY 17, 1951**

p-Joe Sullivan, d-Arthur Herbert; t-Johnny Windhurst.

No matrix number	Pennies from Heaven	Amalgamated

WYNC MUSIC FESTIVAL (12th ANNUAL)   **NEW YORK, FEBRUARY 17, 1951**

p-Joe Sullivan.

No matrix number	Honeysuckle Rose	Amalgamated

Note: Joe talks on this record.

WNYC MUSIC FESTIVAL (12th ANNUAL)   **NEW YORK, FEBRUARY 17, 1951**

p-Joe Sullivan, d-Arthur Herbert, t-Bob Kuh, tb-Sandy Williams, cl-Buster Bailey.

No matrix number	St. Louis Blues	Private tape

GEORGE WETTLING'S DIXIELANDERS (JAZZ BAND) NEW YORK, MARCH 2, 1951

p-Joe Sullivan, d-George Wettling, b-Bob Casey, g-Eddie Condon, c-Wild Bill Davison,
tb-Jimmy Archey, cl-Edmond Hall.

CO 45152	After You've Gone	LP: Columbia CL 6189, CL 2559, Harmony HL 7089, Time-Life STL-J27
CO 45153	Collier's Clambake (Buckin' for a Buck)	LP: Same as above
CO 45154	Collier's Climb (Hi Moon!)	LP: Same as above, not in Time-Life
CO 45155	Rose Room	LP: Same as above, not in Time-Life

JOE SULLIVAN   **SAN FRANCISCO, AUGUST 1951**

Little Rock Getaway	LP: Riverside RLP 158

Duplicated on: LP: Riverside 12-202
<u>New Solos by an Old Master</u>

Gin Mill Blues

That's A Plenty

A Room with a View
Sweet Lorraine

Hangover Blues   LP: Time-Life STL-J27

Little Rock Getaway

Honeysuckle Rose

Summertime

Fido's Fantasy

My Little Pride and Joy

I Cover the Waterfront

Farewell to Riverside

<u>Note</u>:   On first three titles only: d-Smoky Stover, b-Dave Lario.

STUYVESANT CASINO ORCHESTRA   NEW YORK, FEBRUARY 15, 1952

p-Joe Sullivan, d-George Wettling; t-Hot Lips Page, tb-Lou McGarity; cl-Pee Wee
Russell.

No matrix number	Sweet Georgia Brown	Amalgamated
	When My Sugar Walks Down the Street	Amalgamated
	Sweet Sue (two versions)	Amalgamated
	St. Louis Blues	Amalgamated
	Some of these Days	Amalgamated

STUYVESANT CASINO ORCHESTRA   NEW YORK, MARCH 7, 1952

p-Joe Sullivan, d-George Wettling; t-Hot Lips Page, tb-Lou McGarity; cl-Pee Wee
Russell.

No matrix number	Honeysuckle Rose	Amalgamated
	Margie	Amalgamated

STUYVESANT CASINO ORCHESTRA   NEW YORK, MARCH 7, 1952

p-Joe Sullivan, d-George Wettling; t-Hot Lips Page, tb-Lou McGarity; cl-Bob Wilber.

No matrix number	Exactly Like You	Amalgamated

STUYVESANT CASINO TRIO   NEW YORK, MARCH 7, 1952

p-Joe Sullivan, d-George Wettling; ts-Bud Freeman

No matrix number	You Took Advantage of Me	Amalgamated[66]

STUYVESANT CASINO ORCHESTRA   **NEW YORK, MARCH 7, 1952**

p-Joe Sullivan, d-George Wettling; c-Jimmy McPartland; cl-Pee Wee Russell, ts-Bud
Freeman.

No matrix number	Sugar	Amalgamated[66]
	China Boy	Amalgamated

STUYVESANT CASINO ORCHESTRA   **NEW YORK, MARCH 21, 1952**

p-Joe Sullivan, d-George Wettling; c-Jimmy McPartland; cl-Pee Wee Russell, ts-Bud
Freeman.

No matrix number	That's A Plenty	Amalgamated
	Tin Roof Blues	Amalgamated
	Sister Kate	Amalgamated

STUYVESANT CASINO ORCHESTRA   **NEW YORK, 1952**

p-Joe Sullivan, d-Zutty Singleton, sb-Artie Shapiro; t-Wingy Manone; cl-Matty Matlock.

No matrix number	Bluin' the Blues	Amalgamated
	Sudan	Amalgamated
	Dixieland Shuffle	Amalgamated
	Isle of Capri	Amalgamated
	Memphis Blues	Amalgamated
	St. James Infirmary	Amalgamated
	Mama's Gone, Goodbye	Amalgamated
	Alexander's Ragtime Band	Amalgamated
	Home on the Range	Amalgamated
	Early Morning Blues	Amalgamated

JOE SULLIVAN TRIO   **NEW YORK, JUNE 23, 1952**

p-Joe Sullivan, d-George Wettling, b-Bob Casey.

CO 47476	What's Your Name?	LP: Epic LG 1003
CO 47477	An Armful of You	LP: Epic LG 1003
CO 47478	Sold Eclipse	LP: Epic LG 1003
CO 47479	Breezin'	LP: Epic LG 1003 LN 3295, Time-Life STL-J27

Note: LG 1003 is entitled, Fats Waller First Editions. LN 3295 is entitled, The Art of
Jazz Piano.

JOE SULLIVAN TRIO   NEW YORK, SEPTEMBER 29, 1952

p-Joe Sullivan, d-George Wettling, b-Walter Page.

CO 48393	Can't We Get Together?	LP: Epic LG 1003, LN 3295
CO 48394	Never Heard of Such Stuff	LP: Epic LG 1003
CO 48395	There'll Come a Time When You'll Need Me	LP: Epic LG 1003, LN 3295, Time-Life STL-J27
CO 48396	If You Can't Be Good Be Careful	LP: Epic LG 1003

See above note.

JOE SULLIVAN   SAN FRANCISCO, AUGUST 1, 1953

Little Rock Getaway   LP: Rarities No. 31

JOE SULLIVAN   SAN FRANCISCO, AUGUST 8, 1953

Honeysuckle Rose   LP: Rarities No. 31

Note: The above solos appear on an LP entitled Lee Collins/Ralph Sutton Jazzola Six, and the performances of both the ensemble and Sullivan took place at the Hangover Club.

MAX KAMINSKY AND HIS WINDY CITY SIX   NEW YORK, 1954

p-Joe Sullivan, d-George Wettling, b-Jack Lesberg; t-Max Kaminsky, tb-Miff Mole; cl-Pee Wee Russell.

No matrix number	Hot Time in the Old Town	LP: Jazztone J 1208, J 1009
	Tavern in the Town	LP: Jazztone J 1208, J 1009
	Del Mar Rag	LP: Jazztone J 1208, J 1009, Time-Life STL-J27
	Stuyvesant Blues	LP: Jazztone J 1208, J 1009, J 1258
	Mix Max	LP: Jazztone J 1208, J 1009
	Lonesome Road	LP: Jazztone J 1208, J 1009, J 1278
	Never Touched Me	LP: Jazztone J 1208, J 1009, J 1278
	Short Ties & Long Ties	LP: Jazztone J 1208, J 1278

At The Jazz Band Ball   LP: Jazztone J 1208,
                                         J 1278

Fidgety Feet   LP: Jazztone 1208

JOE SULLIVAN   **LOS ANGELES, MID-1955**

  Mr. Piano Man   LP: Down Home MG D-2

  Save It Pretty Mama
  Go Back Where You Stayed Last Night
  In the Middle of a Kiss
  Just Strollin'
  Black and Blue
  Ain't Misbehavin'
  Bush Above Powell
  I've Found a New Baby
  Frolicking Fido
  Keepin' Out of Mischief Now

JOE SULLIVAN   **SAN FRANCISCO, JUNE 25, 1955**

No matrix   Honeysuckle Rose   Amalgamated
number

Note: Intermission piano with Teddy Buckner's band.

JOE SULLIVAN   **SAN FRANCISCO, JULY 16, 1955**

No matrix   Chicago   Amalgamated   LP: Aircheck 10
number

Note: Intermission piano with Teddy Buckner's band.

JOE SULLIVAN   **SAN FRANCISCO, JULY 23, 1955**

No matrix   I Found a New Baby   Amalgamated
number

Note: Intermission piano with Teddy Buckner's band.

JOE SULLIVAN   **SAN FRANCISCO, AUGUST 6, 1955**

No matrix   Ain't Misbehavin'   Amalgamated   LP:Aircheck 10
number

JOE SULLIVAN   SAN FRANCISCO, AUGUST 20, 1955

No matrix   On the Sunny Side of the   Amalgamated
number   Street

<u>Note</u>: Intermission piano with Teddy Buckner's band.

JOE SULLIVAN   SAN FRANCISCO, SEPTEMBER 3, 1955

No matrix   Exactly Like You   Amalgamated
number

<u>Note</u>: Intermission piano with Teddy Buckner's band.

JOE SULLIVAN AND HIS BAND   SAN FRANCISCO, SEPTEMBER 2, 1961

p-Joe Sullivan, d-Bob Osiban, b-Pete Allen; t-Byron Berry, tb-Bob Mielke; cl-Vince
Cattolica.

Fidgety Feet (incomplete)

Baby, Won't You Please Come Home?

You're Driving Me Crazy

Squeeze Me

That's A Plenty

Wolverine Blues

Sweet Lorraine

Love Is Just Around the Corner

Black and Blue

Jazz Me Blues

Chicago

Clarinet Marmalade

A Closer Walk With Thee

Basin Street Blues

Little Rock Getaway

Do You Know What It Means to Miss New Orleans?

Muskrat Ramble

Shim-Me-Sha-Wabble

St. James Infirmary

Sunday

St. Louis Blues

I Can't Get Started

Shine

Note: Recorded on tape by Richard B. Hadlock at On the Levee.

EDDIE CONDON AND OTHERS   **NEW YORK, OCTOBER 30 & 31, 1961**

p-Joe Sullivan, d-Gene Krupa, b-Bob Haggart, g-Eddie Condon; c-Jimmy McPartland, tb-Jack Teagarden; cl-Pee Wee Russell, ts-Bud Freeman.

61-V6-168	Logan Square (voc-Jack Teagarden)	LP: Verve V-8441
	Chicago That Toddling Town	
	After You've Gone (voc-Jack Teagarden)	
	China Boy	
	In the Land of Jazz (vocal trio-Lil Armstrong,	
	Blossom Seeley, Jack Teagarden)	
61-V6-169	Sugar (voc-Jimmy McPartland)	LP: Verve V-8441
	Original Boogie (piano solo-Lil Armstrong)	
	Nobody's Sweetheart	
	Original Rag (piano solo-Lil Armstrong)	
	Wolverine Blues	
	Chicago That Toddling Town (vocal trio-Lil Armstrong	
	Blossom Seeley, Jack Teagarden)	

Note: This record features selections from the NBC Television Series, "America's Music."

JOE SULLIVAN AND HIS BAND   **SAN FRANCISCO, DECEMBER 30, 1961**

p-Joe Sullivan, d-Bob Osibin, b-Walter Roberts; t-Byron Berry, tb-Bob Mielkes; cl-Vince Cattolica.

Shim-Me-Sha-Wabble

High Society

Note: Recorded on tape at the Club Hangover

JOE SULLIVAN   **SAN FRANCISO, APRIL 29, 1963**

I Got It Bad	LP: Pumpkin 112
My Little Pride and Joy	LP: Pumpkin 112
Just Strollin'	LP: Pumpkin 112
Mood Indigo	
What's New?	
Improvisation and Blues	

Just Friends

Liza (Condon composition)   LP: Time-Life STL-J27

My Little Pride and Joy, #2

Forevermore

Note: Recorded on tape by Richard B. Hadlock at the Blackhawk Club.

JACK TEAGARDEN ALL STARS   MONTEREY, CALIFORNIA, SEPTEMBER 20, 1963

p-Joe Sullivan, d-Nick Ceroli, Jimmy Bond; t-Charlie Teagarden, tb & voc-Jack
Teagarden; cl-Pee Wee Russell, bars-Gerry Mulligan, ts (last two sides)-Sleepy
Matsumoto.

Struttin' with Some Barbecue

St. James Infirmary (vocal-J. Teagarden)

I Found a New Baby

New Blues   LP: IAJRC 28

Basin Street Blues (vocal-J. Teagarden)

Sweet Georgia Brown

Blues

Note: Private recording, Sixth Annual Monterey Jazz Festival.

JACK TEAGARDEN ALL STARS   MONTEREY, SEPTEMBER 21, 1963

p-Joe Sullivan, d-Jimmy Bond, Nick Ceroli; t-Charlie Teagarden, tb-Jack Teagarden;
cl-Pee Wee Russell.

Indiana

Casanova's Lament (vocal-J. Teagarden)   LP: Giants of Jazz
                                           GOJ-1026

Note: Private recording, Sixth Annual Monterey Jazz Festival.

JOE SULLIVAN   SAN FRANCISCO, SEPTEMBER 29, 1963

I Found a New Baby   LP: Pumpkin 112

Someday Sweetheart   LP: Pumpkin 112

Wrap Your Troubles in Dreams   LP: Pumpkin 112

Keepin' Out of Mischief Now

Memories of You

I Found a New Baby (another version)

I Got It Bad

Sweet Lorraine

At the Jazz Band Ball

In the Middle of a Kiss (Sullivan)

Basin Street Blues (some of the beginning missing)

Riverboat Shuffle

JOE SULLIVAN   **SAN FRANCISCO, c. 1962-63**

Blues, slow

Blues, fast

Forevermore

Washboard Blues

Original composition

Note: Recorded on tape by Richard B. Hadlock.

JOE SULLIVAN   **SAN FRANCISCO, SEPTEMBER 29, 1963**

Squeeze Me

That's A Plenty

Liza (Condon composition)

Lazy River

Little Rock Getaway

Memories of You

Aunt Hagar's Blues

Note: Recorded on tape by Richard B. Hadlock at the Trident.

JOE SULLIVAN   **SAN FRANCISCO, NOVEMBER 5, 1963**

Blues for McCoys   LP: Pumpkin 112

Honeysuckle Rose

Lady Be Good

Gin Mill Blues

On the Sunny Side of the Street

That's A Plenty

I'm Coming, Virginia

Now That You're Gone

Fidgety Feet

A Room With a View

What Is There to Say?

Begin the Beguine

Liza (Condon composition--incomplete)

Someone to Watch Over Me

China Boy

I've Got the World on a String

Sugar

<u>Note</u>: Recorded on tape by Richard B. Hadlock at the Trident.

JOE SULLIVAN   **SAN FRANCISCO, NOVEMBER 5(?), 1963**

Ain't Misbehavin'   LP: Pumpkin 112

St. Louis Blues   LP: Pumpkin 112

Honeysuckle Rose

Washboard Blues

My Little Pride and Joy

Sister Kate

April in Paris medley

Maple Leaf Rag

Mama Lowdown Blues

I Found a New Baby

Shine

There'll Be Some Changes Made

Save It Pretty Mama

St. Louis Blues

You Go To My Head

Where or When

Georgia on My Mind

<u>Note</u>: Recorded on tape by Richard B. Hadlock at the Trident.

JOE SULLIVAN   **SAN FRANCISCO, NOVEMBER 11, 1963**

Keepin' Out of Mischief Now   LP: Pumpkin 112

I'm Gonna Stomp Mr. Henry Lee   LP: Pumpkin 112

Alexander's Ragtime Band

I Got It Bad

Liza (Condon composition)

Loudmouth Blonde Blues

One Morning in May

Yesterdays

I Can't Get Started

I Didn't Know What Time It Was

Alone Together

Little Rock Getaway

What It There To Say?

Washboard Blues

Someday Sweetheart

Handful of Keys

Liza (Gershwin)

DICK HADLOCK TRIO   SAN FRANCISCO, DECEMBER 31, 1964

p-Joe Sullivan, d-Bob Osibin; ss-Dick Hadlock.

Big Butter and Egg Man

Careless Love

You Took Advantage of Me

I Found a New Baby

Riverboat Shuffle

Embraceable You

Peg O' My Heart/Out of Nowhere

Rose of Washington Square

Someday Sweetheart

Struttin' with Some Barbecue

Indiana

St. Louis Blues

Body and Soul

Medley: I'm Getting Sentimental Over You, Time on My Hands,
   When It's Sleepytime Down South, Moonglow, My Silent Love

Lady Be Good (incomplete)

Note: Recorded on tape at Apostleship of the Sea (Catholic Rescue Mission for Homeless Seamen).

Notes

1. Anonymous, "Joe Sullivan Stirs Breeze in Pittsburgh," *Down Beat* (November 3, 1948).
2. jac, "Spanier, Sullivan Working Together Again at Jazz Ltd.," *Down Beat* (May 20, 1949).
3. Anonymous, "New Jazz Concerts," *Down Beat* (November 24, 1950).
4. John S. Wilson, "Sullivan Piano Shines at N.Y. Dixieland Bash," *Down Beat* (April 21, 1950).
5. Ralph J. Gleason, "Frisco Ops Wondering—Who's Got Joe Sullivan?", *Down Beat* (August 11, 1950).
6. Anonymous, "Pianists, Not Dance Orks, Are Grabbing Limelight," *Down Beat* (August 11, 1950).
7. Anonymous, "Where the Bands are Playing," *Down Beat* (August 25, 1950).
8. Anonymous, "Where the Bands are Playing," *Down Beat* (October 20, 1950).
9. Autographed photograph in the possession of Joe Sullivan's nephew, Daniel O'Sullivan. The date is plainly inscribed.
10. Hal Holly, "The Hollywood Beat," *Down Beat* (May 4, 1951).
11. Anonymous, "Final Results Down Beat 1951 Band Poll," *Down Beat* (December 28, 1951).
12. Ralph J. Gleason, "Swingin' The Golden Gate," *Down Beat* (October 5, 1951).
13. Printed program, San Quentin Prison, sent with letter, dated April 6, 1982, to the author by Larry L. Quilligan, who also enclosed an excellent photograph of this group in action at the Club Hangover.
14. Ralph J. Gleason, Swingin' The Golden Gate," *Down Beat* (November 30, 1951).
15. Anonymous, "Joe Sullivan Joins Satch," *Down Beat* (January 11, 1952).
16. Ralph J. Gleason, "Swingin' The Golden Gate," *Down Beat* (January 11, 1952).
17. Anonymous, "Strictly Ad Lib," *Down Beat* (May 21, 1952).
18. Don Freeman, "We'll Get Along Without Hines' Ego, Says Armstrong," *Down Beat* (February 22, 1952).
19. Ralph J. Gleason, "Swingin' The Golden Gate," *Down Beat* (February 22, 1952).
20. Leonard Feather, "The Blindfold Test," *Down Beat* (April 18, 1952). It is to be regretted that Marian McPartland limited her appraisal of Joe's solo, which he himself regarded as one of his favorites, to a laconic response perhaps conveying a hint of reproach.
21. George Hoefer, "The Hot Box," *Down Beat* (October 22, 1952).
22. George Hoefer, "The Hot Box," *Down Beat* (March 24, 1954).
23. George Avakian, liner notes to *Fats Waller First Editions,* Epic LG 1003 (1952).
24. Anonymous, "Strictly Ad Lib," *Down Beat* (July 29, 1953).
25. Anonymous, "Strictly Ad Lib," *Down Beat* (August 26, 1953).
26. Anonymous, "Strictly Ad Lib," *Down Beat* (September 9, 1953).
27. Anonymous, "Strictly Ad Lib," *Down Beat* (September 23, 1953).
28. Anonymous, "Strictly Ad Lib," *Down Beat* (October 7, 1953).
29. Anonymous, "Down Beat 1953 Poll," *Down Beat* (December 30, 1953).
30. Eli H. Newberger, "Refinement of Melody and Accompaniment in the Evolution of Swing Piano Style," *Annual Review of Jazz Studies 1* (1982).
31. Richard B. Hadlock, *Joe Sullivan—Notes on the Music,* booklet accompanying Time-Life Giants of Jazz STL-J27 (1982).
32. Letter from [name withheld] to Maria Hail (Joe Sullivan's sister), February 5, 1954.
33. Letter from John T. Baker to the author, July 13, 1981.
34. Anonymous, "Strictly Ad Lib," *Down Beat* (October 6, 1954).
35. George Hoefer, "Caught in the Act," *Down Beat* (September 8, 1954).
36. Anonymous, "Strictly Ad Lib," *Down Beat* (October 20, 1954).
37. George Hoefer, "Caught in the Act," *Down Beat* (January 12, 1955).
38. Anonymous, "Strictly Ad Lib," *Down Beat* (July 25, 1955).

39. *TV Guide* (July 30-August 5, 1955) had both an advertisement and a program listing for drama shown on Thursday evening, August 4:

Advertisement:

LIVE FROM HOLLYWOOD

8:30—9:30   Channel 10 61

CLIMAX!

"One Night Stand"

The true story of how Bob Crosby and his famous Bobcats gave a concert to save the life of their beloved piano player.

[List of actors as shown below in the program listing]

your host
BILL LUNDIGAN

Presented by
CHRYSLER CORPORATION

Program Listing

Bob Crosby stars in "One Night Stand," an original story by Bob Crosby and Gil Rodin, Bob's manager. In 1937, jazz pianist Joe Sullivan, member of Crosby's Bobcats, became ill with tuberculosis. This is the true, behind-the-scenes story of his illness and what his fellow musicians did for him. Six of Crosby's original Bobcats play themselves in tonight's presentation.

Bob Crosby . . . . Himself
Joe Sullivan . . . . John Forsythe
Mrs. Sullivan . . . . Cloris Leachman
Gil Rodin . . . . Bob Sweeney
Bob Zurke . . . . Donald Buka
Bobcats . . . . Ray Bauduc, Bobby Haggart, Nappy LaMarr, Matty
Matlock, Eddie Miller, Joe Venuti

40. Emge, "TV Reunites Crosby Ork for 'Joe Sullivan Story,'" *Down Beat* (September 7, 1955).
41. Anonymous, liner notes to *Mr. Piano Man,* Down Home MG D-2 (Mid-1955).
42. Anonymous, "Strictly Ad Lib," *Down Beat* (October 19, 1955).
43. Ralph J. Gleason, "Strictly Ad Lib," *Down Beat* (April 4, 1956).
44. Anonymous, "Strictly Ad Lib," *Down Beat* (June 13, 1956).
45. Anonymous, "Strictly Ad Lib," *Down Beat* (October 17, 1956).
46. Whitney Balliett, *Dinosaurs in the Morning* (Philadelphia and New York: J.B. Lippincott, 1962).
47. John W. Norris, "Chicago and All That Jazz," *Coda* (December 1961).
48. Richard B. Hadlock, "The Return of Joe Sullivan," *Down Beat* (January 2, 1964).
49. These and the other tape recordings made by Richard Hadlock and listed in the discography are now owned by Robert Hilbert, proprietor of Pumpkin Productions, Inc., P.O. Box 7963 (Ludlum Branch), Miami, Florida 33155. Hilbert has (as of October 1983) issued one LP of this Sullivan bonanza and, depending on consumer response, may plan further releases. The jazz community must be forever grateful to enterprising spirits like Robert Hilbert, Bozy White, and Jerry Valburn, who make evanescent material available at considerable expense to themselves in time, effort, and money and with little assurance of any pecuniary reward commensurate with their unique service.
50. Letter from Joe Sullivan to Glen Kilner, April 23, 1962.
51. Letter from John L. Fell to the author, November 23, 1976.
52. Letter from Joe Sullivan to Jack Stine, March 26, 1971.
53. Ralph Gleason, "A Sullivan Postscript," *Jazz & Blues* (October 1973).
54. Richard P. Hadlock, "The Return of Joe Sullivan," *Down Beat* (January 2, 1964).
55. Ken Gallacher, "Joe Sullivan: A Study in Neglect," *Jazz Journal* (April 1967).
56. Anonymous, "Final Bar," *Down Beat* (November 1971).

57. Richard Hadlock, "Joe Sullivan: The Last Days," *Jazz & Blues* (June 1973).
58. Interview with Daniel R. O'Sullivan (Joe's nephew), Stamford, Connecticut (June 5, 1977).
59. Postcard from Joe Sullivan to James D. Shacter (November 14, 1970).
60. Letter from Joe Sullivan to William Cleland (March 4, 1971).
61. Letter from Joe Sullivan to his sister, Maria Hail (April 20, 1971).
62. Letter from Ray Skjelbred to the author (March 18, 1976).
63. Roy Fisher, *Poems 1955-1980* (Oxford and New York: Oxford University Press, 1980); also in Fisher, *The Thing About Joe Sullivan/Poems 1971-1977* (Manchester: Carcanet New Press, 1978).
64. Len Guttridge, "You Have to Drink, Sleep, Live and Love Jazz, Says Joe Sullivan," *Melody Maker* (August 18, 1956). This article, which includes an interview with the articulate pianist, describes an event on a hot summer Sunday afternoon in 1954, when Sullivan played for an audience of aficionados in a club near Washington usually devoted to the gryrations of strippers.
65. All recordings identified as "Amalgamated" were once available from an organization known as Amalgamated Records, which operated out of a post office box number in New York City. One set of these rare disks exists in the Sullivan collection of the late William Cleland. This firm may have functioned in a gray area, but, like other such operations, it provided serious collectors with materials which the more commercially oriented industry has often neglected.
66. Jim Gordon, in a letter of November 14, 1976, to the author, assigns the date of March 3, 1952, to the recordings of "You Took Advantage of Me," "Sugar," and "China Boy." He comments: "Very disappointing & I think Joe had a snoot full." Perhaps the same situation obtains in the 1954 Jazztone session—but the precedent had perhaps been set as far back as 1929 when the famous recording of "Knocking a Jug" was made. On that occasion, the other number attempted, "I'm Gonna Stomp Mr. Henry Lee," was rejected.

A Method for the Computer-Aided Analysis of Jazz Melody in the Small Dimensions

J. Kent Williams

In view of numerous recent applications of computers in musicological research,[1] it would appear that scholars of jazz music could benefit from the development of methodologies and software specifically suited to their needs. One area of nearly universal interest among analytically oriented critics is the structure and style of jazz melody. Studies in this domain frequently involve the comparison on certain objective criteria of melodic lines improvised or composed by a number of musicians. The methodology described in this article was originally developed as part of a larger study of this type, a multidimensional analysis of the thematic repertory of the bebop era.[2] Since the completion of that work, the set of programs described herein has been refined and expanded to incorporate a more appropriate scheme of pitch representation and to accept a broader range of musical data.[3]

One reason for asserting the utility of computer-aided techniques to jazz studies is the relatively homogeneous nature of jazz, especially prior to about 1960. Nearly all of this music shares certain gross characteristics—quadruple meter, standard formal types, harmonic formulae, melodic motives, and voice leading procedures. With the aid of a computer, it is possible to perform a wide range of analytical tasks that are tedious and time-consuming when done by hand. One can consider gross characteristics as control variables and move on to a higher level of analysis of more subtle features within a given analytic category.

In general, three types of musical analysis are possible with the computer. A program or set of programs might utilize all three at various stages. They are:

1. Pattern matching—the testing of data for specific characteristics. A match is successful when these characteristics are found.
2. Sorting—the ranking of data according to a predefined scale (usually alphabetical or numerical order).
3. Calculating—the performance of a wide range of arithmetical and mathematical computations.

Most computer centers have numerous calculating and sorting programs available for use with data which satisfy certain characteristics. Pattern-matching programs, however,

J. Kent Williams teaches music theory, music literature, and jazz studies in the School of Music of the University of North Carolina at Greensboro.

are usually much more specific and demand fundamental analytical decisions. Although a few generalized analysis programs which perform relatively simple music-analytic tasks (i.e., "simple" in *musical* terms) have been developed, it may be necessary to develop one's own if the data is too specialized or if previously developed programs will not provide the answers one is seeking.

After reviewing several studies of jazz melody and various musical analysis programs, I became convinced that a set of computer programs was needed to facilitate the analysis of jazz melody. The programs I have developed are intended primarily for interopus analysis of a large body of music. Several studies of this type have been made recently; two dealt with the music of Charlie Parker.[5]

Both Owens and Koch were concerned with identifying specific melodic devices (motives, scale degrees, scale formations) and generalizing about Parker's habits in specific musical contexts. After transcribing approximately 250 of Parker's nearly 900 known recordings, Owens classified the mature-period solos by key and, within each key group, by harmonic model. He then identified frequently used motives, noted their harmonic context, and compiled motivic catalogs for each subgroup of solos. The various catalogs were compared to demonstrate the effect of various contexts (key, mode, harmonic model) on the melody. Whereas Owens apparently began by identifying motives, Koch seems to have looked first for specific harmonic progressions and chord types and then drew conclusions about the treatment of each. However, there is some discussion of other aspects (e.g., the lowered sixth scale degree, substitute chords, and rhythmic figures).

It is obvious that both studies involved a considerable amount of searching, sorting, and calculating—tasks which a computer can perform with incredible speed and precision when given the proper instructions. The development of a set of programs which will yield output containing answers to substantive questions about musical structure and style is the analyst-programmer's responsibility. It is hoped that the set of programs described below will be capable of providing such information to the students of jazz melody.

Encoding and Proofreading of Data

The first task in any computer-aided analysis project is the encoding of the musical notation. Several languages have been developed for this purpose and their relative merits have been discussed in the literature.[6] The language chosen for this study is MUSTRAN which was developed by Jerome Wenker.[7] It seems best suited for jazz studies because it was developed by an ethnomusicologist and offers a wide variety of symbols used in the transcription of ethnic musics, in addition to those of Western art music. MUSTRAN is extensively supported by hardware and software for encoding, proofreading, transcription, and analysis at the Wrubel Computing Center of Indiana University at Bloomington.

Before it was encoded, a theme was parsed into phrases and/or subphrases. This was done to limit the length of the character strings in the preliminary analysis programs and to help avoid the matching of invalid melodic figures (i.e., those formed by the last notes of one phrase and the first notes of the next) in the pattern-matching program.

The next step was the proofreading of the data. This was done in several ways. The first was the visual comparison of hard copies of the encoded data with the musical score. Second, a program was written to check the data for syntactic accuracy. Although it was helpful in further refining the data, the program could not detect *musical* errors. Pitches could be incorrect in terms of pitch-class or register, durations could be wrong, ties omitted, etc., and the data could still be syntactically correct. Therefore, another program was developed to compare the computer attack-point of the final note with that specified by the encoder. This made it possible to locate some errors in the duration of notes. Remaining errors were detected by the careful proofreading of the output from the pattern-matching program RPAT. Example 1 shows a phrase and the corresponding MUSTRAN code with an explanation of the various data fields.

Preliminary Analysis

The actual processing of data begins with the program REFORM which reformats the data in fixed fields for more efficient processing at later stages. Output from REFORM is fed as input to PRELIM which computes four-character strings representing the melodic line of the phrase. The first string, the "note string," represents pitches by their ordinal position on the piano keyboard (e.g., middle C equals 48, G a perfect fifth above equals

Ex. 1. Specimen phrase and corresponding MUSTRAN code with key to data fields

```
Initial data

CBJOYS32 0,2.5-2,2.5 1.1 F:1/1/27-57

a b   c d     e     f  g h
```

```
Melody and code
```

```
        8C,8F,8C+,/,2C+J,8C+J,8A,3(,16G,16A,16G,3),8F,/,4G,8A,
```

```
Key to data fields
```

a	composer's initials (Clifford Brown)	
b	abbreviation of title (Joyspring)	
c	harmonic model (32-measure, unknown)	
d	location of first note (measure no., attack point)	
e	location of last note (measure no., attack point)	
f	ordinal number of phrase	
g	tonic key and mode (F major)	
h	harmony (1/1/27-57 = I/I/ii7-V7)	

55, etc.). This string is then used to compute a representation of the pitches in terms of their scale-degree function (using integer notation mod_{12} where tonic equals 0, dominant equals 7, etc.) and a string which records the sequence of melodic intervals in increments of a semitone (e.g., ascending major third equals +04, descending minor seventh equals −10).

The precise location of the onset of each pitch is computed by the next stage of PRE-LIM, which uses the measure number and attack-point of the first note and the MUS-TRAN code to compute the measure number and attack-point of every note in the phrase. Measures are numbered from the first full measure of the theme; notes in the measure preceding measure one are assigned measure number zero. Attack-points are computed in terms of their distance in quarter-note beats from the beginning of the measure. Thus, a note beginning on the first beat is assigned an attack-point of 0.0; one which begins on the second half of two is assigned 1.5. The program increments the measure number and resets the attack point to 0.0 each time a bar line is encountered in the code. This insures that any mistakes in duration will not be carried over into the next measure. Example 2 shows the result of processing the specimen phrase through PRELIM. The various strings are labeled to facilitate identification.

Output from PRELIM is fed to REDUX (reduction program) for the next stage of preliminary analysis. REDUX locates complete, unaccented neighbor-tone figures and reduces them to their primary note by deleting the data for the second and third notes of

**Ex. 2. Specimen phrase after processing by preliminary
analysis program PRELIM**

```
Initial data ---------------------------------- Note string

CBJOYS32  0,2.5 - 2,1.5  1.1        F:1/1/27-57 48,53,60,


--------------------- Pitch-class string ----------------

57,55,57,55,53,55,57,; 7-3, 0-4, 7-4, 4-4, 2-4, 4-4, 2-4,


-------------- Interval string -------------------- Measure

0-4, 2-4, 4-4,;+05,+07,-03,-02,+02,-02,-02,+02,+02,; 0-2.5 ,


no.-attack-point string ----------------------------------

  0-3.0 , 0-3.5 , 1-2.5 , 1-3.0 , 1-3.16, 1-3.33, 1-3.5 ,


  ----------------

  2-0.0 , 2-1.5 ,
```

Ex. 3. Neighbor-tone figures reduced at various stages of reduction program REDUX

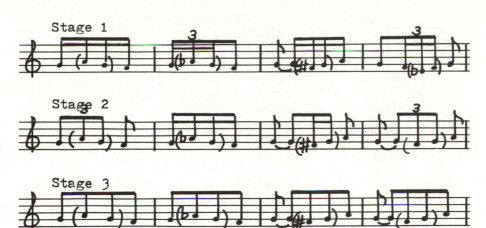

the figure from the appropriate pitch and attack-point strings. The user is able to specify the stages of reduction desired. These stages correspond to the total duration of the neighbor-tone figure and are illustrated in Example 3. The notes which REDUX deletes are enclosed in parentheses.

The rationale for the inclusion of REDUX in the analysis procedure is that comparison of melodic figures is facilitated when the embellishments have been removed. Bebop melodies contain numerous upper neighbor-tone figures. These inverted mordents or "jazz turns" nearly always begin on a strong beat or the strong part of a beat, usually at the beginning of a descending passage. The reduction of the figures to their primary note helps to clarify the basic direction of the melody and to increase the precision of subsequent analysis. Example 4 shows output from REDUX using the specimen phrase.

Searching and Sorting

The output from REDUX may be utilized in various ways. The option chosen here is a combination of the various types of analysis available with a computer (searching, sorting, and calculating) and is intended to serve as a means of classifying the small-dimension melodic gestures of jazz melody. This stage of the analytical process begins with the use of the program RPAT (Rhythmic PATterns), which searches the data for a specific rhythmic pattern and, upon finding a match for that pattern, extracts the corresponding pitch data along with the initial identifying data (title, composer, harmonic model, and the location of the phrase). A record of the match is then printed in fixed-field format. After it is proofread and errors corrected, the list is sorted in a musically significant manner. The output from the sort is then analyzed using various statistical programs and formatted for printing. The printed output serves as a motivic concordance to the themes which are the subject of this study. It enables one to evaluate each rhythm pattern in terms of its association with any one or a combination of the following variables:

Ex. 4. Specimen phrase after processing by program REDUX

```
Initial data ----------------------------------------

CBJOYS32   0,2.5 - 2,2.5    1.1           F:1/1/27-57


Note string ------------ Pitch-class string ---------

48,53,60,57,55,53,55,57,;  7-3, 0-4, 7-4, 4-4, 2-4, 0-4,


--------- Interval string ------------ Measure no. -

2-4, 4-4,;+05,+07,-03,-02,-02,+02,+02,;  0-2.5 , 0-3.0 ,


attack-point string ----------------------------

  0-3.5 , 1-2.5 , 1-3.0 , 1-3.5 , 2-0.0 , 2-1.5 ,
```

frequency of occurrence, melodic contour, composer, harmonic model, position in the phrase, and cumulative interval.

The above description is general and intended to furnish the reader with an overview of the entire analytical process. A more detailed description of the rationale and method for the searching and sorting stage follows. An excerpt from the concordance can be found in Example 8.

The primary basis for the organization of the concordance is shown in Table 1. Here rhythmic patterns which are common in bebop melody are classified. The rows group patterns by the number of notes and the metric position of the interior note(s) of the pattern. The columns group the patterns by the metric position of the first and last notes. Thus, patterns of a given row or column are conceptually equivalent. Those which share the same column begin and end on equivalent attack points within the measure, but differ in terms of their internal attack points. Those sharing the same row are alike in terms of their internal attack points, but differ in terms of the metric position of the first and/or last notes. All of the patterns except those listed as "Additional Patterns" begin and end on a strong beat or a syncopated anticipation of a strong beat. Within a given row, one pattern can be changed into another by shifting the attack point of the first and/or last notes one-half beat.[8]

The "additional patterns" at the end of the list are related to specific patterns above. 1SA1, 1SA2, and 1SA3[9] all begin with 1SA, but have another note added. 2SW is merely 2SS or 2SA with the last note omitted. 6SW is related in the same manner to 6SS and 6SA. 9SU and 9AU are merely 9SS and 9AS respectively, but with an extra note at the end. This two eighth-note figure is called 1SU in the table. 13US can be derived from 12SS by reversing the position of the triplet group and the two eighth notes. Since it occurs both with and without the initial eighth note on a strong beat, it was decided to omit the initial

Table 1. Classification of Rhythmic Patterns

Table 1 (continued)

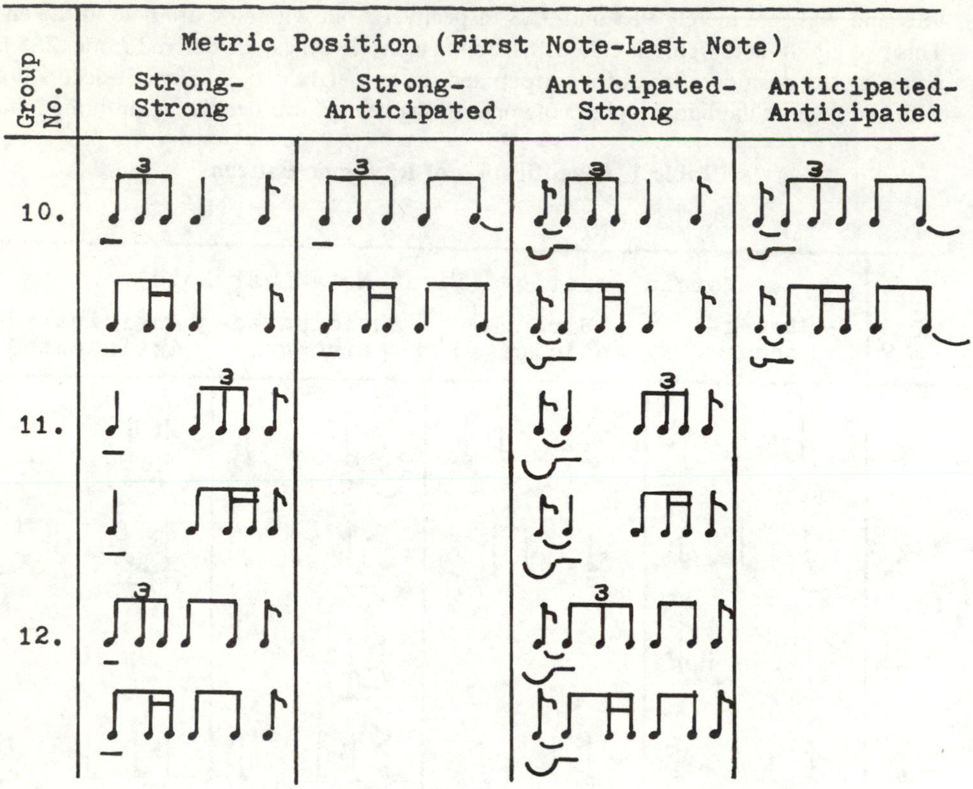

Additional Patterns

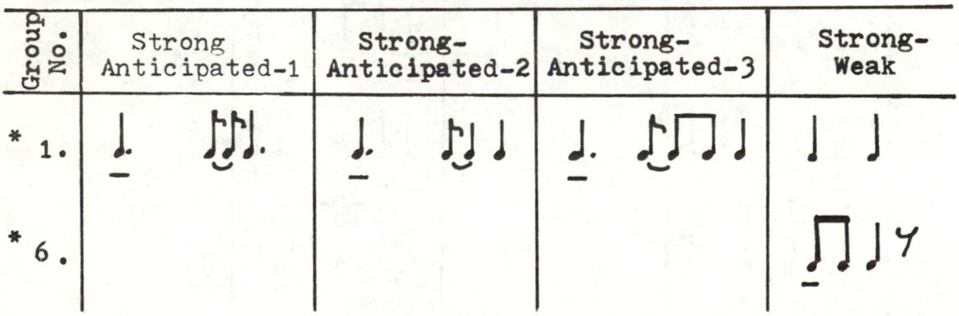

Table 1 (continued)

Additional Patterns (continued)

Group No.	Strong-Upbeat	Anticipated-Upbeat	Upbeat-Strong	Upbeat-Anticipated
*1.	♫ 𝄽 ♪			
*9X.	♫♫ ♫♪	♫♫ ♫♪		
13.				♪ ♫♫♪

*The group numbers which are marked with an asterisk duplicate those assigned to the patterns at the beginning of the table. This is intentional and points up the close relationship of the "additional patterns" to their correspondents in the first group.

eighth in the specification to the computer. This would enable the matching of both variants—those with and those without the initial eighth:

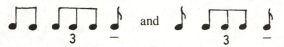

Crucial to an understanding of the searching and pattern-matching process is the idea that, in the computer program RPAT, the rhythmic pattern to be found is defined as a series of attack-points and not as a series of note-values. The attack-point definition has two advantages. First, it permits the matching of any and all rhythmic patterns which are the same in terms of attack-points, but which may differ in terms of note-values. Second, it permits the specification of the metric position of the rhythmic pattern. To illustrate, pattern 7SS was defined as either the attack-point string '0 ,0.5 ,1.5 ,2. ,' or '2. ,2.5 ,3.5 ,0. ,'. Example 5a shows patterns that *would* be matched by RPAT; 5b shows some which *would not* be matched.

The patterns are given in musical notation in Table 1. The notation shown should be regarded as the most frequently used, but not necessarily the only realization of the pattern.[10] The position of the strong beat is shown by the accent mark under one of the notes. A plain accent mark (—) indicates the note falls on the first or third beat of the measure. An unaccent preceding and connected to an accent (‿⌐) indicates a fusing of the syncopated anticipation to the next strong beat.[11]

Ex. 5. Valid and invalid examples of Pattern 7SS

The duration of the final note of the rhythmic patterns as shown in Table 1 is, in some cases, significant. If the last note is longer than an eighth note, the computer matched only those patterns which had a final note-value or note-plus-rest-value at least as long as that shown. In other words, the note following the pattern could not occur before the release of the final note of the pattern. If a tie begins at the last note of the pattern, a note does not occur on the next strong beat. The tie is provided to show that the final note is a syncopated anticipation of the next strong beat.

A run of the computer program RPAT produces a list of records of the matches found. Each record gives the title, composer, and harmonic model of the theme, the location of the phrase which contains the pattern, the location of the pattern, the cumulative interval (pitch interval between the first and last notes) of the pattern, the complete interval sequence, the tonic key and mode, and the scale-degree function (in integer notation mod_{12}) and register of each note. Example 6 shows a passage from Barney Kessel's "Swedish Pastry" containing pattern 4SA. The record of that match is given below the musical notation with the various data fields bracketed and labeled.

Ex. 6. Record of match for Pattern 4SA

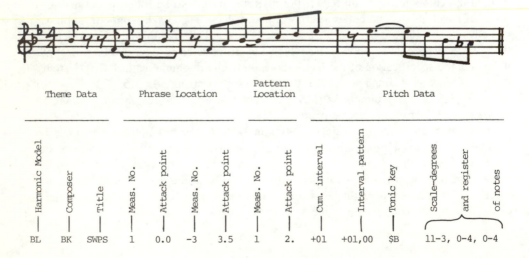

Theme Data			Phrase Location				Pattern Location					Pitch Data		
Harmonic Model	Composer	Title	Meas. No.	Attack point	Meas. No.	Attack point	Meas. No.	Attack point	Cum. interval	Interval pattern	Tonic key	Scale-degrees and register		of notes
BL	BK	SWPS	1	0.0	-3	3.5	1	2.	+01	+01,00	$B	11-3, 0-4, 0-4		

Ex. 7. Pattern 5AS divided between two statements of Pattern 6SA

After a successful run of the program, the list of records is proofread by verifying each in the musical score. Besides checking the accuracy of the list, the proofreading also serves as an additional means of locating errors in the original encoded data. Some of the lists contained records of matches which would probably be ruled invalid by a human analyst since the rhythmic pattern was divided between two more obvious musical motives. This usually occurred in cases where the pattern contained a longer note-value before its final note. The longer note (or combined note-plus-rest) functioned more as a point of closure than as a point of continuity and, as a result, other rhythmic patterns emerged more clearly. For example, pattern 5AS was matched in the first measure of the Parker blues "Au Privave." It is obvious that 5AS occurs coincidentally between two statements of 6SA and the latter is the dominant grouping in this passage (see Example 7). Records of dubious matches such as this were marked by placing an asterisk in column nine, immediately following the title abbreviation.

Once the accuracy of a list is verified and the doubtful records are marked the list is sorted. After considerable experimentation, the following sorting procedure was chosen as the one which yielded the most significant musical results:[12]

1. *Basic melodic contour*—the direction only of each pitch interval, repeated pitches preceding ascending intervals and ascending intervals preceding descending.
2. *Cumulative interval*—the direction and size of the pitch interval between the first and last notes of the pattern, directions ordered the same as above, numbers in ascending order.
3. *Interval pattern*—the direction and size of the pitch intervals, same order as above.
4. *Harmonic model*—as given by the abbreviation in columns 1-2 which is based on the developed classification scheme.
5. *Pattern location*—as given by the measure number and attack-point of the first note of the pattern.

The result of this sorting procedure can be seen in Examples 8 and 9. Example 8 is a list of matches for pattern 2SS. Changes of melodic contour are separated by two extra blank lines. Within a given contour, changes in the value of the cumulative interval from zero to a positive number or from a positive to a negative number are separated by one additional blank line.

Example 9 is a notated realization of the list displayed in Example 8. Numerals above the staff show the ordinal position of the pattern in Example 8. In those cases where the

Ex. 8. Sample list of matches for Pattern 2SS from concordance of motives

```
 1.  32TMWHOK  9,0.0 -11,1.5 10,2.    00; 00, 00,  F: 2-5, 2-5, 2-5,

 2.  CWTDOURD  4,3.0 - 8,1.5  6,0.    00; 00, 00, $A: 0-4, 0-4, 0-4,

 3.  CWTDOURD 12,3.0 -16,1.5 14,0.    00; 00, 00, $A: 0-4, 0-4, 0-4,

 4.  36TMINTR 32,3.5 -35,3.0 34,0.    00; 00, 00, $D: 3-4, 3-4, 3-4,

 5.  LBTDLADY  1,0.5 - 4,0.0  1,2.    00; 00, 00,  C: 7-4, 7-4, 7-4,

 6.  LBTDLADY  5,0.5 - 8,0.0  5,2.    00; 00, 00,  C: 7-4, 7-4, 7-4,

 7.  RSTMLETS  1,0.0 - 4,0.0  1,0.    00; 00, 00, $E:11-3,11-3,11-3,

 8.  RSTMLETS  1,0.0 - 4,0.0  2,0.    00; 00, 00, $E: 0-4, 0-4, 0-4,


 9.  RRXGDXDK 18,3.5 -19,3.5 19,0.   +02; 00,+02, $B: 9-3, 9-3,11-3,

10.  RRDBWEE   5,0.0 - 7,3.0  5,0.   +04; 00,+04, $B: 0-3, 0-3, 4-3,

11.  RRDBWEE   5,0.0 - 7,3.0  7,0.   +04; 00,+04, $B: 7-3, 7-3,11-3,


12.  BLMDSOLR  1,1.5 - 3,3.5  3,0.   -01; 00,-01, CM:10-4,10-4, 9-4,

13.  BLMDSOLR  5,1.5 - 7,3.5  7,0.   -01; 00,-01, CM: 8-4, 8-4, 7-4,

14.  32CBTICA  0,3.5 - 2,1.5  1,2.   -02; 00,-02, $B:11-3,11-3, 9-3,

15.  RRCPCHBU  2,0.0 - 4,0.0  2,2.   -02; 00,-02,  F: 4-4, 4-4, 2-4,

16.  EXTMIMNU  4,3.5 - 8,0.0  6,2.   -04; 00,-04,  F: 4-4, 4-4, 0-4,

17.  BLXGLONG* 8,3.5 -10,2.0  9,2.   -06; 00,-06, $B: 7-4, 7-4, 1-4,


18.  HTSGATAS 16,2.5 -19,3.5 17,0.   +10;+10, 00, AM:10-3, 8-4, 8-4,

19.  LGDBMOVE 17,0.0 -20,1.0 19,0.   +12;+12, 00, $B: 5-3, 5-4, 5-4,


20.  36SRAIRE 32,2.0 -35,1.0 32,2.   +02;+01,+01, FM: 5-4, 6-4, 7-4,

21.  RRMDTHEM  6,2.5 - 8,1.5  7,2.   +02;+01,+01, $B: 5-3, 6-3, 7-3,
```

Ex. 8 (continued)

```
22.  BLDGCHMP  0,3.0 -  3,3.0  1,2.  +03;+01,+02, $A: 3-4, 4-4, 6-4,

23.  BLDGCHMP  4,3.0 -  7,3.0  5,2.  +03;+01,+02, $A: 3-4, 4-4, 6-4,

24.  BLDGCHMP  8,3.0 -11,3.0  9,2.  +03;+01,+02, $A: 3-4, 4-4, 6-4,

25.  HTSGTOOT 17,1.5 -20,2.0 18,2.  +03;+01,+02,  F: 7-4, 8-4,10-4,

26.  RSTMLETS  1,0.0 -  4,0.0  3,0.  +03;+01,+02, $E: 4-4, 5-4, 7-4,

27.  32GWGDCH  1,0.0 -  4,1.5  3,0.  +03;+02,+01, $A: 7-3, 9-3,10-3,

28.  AGJJCOFF  1,0.0 -  4,1.5  2,2.  +03;+02,+01,  F: 9-4,11-4, 0-5,

29.  RSCPYARD  1,0.5 -  3,3.5  1,2.  +03;+02,+01,  C: 7-4, 9-4,10-4,

30.  RSTMLETS  1,0.0 -  4,0.0  3,2.  +03;+02,+01, $E: 7-4, 9-4,10-4,

31.  RSTMLETS  1,0.0 -  4,0.0  2,2.  +04;+02,+02, $E: 0-4, 2-4, 4-4,

32.  LGDBMOVE  5,0.0 -  8,1.0  7,0.  +08;+03,+05, $B: 4-3, 7-3, 0-4,


33.  BLHMSKNK  9,0.0 -12,1.0 11,0.   00;+01,-01,  F:11-3, 0-4,11-3,

34.  BSTMINWB 17,0.0 -19,0.0 18,0.   00;+02,-02, $A: 0-4, 2-4, 0-4,


35.  SDTDTADD  5,3.5 -  8,2.5  7,2.  +01;+03,-02, $D: 1-4, 4-4, 2-4,

36.  32FNBPRN  4,3.0 -  7,0.0  5,0.  +02;+03,-01,  F: 7-4,10-4, 9-4,

37.  32TMOFMI 17,0.0 -24,1.0 20,0.  +02;+04,-02, GM: 9-3, 1-4,11-3,

38.  32FNBPRN  4,3.0 -  7,0.0  6,0.  +05;+06,-01,  F: 2-4, 8-4, 7-4,

39.  32CBALLW  3,1.5 -  4,2.5  4,0.  +07;+10,-03,  F:11-3, 9-4, 6-4,

40.  AGJJCOFF  9,0.5 -12,1.5  9,2.  +08;+09,-01,  F: 3-4, 0-5,11-4,


41.  RRHJOPUS 12,3.5 -15,3.5 14,0.  -01;+10,-11, $B: 6-3, 4-4, 5-3,


42.  HSTDOURD 16,3.5 -20,1.5 19,2.  -02;-02, 00, $A: 2-4, 0-4, 0-4,

43.  BLXGINDX  1,0.0 -  4,1.0  3,0.  -04;-04, 00, $B: 4-4, 0-4, 0-4,
```

Ex. 8 (continued)

```
44.  BLXGINDX  5,0.0 - 8,1.0  7,0.  -04;-04, 00, $B: 4-4, 0-4, 0-4,

45.  BLXGINDX  9,0.0 -12,1.0 11,0.  -04;-04, 00, $B: 4-4, 0-4, 0-4,

46.  34SGCOMX 20,0.5 -24,1.5 23,0.   00;-01,+01, $B: 5-4, 4-4, 5-4,

47.  LHCBTICA 23,0.0 -24,1.5 23,2.   00;-01,+01, $B: 2-3, 1-3, 2-3,

48.  32FNBPRN  0,2.0 - 3,3.5  2,2.   00;-02,+02,  F: 2-4, 0-4, 2-4,

49.  32BPTEFU 16,3.0 -24,0.0 18,2.   00;-02,+02, DM: 7-4, 5-4, 7-4,

50.  BLWGTWST  4,3.0 - 9,1.5  5,2.   00;-02,+02, $B:11-3, 9-3,11-3,

51.  LGXGDXRF  5,0.0 - 7,1.5  5,0.   00;-02,+02,  G: 7-4, 5-4, 7-4,

52.  BLCBSAND  8,0.5 -10,3.5 10,0.   00;-03,+03, $E:10-3, 7-3,10-3,

53.  LGXGDXRF  1,0.0 - 3,1.5  1,0.   00;-03,+03,  G: 7-4, 4-4, 7-4,

54.  LGXGDXRF  1,0.0 - 3,1.5  2,2.   00;-04,+04,  G: 7-4, 3-4, 7-4,

55.  RRXGDXDI  1,0.0 - 4,1.5  2,0.   00;-04,+04, $D: 0-5, 8-4, 0-5,

56.  RRXGDXDI  5,0.0 - 8,1.5  6,0.   00;-04,+04, $D: 0-5, 8-4, 0-5,

57.  LGDBMOVE  1,0.0 - 4,3.0  1,0.   00;-05,+05, $B: 0-4, 7-3, 0-4,

58.  RRXGDXDI  1,0.0 - 4,1.5  1,2.   00;-05,+05, $D: 0-5, 7-4, 0-5,

59.  RRXGDXDI  1,0.0 - 4,1.5  3,2.   00;-05,+05, $D: 0-5, 7-4, 0-5,

60.  RRXGDXDI  5,0.0 - 8,1.5  5,2.   00;-05,+05, $D: 0-5, 7-4, 0-5,

61.  RRFNEBPB 17,0.0 -18,3.0 17,0.   00;-12,+12, $B: 4-4, 4-3, 4-4,

62.  RRFNEBPB 19,0.0 -20,3.0 19,0.   00;-12,+12, $B: 3-4, 3-3, 3-4,


63.  LBTDLADY  9,0.5 -10,1.5  9,2.  +01;-01,+02,  C: 9-4, 8-4,10-4,

64.  LBTDLADY 11,0.5 -12,1.5 11,2.  +01;-01,+02,  C:10-4, 9-4,11-4,

65.  32TMOFMI  1,0.0 - 3,0.5  1,2.  +01;-02,+03, GM: 9-3, 7-3,10-3,

66.  32BPTEFU 16,3.0 -24,0.0 20,2.  +01;-02,+03, DM: 2-4, 0-4, 3-4,
```

Ex. 8 (continued)

```
67.  RSTMLETS  1,0.0 -  4,0.0  1,2.  +01;-02,+03, $E:11-3, 9-3, 0-4,
68.  AGJJCOFF 13,0.5 -16,1.5 13,2.  +01;-04,+05,  F: 8-4, 4-4, 9-4,
69.  RRGMFIVE  2,3.5 -  4,1.5  3,2.  +01;-04,+05,  C: 4-4, 0-4, 5-4,
70.  BLSSBUBL  1,0.0 -  2,3.5  1,2.  +02;-01,+03, $B: 5-4, 4-4, 7-4,
71.  BLSSBUBL  5,0.0 -  6,3.5  5,2.  +02;-01,+03, $B: 5-4, 4-4, 7-4,
72.  BLSSBUBL  9,0.0 -10,3.5  9,2.  +02;-01,+03, $B: 5-4, 4-4, 7-4,
73.  RRXGDXDK  1,0.0 -  3,1.5  2,2.  +02;-02,+04, $B: 2-4, 0-4, 4-4,
74.  RRGMFIVE  0,3.5 -  2,1.5  1,2.  +02;-03,+05,  C: 7-4, 4-4, 9-4,
75.  RSACFAST  1,0.0 -  3,1.5  2,2.  +02;-03,+05,  C: 7-4, 4-4, 9-4,
76.  RRXGDXDI  5,0.0 -  8,1.5  7,2.  +04;-05,+09, $D: 0-5, 7-4, 4-5,
77.  HSTDSYMP 21,0.0 -24,3.0 23,2.  +07;-01,+08, $B: 9-3, 8-3, 4-4,
78.  SDTDTADD  1,0.0 -  5,1.5  1,0.  +07;-03,+10, $D: 7-4, 4-4, 2-5,

79.  PACPKLAC  1,0.0 -  4,1.5  2,2.  -01;-04,+03, $B: 3-3,11-2, 2-3,
80.  RRDBWEE   3,0.0 -  4,3.0  3,0.  -02;-06,+04, $B:11-3, 5-3, 9-3,
81.  BLWGTWST 10,0.5 -11,2.0 11,0.  -03;-05,+02, $B: 0-4, 7-3, 9-3,
82.  RRHMCRIN 16,2.5 -19,2.0 19,0.  -03;-05,+02,  C: 9-4, 4-4, 6-4,
83.  32TMWHOK 12,2.0 -15,1.5 12,2.  -03;-12,+09,  F: 2-5, 2-4,11-4,
84.  RRHMCRIN  4,3.0 -  6,1.5  5,0.  -05;-06,+01,  C: 0-5, 6-4, 7-4,
85.  RRCPCONS  0,3.0 -  3,2.0  3,0.  -05;-07,+02,  C: 7-4, 0-4, 2-4,

86.  32CBTICA  2,2.5 -  4,1.5  3,2.  -03;-01,-02, $B: 5-3, 4-3, 2-3,
87.  THDRPRAL  0,3.5 -  4,2.5  2,0.  -03;-01,-02, $A: 5-4, 4-4, 2-4,
88.  32HMTURN  9,0.0 -10,3.0  9,0.  -03;-02,-01,  C:11-4, 9-4, 8-4,
```

Ex. 8 (continued)

```
89.   32BPTEFU 16,3.0 -24,0.0 18,0.   -03;-02,-01, DM:10-4, 8-4, 7-4,

90.   32BPTEFU 16,3.0 -24,0.0 20,0.   -03;-02,-01, DM: 5-4, 3-4, 2-4,

91.   LBMDHALF  1,0.5 - 3,2.5  3,0.   -03;-02,-01,  C:10-4, 8-4, 7-4,

92.   LGXGDXRF  5,0.0 - 7,1.5  6,2.   -03;-02,-01,  G: 7-4, 5-4, 4-4,

93.   THDRPRAL  0,3.5 - 4,2.5  2,2.   -03;-02,-01, $A: 2-4, 0-4,11-3,

94.   RRDGOW   18,3.5 -20,1.5 19,2.   -04;-02,-02, $B: 6-4, 4-4, 2-4,

95.   32JLROUG 17,0.  -18,2.0 18,0.   -05;-02,-03,  C: 1-4,11-3, 8-3,

96.   BLCBSAND  8,0.5 -10,3.5  9,2.   -05;-03,-02, $E: 3-4, 0-4,10-3,
```

same interval pattern occurs more than once, only one example was notated. Three types of bar lines are used to delineate the pitch-contour classification scheme. Double bars separate changes of contour, single bars separate a change of the direction of the cumulative interval, and dotted bar lines separate patterns which share the same contour and cumulative interval direction.

In his review of thematic indices, Boody observes that:

> The majority of projects reported here have adopted a sorting algorithm that ignores repeated pitches, ignores rhythm, organizes output according to interval size, and treats intervals without respect to whether they are major, minor, diminished, augmented, or perfect. Though this sorting algorithm has proven very popular, it is not necessarily the best or the only possibility. Two factors make it common in the table: (1) The items mentioned . . . all use the set of programs developed by Lincoln and reported widely. . . . (2) Most of these items and all of the others using this sorting procedure catalog Renaissance music where this particular sort allows location of thematic material that has been borrowed and altered with respect to mode or repetition of pitches. Such a sorting method is ideal for that material. It would not do nearly as well for cataloging music from the eighteenth and nineteenth centuries where specific intervals and repeated notes become much more important.[13]

The sorting procedure utilized in this study does not need to account for rhythm since a given list contains records of only one rhythmic pattern. The sort takes place *within* a given rhythmic pattern, first by melodic contour and then by the harmonic model and the location of the rhythmic pattern within that harmonic model. It would, of course, be possible to add a pattern-identification number to each record and then merge a list with others if one wished to group the patterns at some higher level of analysis.

The three-stage approach to sorting melodic contours permits the classification of homo-rhythmic melodic figures first by their basic shape, then by their cumulative interval, and finally by their specific interval pattern. The procedure is both general and highly specific and, thus, more capable of yielding significant information than the sorting procedure which Boody describes. The new approach also seems more compatible with tradi-

Ex. 9. Notation of representative cases from Example 8

tional, nonautomated approaches to melodic analysis, especially those which emphasize curvilinear aspects.[14]

It is important to point out that the lists of rhythmic patterns which make up the concordance of motives are not mutually exclusive. This is because the searches for patterns one through nine were conducted using data which had been processed through stages one and two of the neighbor-tone reduction program, while patterns ten through thirteen were sought in data which had been processed through only the first stage. Such a policy enabled the matching of a greater number of patterns from groups one through nine. If a passage contained a neighbor-tone figure which would be reduced by stage two of RE-DUX, that figure would be matched twice—once with the neighbor-tone figure and once without. For example, pattern 5SS was found at the beginning of the third measure of Parker's "Donna Lee." A record for this match occurs at item number 149 in the list for pattern 5SS. The computer, on another run, matched pattern 12SS at the same location and the match is recorded as item number 65 on its list. Example 10 shows the passage and the record of each match as it appears in the concordance.

Analysis of the Concordance of Motives

Previous studies of jazz melody have devoted much attention to aspects of harmony. This is understandable since the theory of tonal harmony is more fully developed and more widely accepted than any theory of melody. Analysts of melody are apparently drawn to harmonic concepts because they are available and more familiar than concepts associated with melody. Jazz musicians are especially prone to think of melody in terms

Ex. 10. Records of matches of Patterns 5SS and 12SS at the same location in "Donna Lee"

Pattern 5SS

149. INCPDNLE 1,1.5 - 4,0.5 3,0. -04;-01,-02,-01,
      $A:10-3, 9-3, 7-3, 6-3,

Pattern 12SS

 65. INCPDNLE 1,1.5 - 4,0.5 3,0. -04;+02,-02,-01,-02,-01,
      $A:10-3, 0-4,10-3, 9-3, 7-3, 6-3,

of harmony since, in the process of learning to improvise, they spend countless hours practicing the standard harmonic formulas.

While one cannot deny the importance of harmony to melody in the jazz music of the late 40s and early 50s, it is essential to remember that harmony and melody are musical parameters which are both separate and related. While melody can be thought of as figures drawn in musical space, harmony serves as the ground which throws these figures into greater relief and endows them with more potential for expression. For purposes of analysis, it is sometimes helpful to separate the figure and the ground so that each may be studied in greater detail. One may discover, for example, that essentially the same melodic figure occurs in varied harmonic contexts or, conversely, that a given harmonic context supports a variety of melodic figures.

If one aspect has been emphasized at the expense of the other by analysts of jazz, it has been harmony at the expense of melody. A legacy of this approach is the description of melodies in terms of chord tones and nonchord tones. While the vocabulary used in this type of analysis has certain implications with respect to the linear design of a melodic figure (e.g., "passing-tone" implies unidirectional motion), these terms are, at best, imprecise in this regard. They can provide us with no more than a vague and narrowly focused image of the pitch contour aspect of a melodic line.

A precise description of melodic contour entails specification of both the horizontal and vertical dimensions. The former can be represented as a series of attack-points, the latter as a series of pitch intervals.[15] They can be represented as numerical data, the manipulation and analysis of which are easily done with a digital computer. Perhaps the advent of computer-aided analytical techniques will prompt analysts of melody to devote more attention to melodic contour.

Patterns with more than two notes have a distinctive contour which is a product of their interval succession and their cumulative interval. A three-note pattern such as 1SA1 has two intervals and each of these intervals may take one of three possible directions: up, down, or repeated. For the purpose of this study, these directions will be abbreviated by the letters, U, D, and R. For example, RR will indicate a three-note or two-interval pattern which shows no change of pitch; DU will indicate a descending interval followed by an ascending one. If a pattern contains one or more ascending intervals and one or more descending intervals, it will be necessary to indicate the direction of the cumulative interval, since this property cannot be inferred from the directions of the constituent intervals themselves. To illustrate, a contour of DU could have an interval pattern of -02, $+07$ or -09, $+01$. In the first instance the cumulative interval would be $+02$, but in the second instance it would be -08. Obviously, the shape of these two patterns is markedly different. Therefore, to be more precise, in those cases where the direction of the cumulative interval cannot be inferred from the interval pattern, it will be indicated by an additional R, D, or U following a hyphen. The contour of the first pattern $(-02, +07)$ would be abbreviated DU-U and that of the second pattern $(-09, +01)$ would read DU-D.

The number of possible contours which a rhythmic pattern may assume is a function of the number of possible directions and the number of intervals in the pattern. It has already been noted that there are three possible directions—up, down, and repeated—so the number of contours may be computed by the formula $C = 3^n$, where C represents the number of contours and n the number of intervals. Thus, a three-note pattern would have 3^2 or 9 possible contours, a four-note pattern would have 3^3 or 27, and a five-note pattern would have 3^4 or 81. Each of these figures tells only the number of *basic* contours, that is, the direction of the various intervals which constitute the pattern. They do not tell the direction of the cumulative interval which is crucial for a precise description of contour with those patterns containing at least one ascending and at least one descending interval. Specification of the direction of the cumulative interval adds to the number of possible contours.

The system described above will be used to classify rhythmic patterns having three or more notes according to their pitch contour. The term "motive" will be used to describe a unique association of rhythm and pitch contour. Because it implies no additional restrictions such as further development or rhythmic closure, this definition of the term is broader than that which is frequently stated or implied by other writers.[16]

In the ensuing analysis of rhythmic patterns, tonal considerations will, as a rule, be discussed after contoural ones. The contour-first approach allows one to isolate the various melodic gestures in terms of their pitch contour and then concentrate on similarities and differences in terms of their tonal attributes.

The final stage of the method under discussion is the analysis of the concordance of motives using packaged statistical programs. This enables one to characterize the style of this (or any other) body of melody in terms of varying degrees of association between the following variables: rhythmic pattern, pitch contour, cumulative interval, position in phrase, and composer. Since the possible combinations of these variables are numerous (and not equally worthy of investigation), I will illustrate the method using the pair discussed above: rhythmic pattern and pitch contour.

A crosstabulation table is a two-dimensional matrix which gives the distribution of data

Table 2. Crosstabulation of Rhythmic Pattern by Pitch Contour for Three-Note Patterns

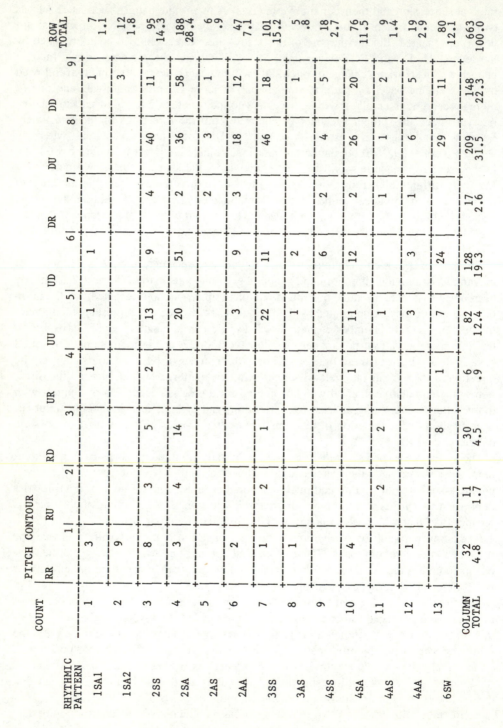

RHYTHMIC PATTERN	COUNT	RR	RU	RD	UR	UU	UD	DR	DU	DD	ROW TOTAL
1SA1	1	3			1	1	1			1	7 / 1.1
1SA2	2	9								3	12 / 1.8
2SS	3	8	3	5	2	13	9	4	40	11	95 / 14.3
2SA	4	3	4	14		20	51	2	36	58	188 / 28.4
2AS	5							2	3	1	6 / .9
2AA	6	2		1		3	9	3	18	12	47 / 7.1
3SS	7	1	2			22	11		46	18	101 / 15.2
3AS	8	1				1	2			1	5 / .8
4SS	9				1		6	2	4	5	18 / 2.7
4SA	10	4	2		1	11	12	2	26	20	76 / 11.5
4AS	11					1		1	1	2	9 / 1.4
4AA	12	1				3	3	1	6	5	19 / 2.9
6SW	13			8	1	7	24		29	11	80 / 12.1
COLUMN TOTAL		32 / 4.8	11 / 1.7	30 / 4.5	6 / .9	82 / 12.4	128 / 19.3	17 / 2.6	209 / 31.5	148 / 22.3	663 / 100.0

PITCH CONTOUR

in terms of either or both of a pair of variables. For example, Table 2 shows how the three-note patterns in the concordance are distributed in terms of rhythm, basic pitch contour, and, thus, motivic identity (i.e., the unique association of a specific rhythmic pattern and a basic pitch contour). The table is comprised of thirteen rows and nine columns which intersect to form 117 cells. As indicated by the headings, the rows represent rhythmic patterns and the columns represent basic pitch contours. Numbers within each cell give the absolute frequency of the various combinations of rhythmic pattern and pitch contour, and the totals of these numbers are shown in terms of both absolute and relative frequency (i.e., percent) at the right of each row and the bottom of each column. The row and column totals each add up to the total number of 663 cases (three-note patterns) which is given at the lower right corner of the table.

When studying a crosstabulation table, it is usually best to proceed from the general to the specific. In this regard, one would begin by noting the total number of cases and then continue by observing the distribution of cases in terms of each of the criterion variables. For example, the row totals indicate that Pattern 2SA is the most frequent of the three-note rhythmic figures (188 times or 28.4 percent of the total) and that Pattern 3AS is the least frequent (5 times or 0.8 percent). The column totals reveal basic contour DU to be the most characteristic (209 times or 31.5 percent) and UR to be the least characteristic (6 times or 0.9 percent). In each case, the distribution is highly skewed in favor of a few values.

More specific information can be gained by studying the distribution of cases within a particular row or column. For example, one can learn by studying column one that a slight majority (17) of the 32 examples of the RR contour assumed a rhythmic configuration of 1SA2 or 2SS. Likewise, a perusal of row one indicates that the most favored pitch contour for rhythmic pattern 1SA1 was RR.

Although a musically sophisticated person might characterize as trivial the observation that bebop is a highly stylized body of melody, one would be hard pressed without the aid of a computer to state exactly *how stylized* it is and to delineate the precise nature of that style. An overall feeling for the degree of association between rhythmic pattern and pitch contour can be gained by noting the highly skewed distribution of cases among the cells of Table 2. In more precise terms, this quality can be expressed by a statistic known as Kendall's Tau. The measure of significance for the Tau value of this table indicates that the probability of the same distribution occuring at random is 343 chances in ten thousand.

The precise nature of rhythmic pattern-pitch contour association can be seen by comparing the numbers within the various cells. From this one learns that the ten most characteristic three-note patterns in order of decreasing frequency are 2SA-DD, 2SA-UD, 3SS-DU, 2SA-DU, 6SW-DU, 4SA-DU, 3SS-UU, 2SA-UU and 4SA-DD (tied for eighth), and 3SS-DD.

Table 3 provides more insight into the bebop style by showing the breakdown of the UD and DU pitch contours into the three possible cumulative interval directions. The table consists of twelve matrices, one for each rhythmic pattern which assumed either or both of the two basic contours UD and DU. (Rhythmic pattern 1SA2 assumed neither contour so it is omitted). A key to the four numbers contained within each cell is given at the upper left corner of each matrix.

Table 3. Crosstabulation of Cumulative Interval Direction by Pitch Contour for Three-Note Patterns

```
        PATTERN 1SA1

                          CONTOUR
                  COUNT  I
                  ROW PCT IUD           ROW
                  COL PCT I             TOTAL
                  TOT PCT I      6  I
        CUMDIR    --------I--------I
                     1  I      1  I      1
        UP            I  100.0  I  100.0
                      I  100.0  I
                      I  100.0  I
                     -I--------I
                  COLUMN         1         1
                  TOTAL      100.0     100.0
```

```
        PATTERN 2SS
                          CONTOUR
                  COUNT  I
                  ROW PCT IUD          DU          ROW
                  COL PCT I                        TOTAL
                  TOT PCT I      6  I      8  I
        CUMDIR    --------I--------I--------I
                    -1  I      1  I      7  I      8
        DOWN          I  12.5  I  87.5  I  16.3
                      I  11.1  I  17.5  I
                      I   2.0  I  14.3  I
                     -I--------I--------I
                     0  I      2  I     17  I     19
        REPEATED      I  10.5  I  89.5  I  38.8
                      I  22.2  I  42.5  I
                      I   4.1  I  34.7  I
                     -I--------I--------I
                     1  I      6  I     16  I     22
        UP           I  27.3  I  72.7  I  44.9
                      I  66.7  I  40.0  I
                      I  12.2  I  32.7  I
                     -I--------I--------I
                  COLUMN         9        40        49
                  TOTAL      18.4      81.6     100.0
```

Table 3 (continued)

```
PATTERN 2SA

                        CONTOUR
              COUNT  I
              ROW PCT IUD          DU          ROW
              COL PCT I                        TOTAL
              TOT PCT I     6   I     8   I
CUMDIR        --------I--------I--------I
                 -1   I    31   I    18   I    49
     DOWN           I  63.3   I  36.7   I  56.3
                    I  60.8   I  50.0   I
                    I  35.6   I  20.7   I
              -I--------I--------I
                  0   I     2   I     2   I     4
     REPEATED       I  50.0   I  50.0   I   4.6
                    I   3.9   I   5.6   I
                    I   2.3   I   2.3   I
              -I--------I--------I
                  1   I    18   I    16   I    34
     UP             I  52.9   I  47.1   I  39.1
                    I  35.3   I  44.4   I
                    I  20.7   I  18.4   I
              -I--------I--------I
              COLUMN      51        36        87
              TOTAL     58.6      41.4     100.0




     PATTERN 2AS

                        CONTOUR
              COUNT  I
              ROW PCT IDU          ROW
              COL PCT I            TOTAL
              TOT PCT I     8   I
CUMDIR        --------I--------I
                 -1   I     1   I     1
     DOWN           I 100.0   I  33.3
                    I  33.3   I
                    I  33.3   I
              -I--------I
                  1   I     2   I     2
     UP             I 100.0   I  66.7
                    I  66.7   I
                    I  66.7   I
              -I--------I
              COLUMN       3         3
              TOTAL     100.0     100.0
```

Table 3 (continued)

PATTERN 2AA

```
                    CONTOUR
           COUNT  I
           ROW PCT IUD          DU        ROW
           COL PCT I                      TOTAL
           TOT PCT I    6  I     8  I
CUMDIR     --------I--------I--------I
              -1 I     1  I    12  I     13
           DOWN  I   7.7  I  92.3  I    48.1
                 I  11.1  I  66.7  I
                 I   3.7  I  44.4  I
                -I--------I--------I
               0 I     0  I     3  I      3
           REPEATED I 0.0 I 100.0 I    11.1
                 I   0.0  I  16.7  I
                 I   0.0  I  11.1  I
                -I--------I--------I
               1 I     8  I     3  I     11
           UP    I  72.7  I  27.3  I    40.7
                 I  88.9  I  16.7  I
                 I  29.6  I  11.1  I
                -I--------I--------I
           COLUMN      9        18       27
           TOTAL    33.3      66.7    100.0
```

PATTERN 3SS

```
                    CONTOUR
           COUNT  I
           ROW PCT IUD          DU        ROW
           COL PCT I                      TOTAL
           TOT PCT I    6  I     8  I
CUMDIR     --------I--------I--------I
              -1 I     3  I    22  I     25
           DOWN  I  12.0  I  88.0  I    43.9
                 I  27.3  I  47.8  I
                 I   5.3  I  38.6  I
                -I--------I--------I
               0 I     0  I    11  I     11
           REPEATED I 0.0 I 100.0 I    19.3
                 I   0.0  I  23.9  I
                 I   0.0  I  19.3  I
                -I--------I--------I
               1 I     8  I    13  I     21
           UP    I  38.1  I  61.9  I    36.8
                 I  72.7  I  28.3  I
                 I  14.0  I  22.8  I
                -I--------I--------I
           COLUMN     11        46       57
           TOTAL    19.3      80.7    100.0
```

Table 3 (continued)

PATTERN 3AS

```
                        CONTOUR
              COUNT   I
              ROW PCT IUD              ROW
              COL PCT I                TOTAL
              TOT PCT I       6  I
CUMDIR        --------I--------I
              1    I     2  I         2
    UP             I 100.0  I 100.0
                   I 100.0  I
                   I 100.0  I
                  -I--------I
              COLUMN        2         2
              TOTAL     100.0     100.0
```

PATTERN 4SS

```
                        CONTOUR
              COUNT   I
              ROW PCT IUD        DU          ROW
              COL PCT I                       TOTAL
              TOT PCT I     6  I     8  I
CUMDIR        --------I--------I--------I
             -1    I     5  I     4  I         9
   DOWN            I  55.6  I  44.4  I      90.0
                   I  83.3  I 100.0  I
                   I  50.0  I  40.0  I
                  -I--------I--------I
              1    I     1  I     0  I         1
    UP             I 100.0  I   0.0  I      10.0
                   I  16.7  I   0.0  I
                   I  10.0  I   0.0  I
                  -I--------I--------I
              COLUMN        6         4        10
              TOTAL      60.0      40.0     100.0
```

Table 3 (continued)

PATTERN 4SA

```
                          CONTOUR
              COUNT   I
              ROW PCT IUD          DU              ROW
              COL PCT I                            TOTAL
              TOT PCT I      6  I       8  I
    CUMDIR    --------I--------I--------I
                  -1  I      5  I      15  I         20
        DOWN        I   25.0  I   75.0  I         52.6
                    I   41.7  I   57.7  I
                    I   13.2  I   39.5  I
                  -I--------I--------I
                   0  I      2  I       3  I          5
    REPEATED        I   40.0  I   60.0  I         13.2
                    I   16.7  I   11.5  I
                    I    5.3  I    7.9  I
                  -I--------I--------I
                   1  I      5  I       8  I         13
        UP          I   38.5  I   61.5  I         34.2
                    I   41.7  I   30.8  I
                    I   13.2  I   21.1  I
                  -I--------I--------I
              COLUMN       12         26             38
              TOTAL      31.6       68.4          100.0
```

PATTERN 4AS

```
                          CONTOUR
              COUNT   I
              ROW PCT IDU          ROW
              COL PCT I            TOTAL
              TOT PCT I      8  I
    CUMDIR    --------I--------I
                   0  I      1  I          1
    REPEATED        I  100.0  I      100.0
                    I  100.0  I
                    I  100.0  I
                  -I--------I
              COLUMN        1             1
              TOTAL      100.0         100.0
```

Table 3 (continued)

PATTERN 4AA

```
                        CONTOUR
              COUNT  I
              ROW PCT IUD          DU          ROW
              COL PCT I                        TOTAL
              TOT PCT I     6  I      8  I
CUMDIR        --------I--------I--------I
                  -1  I     2  I      5  I     7
DOWN                  I  28.6  I   71.4  I  77.8
                      I  66.7  I   83.3  I
                      I  22.2  I   55.6  I
                      -I--------I--------I
                   0  I     1  I      0  I     1
REPEATED              I 100.0  I    0.0  I  11.1
                      I  33.3  I    0.0  I
                      I  11.1  I    0.0  I
                      -I--------I--------I
                   1  I     0  I      1  I     1
UP                    I   0.0  I  100.0  I  11.1
                      I   0.0  I   16.7  I
                      I   0.0  I   11.1  I
                      -I--------I--------I
                 COLUMN      3         6          9
                 TOTAL    33.3      66.7      100.0
```

PATTERN 6SW

```
                        CONTOUR
              COUNT  I
              ROW PCT IUD          DU          ROW
              COL PCT I                        TOTAL
              TOT PCT I     6  I      8  I
CUMDIR        --------I--------I--------I
                  -1  I     8  I      6  I    14
DOWN                  I  57.1  I   42.9  I  26.4
                      I  33.3  I   20.7  I
                      I  15.1  I   11.3  I
                      -I--------I--------I
                   0  I     7  I     12  I    19
REPEATED             I  36.8  I   63.2  I  35.8
                      I  29.2  I   41.4  I
                      I  13.2  I   22.6  I
                      -I--------I--------I
                   1  I     9  I     11  I    20
UP                    I  45.0  I   55.0  I  37.7
                      I  37.5  I   37.9  I
                      I  17.0  I   20.8  I
                      -I--------I--------I
                 COLUMN     24        29         53
                 TOTAL    45.3      54.7      100.0
```

Ex. 11. Ten most characteristic three-note motives

Example 11 is a listing in musical notation of the ten most characteristic three-note motives in the analytical sample of two hundred themes. In those cases where the basic contour is UD or DU the final note indicates the most characteristic cumulative interval. Table 4 provides a summary of the most typical rhythmic pattern-pitch contour associations for three-note motives.

Table 4. Summary of Rhythmic Pattern-Pitch Contour Association for Three-Note Patterns

Rhythmic Pattern#	First			Second			Third			Sum of Cases	
	Basic Contour	Abs. Freq.	Rel. Freq.	Basic Contour	Abs. Freq.	Rel. Freq.	Basic Contour	Abs. Freq.	Rel. Freq.	Sum	% of Total
1SA1(7)	RR	3	42.9	UR	1	14.3	----------------			7	100.0
				UU	1	14.3					
				UD	1	14.3					
				DD	1	14.3					
1SA2(12)	RR	9	75.0	DD	3	25.0	----------------			12	100.0
2SS(95)	DU	40	42.1	UU	13	13.7	DD	11	11.6	64	67.4
2SA(188)	DD	58	30.9	UD	51	27.1	DU	36	19.1	145	77.1
2AS(6)	DU	3	50.0	DR	2	33.3	DD	1	16.7	6	100.1
2AA(47)	DU	18	38.3	DD	12	25.5	UD	9	19.1	39	90.0
3SS(101)	DU	46	45.5	UU	22	21.8	DD	18	17.8	86	85.1
3AS(5)	UD	2	40.0	RR	1	20.0	----------------			5	100.0
				UU	1	20.0					
				DD	1	20.0					
4SS(18)	UD	6	33.3	DD	5	27.8	DU	4	22.2	15	83.3
4SA(76)	DU	26	34.2	DD	20	26.3	UD	12	15.8	58	76.3
4AS(9)	RU	2	22.2	UU	1	11.1	----------------			9	100.0
	RD	2	22.2	DR	1	11.1					
	DD	2	22.2	DU	1	11.1					
4AA(19)	DU	6	31.6	DD	5	26.3	UU	3	15.8	17	89.5
							UD	3	15.8		
6SW(80)	DU	29	36.3	UD	24	30.0	DD	11	13.8	64	80.0

*Three-note patterns have nine possible basic contours.

#The number in parentheses is the total number of valid cases for that rhythmic pattern.

The fact that a computer can generate tables such as those shown above in just a few seconds often tempts the novice analyst to go "fishing" for significant associations of any and all possible pairs of variables. Yielding to this temptation, however, may capsize one's analytical boat and drown one in a sea of matrix cells. It is, therefore, crucial in this type of work to formulate analytical hypotheses carefully, taking into account and building upon the wisdom of conventional theory and analysis. Once this is done, computer programs to test those hypotheses can be selected or written, the data can be processed, and the results analyzed.

As with many fields of intellectual endeavor, the potential benefits of computer-aided analysis to jazz studies are great. However, if our recent experiences with computers have taught us anything, it is that these rewards will not be realized until the incredible speed of the computer is harnessed to human minds which are both musically informed and intellectually creative.

Notes

1. A critical review of these studies can be found in Charles Boody, "Non-compositional Applications of the Computer to Music: An Evaluative Study of Materials Published in America Through June of 1972" (Ph.D. dissertation, University of Minnesota, 1972), chapter 3. Also see Stefan Kostka, *A Bibliography of Computer Applications in Music* (Hackensack, N.J.: Joseph Boonin, 1974).
2. See my dissertation, "Themes Composed by Jazz Musicians of the Bebop Era: A Study of Harmony, Rhythm, and Melody," 2 vols. (Indiana University, 1982) (UMI No. 8308888).
3. A complete description and listing of these programs is available from the author.
4. E.g., Dorothy Susan Gross, "A Set of Computer Programs to Aid in Musical Analysis" (Ph.D. dissertation, Indiana University, 1975).
5. Thomas Owens, "Charlie Parker: Techniques of Improvisation" (Ph.D. dissertation, University of California at Los Angeles, 1974) and Lawrence O. Koch, "Ornithology: A Study of Charlie Parker's Music," *Journal of Jazz Studies* 2 (December 1974): 61-87 and 2 (June 1975): 61-93, and 115-119.
6. A good overview of this topic can be found in Boody, "Non-compositional Applications of the Computer to Music," and Ann Kariger Blombach, "A Conceptual Framework for Use of the Computer in Music Analysis" (Ph.D. dissertation, Ohio State University, 1976).
7. See his articles, "A Computer-Oriented Music Notation Including Ethnomusicological Symbols," *Musicology and the Computer,* ed. Barry S. Brook (New York: City University of New York Press, 1970), pp. 91-129 and "Mustran II: A Foundation for Computational Musicology," *Computers in the Humanities,* ed. J. L. Mitchell (Minneapolis: University of Minnesota Press, 1974), pp. 267-80.
8. Although a syncopated anticipation is usually written on the second half of the previous beat, the actual placement in performance varies with the tempo. Fundamental to the entire classification scheme is the idea that the syncopated notes in jazz melody are placed slightly *before* the beat where they would "normally" fall. For corroboration of this view see Feather, *Inside Jazz,* 17, p. 62, and Billy Taylor, *How to Play Bebop Piano* (New York: Charles Hansen Music and Books, 1974), Ex. 19 and 21, pp. 14-15.
9. The patterns will be referred to by their row number, followed by a two-letter abbreviation of their column heading, e.g., the pattern in the "*Strong-Anticipated*" column of row two will be called 2SA.
10. The variations in notation occur when a note longer than an eighth-note is written sometimes as a note-value and other times as a combined note-and-rest value.
11. The terminology and symbols are those used in Grosvenor Cooper and Leonard Meyer, *The Rhythmic Structure of Music* (Chicago: The University of Chicago Press, 1960).
12. The writer is at least partially indebted to Benjamin Suchoff's article, "Computerized Folk Song Research and the Problem of Variants," *Computers and the Humanities* 2 (1967-68): 155-58, for this sorting procedure.

13. Boody, "Non-compositional Applications," pp. 54-55.
14. For a critical review of these approaches, see Eugene Narmour, "The Melodic Structure of Tonal Music" (Ph.D. dissertation, The University of Chicago, 1974), I, chapter 1.
15. In the horizontal dimension, a mere listing of the durations of notes will not suffice since it ignores the metric position of those notes. The rationale for the attack-point specification has been stated earlier. Interval representation of the vertical (pitch) dimension is more general than specific pitches or scale degrees. However, the latter are also available for greater specificity at later stages of analysis.
16. Broad and narrow definitions of the term "motive" are implied in two recent analytical studies of major jazz musicians. Thomas Owens uses the term in a broad sense in his study of Charlie Parker's improvised solos. The 64 motives which he illustrates vary in length from two notes to a dozen or more. Many of the longer motives are combinations of shorter ones. Several of the shorter motives would be called ornaments of figures by other writers. See Owens, "Charlie Parker: Techniques of Improvisation," I, chapter 3, and II, pp. 1-10. A narrower definition of the term is implied by Charles Clement Blancq III in "Melodic Improvisation in American Jazz: The Style of Theodore 'Sonny' Rollins, 1951-1962" (Ph.D. dissertation, Tulane University, 1977). Blancq notes that "motivic construction represents a notable advance in the art of jazz improvisation, but in Parker's music it sometimes results in a melodic line of many separate and only remotely related melodic fragments. This is because the motives were not developed in a continuous or extended way as they were in European music but were 'recalled' from time to time as a particular harmonic situation occurred or as inspiration dictated" (pp. 28-29). See also pp. 78-79, especially note 74.

The Jazz Avant-Garde and the Jazz Community: Action and Reaction

Ronald M. Radano

Although the social and cultural life of jazz has become an increasingly popular topic in sociology and related fields, few studies can surpass Alan Merriam's and Raymond Mack's classic work "The Jazz Community."[1] In their article, the authors discuss the society-enforced yet self-imposed isolation of the mid-1950s jazz musician. They also describe the deviant behavior, esoteric language, and eccentric dress that represented the musician's reaction to this isolation. Merriam and Mack create a vivid picture of the jazz musician's often frustrating life, his helplessness, and his narrow outlook on society. They explain that the jazz community was not necessarily confined to the musicians themselves; the families of the musicians and the members of the audience were all considered part of the jazz community.

Merriam's and Mack's portrayal of the 1950s jazz community can be used with some modification to describe the 1960s jazz mainstream, but it falters when applied to the jazz avant-garde. As supporters of a politically radical black nationalist movement and progenitors of a century-long trend to reorder the direction of western art, many avant-garde jazzmen—particularly those at the helm of its aesthetic direction—struck a pose markedly different from that of their mainstream counterparts.[2] These avant-garde jazz musicians were sometimes better educated and often better versed in the social and political events of contemporary American society. And as their movement gained momentum during the decade, it attracted an ever-increasing corps of artistically and intellectually advanced musicians.[3]

But we cannot say that the way of being of the avant-garde jazz musicians was completely unrelated to the behavioral model described by Merriam and Mack. Their training in jazz and their status as performers of improvised music cast them into a socially prescribed mold associated with blackness and corruption. Further, their stance as avant-garde artists[4] with political motivations contributed to their posture and code of behavior as social deviants, and thus their alignment with the jazz community. Nonetheless, while the 1960s jazz avant-garde conformed in some ways to the mold of the jazz community,

Ronald M. Radano is a doctoral candidate in musicology and ethnomusicology at the University of Michigan, completing a dissertation on the music of Anthony Braxton.

its position in it was never a comfortable fit. For the purposes of this discussion, then, we may think of the jazz avant-garde and the jazz mainstream as two subgroups interacting in the same community—one dominant, the other only tentatively affiliated—each with its own kinds of musicians, audiences, critics, and agencies.

The division between the jazz avant-garde and the jazz mainstream is not this author's creation but stems from the expressed views of the musicians and critics themselves. For the traditionalists, the music of the jazz avant-garde seemed separate from the mainstream style. It was, for them, a mutation, a fluke, a spurious and perverted parody of the "real" jazz form. Ira Gitler's claim that the jazz avant-garde was "getting away from musical values that have been established for centuries"[5] voiced a sentiment popular among the critical and musical establishments. The mainstream camp shared another more specific objection: avant-garde jazz was not based on a harmonic progression, it did not rely on modes or scales, it was not tempered in pitch, and it did not always follow a strict rhythm. Therefore, this music, which flouted the conventions of traditional jazz, was not jazz.

The hostile reaction by the jazz community was understandable. Not only did the music sound foreign, but the musicians acted foreign. The hard-edged radicalism of some of the avant-garde jazz musicians surely produced fear and misunderstanding in many traditional jazz lovers, and the superior, self-righteous attitudes of these musicians only intensified the mainstream's contempt. As we will see, the contemporary source of this controversy can be traced to Ornette Coleman and Cecil Taylor, two seminal figures of the jazz avant-garde, whose first radical departures met with an unwelcoming reception from the jazz community.[6]

Cecil Taylor and Ornette Coleman

Two landmark performances signified a turning towards the jazz avant-garde: Cecil Taylor's appearance in 1957, and Ornette Coleman's New York debut in 1959, both at the Five Spot Cafe, a small club on Manhattan's Lower East Side. These events introduced the New York jazz community to an early form of avant-garde jazz, a style that lay between traditional tonal jazz and the marginally tonal music based on collective improvisation that would appear a few years later. The performances at the Five Spot were significant in two respects. Musically, they represented early efforts by Taylor and Coleman that eventually led to a more abstract form, and socially, they introduced a new, revolutionary music to responsive New York literati and to a somewhat less responsive New York jazz community.

The initial critical reaction to Taylor was one of curiosity. While his improvisations did not always appeal to traditional musicians, Taylor was not at first highly controversial. Rather he was considered exotic—an obviously gifted musician but one who did not seem to fit into the jazz subculture.[7] Furthermore, the press coverage of Taylor was generally favorable. Gunther Schuller's and Larry Gushee's *Jazz Review* analyses from 1959 and 1960, Whitney Balliett's *New Yorker* review from August 1958, and Bill Coss's sympathetic article in *Down Beat* from 1961 portrayed Taylor as an artist of high potential—a portrayal that he and his champions preferred to ignore.[8]

For Coleman, the initial critical reaction was also generally supportive. He was just what the community was looking for: a stylist who would point the way for future musical developments. After his Five Spot engagement, he was acclaimed by much of the jazz press and community as the new creative fountainhead of jazz. Leonard Bernstein called him "the greatest innovator in jazz since Charlie Parker."[9] Martin Williams predicted that his work would "affect the whole character of jazz profoundly and pervasively."[10] Many respected musicians, including George Russell, Julian Adderley, Percy Heath, and John Lewis, supported him. Even the critics for *Down Beat,* the bastion of traditional jazz criticism, lauded Coleman. Critic John Tynan, in his two-and-a-half page article from 1960, wrote: "Ornette is heart and soul an artist following the star of his own musical and esthetic convictions."[11] Another *Down Beat* critic, Ira Gitler, who, as noted before, would later become an opponent of the jazz avant-garde, voted Coleman the second new star on alto saxophone in 1960.[12] Two weeks before Tynan's review, Leonard Feather invited the young Coleman to participate in his record-identification column, "The Blindfold Test"—an opportunity usually reserved for established members of the community.[13]

Of course many other community members were disturbed by Coleman. Dexter Gordon's dismissal of Coleman from a playing session is often cited as an example of conflict between the mainstream and the avant-garde.[14] Other mainstream figures like Zoot Sims and Ruby Braff also criticized his playing.[15] But for many musicians and much of the critical community, Coleman was the founder of a new style, a much needed creative charge that would revitalize the development of jazz.

Emerging Hostility to the Avant-Garde

Within the next two years, however, the tolerance for Taylor and the expressed enthusiasm for Coleman had disappeared. Both musicians, along with the saxophonists John Coltrane and Eric Dolphy, who remained on the fringe of the avant-garde, were now being maligned as jazz executioners—the creators of what Leonard Feather described as "anti-jazz."[16] Another *Down Beat* critic, Don DeMicheal, in his review of Coleman's album *This is Our Music* (1960), has this reaction:

> The technical abominations of his playing aside—and his lack of technical control is abominable—Coleman's music, to me has only two shades: a maudlin, pleading lyricism and a wild ferocity bordering on bedlam. His is not musical freedom; disdain for principles and boundaries is synonymous not with freedom but with anarchy. . . . If Coleman is to be a standard of excellence in jazz . . . then the work of Lester Young, Louis Armstrong, Charlie Parker, Duke Ellington, and all the other jazzmen who have been accepted as important artists must be thrown on the trash heap.[17]

Still another *Down Beat* critic, John Tynan, the creator of the "anti-jazz" epithet, expressed disgust with Coleman's *Free Jazz* (1960) just ten months after his favorable review quoted above:

> Where does neurosis and psychosis begin? The answer must lie somewhere within this maelstrom [of Coleman's music] . . . . Collective improvisation? Nonsense. The only semblance of collectivity lies in the fact that these eight nihilists were collected together in one studio at one time and with one common cause: to destroy the music that gave them birth.[18]

Why had the critical reaction shifted course? There seems to be a simple answer. The change in the community's attitude reflected a major change in the music. During this time, Coleman had discarded his more or less modal vocabulary in favor of a freer, more extended form of collective improvisation that characterized the jazz avant-garde of the 1960s.[19] Moreover, Coltrane's and Dolphy's long-winded, high-register experiments caused the critics to group them with the jazz avant-garde.

The hostile reaction of the critical establishment was more or less to be expected. After all, jazz had changed dramatically. It was no longer music offering immediate gratification but had been transformed into a loud, raucous, and, for the uninitiated listener, nonsensical or simply "unmusical" noise. Furthermore, avant-garde jazz was quite removed from the critics' experience. Although these writers were frequently aware of outside artistic and intellectual trends, their tastes were founded on mainstream jazz. For many of them, jazz had established a fixed line of development. It had an identifiable sound, a tradition, a style, and anything that deviated from this set character was simply no longer jazz.

Many critics eventually did try to understand avant-garde jazz. For instance, in 1962 DeMicheal, by then the editor of *Down Beat,* organized an interview with Coltrane and Dolphy to let them discuss the new course their music was taking.[20] Far-sighted critics like Martin Williams continued to write sensible, even-handed reviews of avant-garde musicians. Thus, by the mid-1960s, most traditional critics had come to terms with the music of the jazz avant-garde. While many musicians and critics still disliked the music, the shriller diatribes dwindled and were gradually replaced by a more judicious perspective.

Racial Aspects of the Avant-Garde Reaction

However (and perhaps ironically), avant-garde musicians were unconcerned with these developments in jazz criticism. Indeed, from the avant-garde's point of view, its music was an art form that heralded the coming of the "new" black society, and the opinions of a primarily white, middle-brow establishment were at best irrelevant. More often, criticism of any sort—even objective criticism—was viewed as an attack against their socially and musically vital artistic goals. If they, the members of the jazz avant-garde, were the "priests and mythmakers of black culture,"[21] then the white establishment critics were the saboteurs, the enemy. Thus, the jazz avant-garde, bent on the recognition of its art, began an ambitious, hard-line campaign against all those who opposed its music, a campaign that split the community into two hostile camps.

From the beginning, virtually all protests by the jazz avant-garde were racially inspired. Regardless of the topic, avant-garde spokesmen who appeared in print in jazz magazines inevitably seemed to base their arguments on racial oppression by a dominant white society. "Racism" became the collective cry, the watchword for the avant-garde jazz community. Any type of opposition, whether directed towards a group or an individual, met with the wrath of the jazz avant-garde, who branded as "racist" the entire jazz establishment. Clubs, the traditional showcases for jazz, were now no more than "crude stables" to Archie Shepp[22] or "whorehouses" to Ornette Coleman.[23] For these musicians, the clubs were a kind of anachronistic slave market in which the owners were the distributors of the "merchandise." Furthermore, according to many spokesmen for the avant-garde, their fate as artists and their chances of survival were at the mercy of these "slave drivers." Ornette Coleman, referring to the club owners' treatment of musicians, stated: "It's bad enough to let talent go to waste but it's worse to let it starve."[24] Record companies were also seen as part of a conspiracy to stifle the recognition of the new jazz. The companies, Andrew Cyrille contended, "owned the music and blacks play it."[25] Taylor supported this notion and proposed a national boycott to "take the music away from the people that own it."[26]

The primary spokesman for the jazz avant-garde was the tenor saxophonist Archie Shepp. Shepp was an articulate, well-educated Marxist who claimed to speak for all black people. He was, or at least hoped to be, in LeRoi Jones's phrase, "the poet of the black nation."[27] Shepp sought to embody the avant-garde artist: arrogant and self-righteous. At the same time, he sought to model himself after other black spokesmen of the day. He was convinced of his value to the black community, and continually spoke out in its behalf. The following example illustrates Shepp's language of protest, a language that surely frightened many conservative members of the jazz community:

> Give me leave to state this unequivocal fact: jazz is the product of the whites—the ofays— too often my enemy. It is the progeny of the blacks—my kinsmen. By this I mean: you own the music, and we make it. By definition then, you own the people who make the music . . . . I give you, then, my brains back, America. You have had them before, as you had my father's, as you took my mother's: in outhouses, under the back porch, next to the black snakes who should have bitten you then . . . don't you ever wonder just what my collective rage will—as it inevitably will be—unleashed? (sic) Our vindication will be black as the color of suffering is black, as Fidel is black, as Ho Chi Minh is black. It is thus that I offer my right hand across the worlds of suffering to black compatriots every-where.[28]

The wrath of Shepp and his cohorts in the avant-garde continued throughout the decade. These knights of the avant-garde cause preached their extremist doctrines in issue after issue of the major publications of the jazz community. No comment critical of them was overlooked by these protectors of the avant-garde domain. Even a hint of criticism would bring forth an immediate counter-attack. For example, Martin Williams, in his May 1, 1969, *Down Beat* review of a Cecil Taylor performance, brusquely remarked about the lifelessness of the final work. In the June 26 issue of *Down Beat*, Taylor's bassist Buell Neidlinger published a caustic reply.

In a way, the musicians functioned as a kind of literary vigilante group, the bulwark of the avant-garde who contradicted any assertion that questioned their artistic-social cause. In another way, the attacks on the establishment seemed to function as an outlet of frustra-tion for the avant-garde. The jazz establishment provided the avant-garde with a scape-goat, an excuse for the latter's lack of recognition by both the black and the jazz com-munities. The frequent appearances of these racially charged verbal onslaughts, moreover, functioned in ways not always intended by the avant-garde musicians. It seems as though their controversial statements might have helped to sell the publications in which they appeared. Controversy is the key to any interesting news item and the colorful, exciting antics of the mostly black members of the avant-garde proved to be a source of entertainment as well as a means for some white readers to deal with their own feelings of guilt. Archie Shepp, in particular, was a big attraction. His photogenic face, vivid writing style, and radical message made him good copy—a marketable commodity for the press.[29] Furthermore, the concerns of these public figures of the jazz avant-garde were not only collective concerns. A performer's appearance in a major jazz journal, whether as a highly praised talent or as a bitter and resentful radical, still brought public notice and could help boost record sales.

Non-Musician Supporters of the Avant-Garde

By the mid-1960s, after the jazz avant-garde had established itself as a viable artistic movement, another faction emerged in full force in the jazz press: the radical critic-polemicists. Rarely did these critics offer objective analysis. Rather they served as champions of the avant-garde, offering blind-faith support to the movement. Often the polemicists themselves—notably LeRoi Jones (later Imamu Amiri Baraka)—were black nationalist spokesmen who used the avant-garde movement as a forum for broadcasting their controversial beliefs. Harvey Pekar offers this insightful analysis of the radical polemicists at the height of their influence:

> Reading some pro-"new thing" critics, one gets the impression that almost every performer connected with the avant-garde is a genius. But there are *poor* musicians connected with the movement . . . who try to mask their lack of inventiveness by playing a bushelful of notes and freak noises. Complexity and intensity, however, are [not] the same as ingenuity. Banal, sloppily constructed solos remain such even when played with vigor.[30]

The initial groundwork for radical criticism was supplied by LeRoi Jones, the poet and playwright. His polemics possessed all the venom and anger of the jazz avant-garde's musician-spokesmen. For Jones, the primary concern seemed not so much the music as the vision of a black nation. Anyone who stood in his way, whether it be the "feeble-minded ofays"[31]—his epithet for the critics—or politically neutral musicians—for example, white saxophonist Frank Smith[32]—was targeted for heavy verbal assaults. In a 1980 *Down Beat* interview, the white pianist Burton Greene, a prime-mover in the 1960s jazz avant-garde, provided this general description of the black polemicists' tactics:

> The music was the thing that guys like LeRoi Jones used as their banner, saying "this is completely ours, and those white m.f.s. they haven't done anything." Those of us who were involved with the founding of that music were the victims of history.[33]

At times the polemic of the white radical critics equalled or surpassed that of Jones. Among these critics, unquestionably the most hostile, and as a result the most widely known and read, was Frank Kofsky. After beginning his critical career in the early 1960s as a *Down Beat* record reviewer, Kofsky later became popular as a principal writer for Pauline Rivelli's *Jazz,* a left-of-center journal that stood in opposition to the more conservative mainstay of the jazz community, *Down Beat.* Kofsky feared no one and would often embark on lengthy diatribes that sought to discredit much of the critical establishment. In one instance, for a period of seven months (May to November, 1965), he continually traded blows with many of the chief voices of the critical community: John Mehegan, Martin Williams, and Ira Gitler.[34] The following example, taken from Kofsky's book *Black Nationalism and the Revolution in Music,* demonstrates the polemic stance that intensified the break between the jazz mainstream and the jazz avant-garde:

> I believe that the editorial staff of *Down Beat* is thoroughly ingrained with the precepts of white supremacy—so much so, indeed, that they are an integral part of the magazine's

frame of reference which can be taken for granted without continual reiteration. That is why black nationalism, as well as other forms of radicalism, which threaten to disrupt the status quo, are anathema to its editors, why they are at such pains to discredit all radical ideologies.[35]

Thus, if the musician-spokesmen were the guardians of the jazz avant-garde, then it would seem the polemicists worked hand in hand with them. In writings of both groups, based on rage rather than rationality, these angry critics and musicians claimed to carry the torch for the new black society. They declared themselves dedicated to restoring "blackness" to jazz, to toppling the power structure of clubs and record companies, and to bringing to the black population a music that they considered rightfully its own.

Yet while the efforts of the avant-garde musicians and critics seemed sincere, what they failed to recognize—or refused to admit—was the elitist character of avant-garde jazz. By nature, avant-garde jazz is not music for the masses—black or white. It is an art form enjoyed by the more sophisticated members of American society. While a more accessible version of avant-garde jazz would later reach the popular ear, it was, and still is in its "purest" form, inaccessible to the masses. Musical norms operate like all other social norms—they change slowly. And the acceptance of the abstract music of the jazz avant-garde could not be forced; only gradually could it reach popular tastes. Indeed the club owners and record companies, no matter how corrupt or honest, were not the cause of the jazz avant-garde's lack of success. The real culprit was jazz itself. While the avant-garde musicians identified with jazz and the jazz community, they themselves remained a separate community. In musical style and personal and political character, the members of the avant-garde were a different kind of musician who rested precariously on the fringe of the jazz community. Nor did they identify with the "downtown" experimentalist school under the aesthetic leadership of John Cage. Although partly recognized by this elite group of artists and the patrons of these artists, the musicians of the jazz avant-garde did not receive the same level of recognition as their non-jazz avant-garde counterparts. If one were to use the terms of H. Wiley Hitchcock, the members of the jazz avant-garde were "cultivated" musicians trapped in a "vernacular" milieu.[36] Consequently, they were forced to contend with the same problems of limited social acceptance that hounded all segments of the jazz community.

Notes

1. Alan Merriam and Raymond Mack, "The Jazz Community," *Social Forces* 38 (March 1960): 211-222.
2. It is noteworthy that many jazz-related avant-garde musicians like Archie Shepp took offense to the term "jazz" and opted instead for the more generic "black music," while others, like some members of the Association for the Advancement of Creative Musicians, preferred the somewhat pretentious "creative music." Ornette Coleman has complained: "I still have that 'black jazz' image; I'm an entertainer who's supposed to exist on a certain level and that's it." Valerie Wilmer, *As Serious as Your Life* (Westport, Connecticut: Lawrence Hill, 1980), p. 71.
3. In the early part of the movement, the broad-thinking members of the avant-garde were limited to a small group of influential musicians. Men like Archie Shepp, Marion Brown, Cecil Taylor, Roswell Rudd, and Sam Rivers were articulate and college educated, and may represent the first intellectuals of the jazz avant-garde. By the 1970s, however, the jazz avant-garde had developed a large corps of self-conscious artists who, like Anthony Braxton and Karl Hans Berger, had developed sophisticated aesthetic doctrines that rank with those of Cowell, Cage, Babbitt, and other American composers of our time.

4. For a detailed discussion of this stance, see Renato Poggioli, *The Theory of the Avant-Garde* (Cambridge: Belknap Press, 1968).
5. Frank Kofsky, *Black Nationalism and the Revolution in Music* (New York: Pathfinder Press, 1970), p. 71.
6. The political side of Taylor and Coleman was not evident until 1964 or 1965, when black nationalism and racial violence had a national impact.
7. In *The Encyclopedia of Jazz,* 2nd ed., rev. (New York: Bonanza Books, 1960), Leonard Feather gives us what was probably a fairly typical assessment of Taylor by most critics at the time: "Taylor is considered by several leading critics to be among the advance guard of a new jazz era, though some musicians have dismissed his work as an unhappy attempt to blend Bartók and Stravinsky with jazz. Nevertheless, he is clearly aware of the techniques and the folk heritage of jazz and shows some ties to the ideas of Ellington and Monk. His execution is most impressive and his ideas are strikingly original."
8. Taylor was known for casting blame on the establishment for his lack of recognition. In one instance, he stated that club owners do not hire avant-garde musicians because if the clubs were to operate at full capacity—as they would with the introduction of the new jazz—then it would lead to the overthrow of the status quo. See Frank Kofsky, *Black Nationalism and the Revolution in Music,* p. 144.
9. George Hoefer, "The Hot Box," *Down Beat* (January 21, 1960): 42.
10. Martin Williams, *Jazz in Transition* (New York: Oxford University Press, 1971), p. 47.
11. John Tynan, "Ornette: The First Beginning," *Down Beat* (July 21, 1960): 32.
12. Ira Gitler, "Caught in the Act," *Down Beat* (February 16, 1961): 47. Gitler expressed second thoughts about his vote in the same article.
13. Leonard Feather, "The Blindfold Test," *Down Beat* (January 7, 1960): 39.
14. James Lincoln Collier, *The Making of Jazz* (Boston: Houghton Mifflin, 1978), p. 462.
15. Braff said of Coleman's "Mind and Time" from *Tomorrow is the Question* (Contemporary M 3569): "Once I heard Charlie Parker sound a little bit like that when he was completely sick—as sick as he could possibly be. . . . It sounds like utter confusion and madness—terrible!" Leonard Feather, "The Blindfold Test" *Down Beat* (January 21, 1960): 37.
16. The term was coined by John Tynan in his *Down Beat* reviews of November 23, 1961 and January 18, 1962. Feather further popularized it in his *Show* article, "Jazz: Going Nowhere" (January 1962): 12-14, and in his *Down Beat* article a month later (February 15, 1962): 40.
17. Don DeMicheal, "Spotlight Review," *Down Beat* (May 11, 1961): 25.
18. John Tynan, "Record Review," *Down Beat* (January 18, 1962): 28. Side-by-side with this review appeared Pete Welding's "excellent" rating of the same album.
19. Loosely tonal, "free" improvisation is also evident on Coleman's records from 1959: *Tomorrow is the Question* (Contemporary M 3569) and *Change of the Century* (Atlantic 1327). A marked change is noted when these recordings are compared to the 1958 tonal works from *Something Else!* (Contemporary M 3551). More extensive examples of Coleman's marginally tonal music did not appear on record until 1960. Taylor's music was, at times, non-tonal as early as 1958, notably on his album *Love For Sale* (United Artists UAS 5046).
20. Don DeMicheal, "John Coltrane and Eric Dolphy Answer the Critics," *Down Beat* (April 12, 1962): 20-23.
21. Roland Snellings, "We Must Create a National Black Intelligentsia in Order to Survive," in *Black Nationalism in America* (New York: Bobbs-Merrill, 1970), p. 454.
22. Archie Shepp, "An Artist Speaks Bluntly," *Down Beat* (December 16, 1965): 11.
23. A.B. Spellman, *Four Lives in the Bebop Business* (New York: Pantheon, 1966), p. 139.
24. Leroi Jones, *Black Music* (New York: William Morrow and Company, 1967), p. 98.
25. Valerie Wilmer, *As Serious as Your Life,* p. 225.
26. Frank Kofsky, *Black Nationalism and the Revolution in Music,* p. 144.
27. Leroi Jones, *Black Music,* p. 176.
28. Archie Shepp, "An Artist Speaks Bluntly," p. 11.
29. Bill Dixon, co-founder of the New York-based Jazz Composer's Guild, claimed that Shepp was selected by the press as a spokesman. See Roger Riggins, "Bill Dixon: Intents of an Innovator," *Down Beat* (August 1980): 30-32.

30. Harvey Pekar, "The Critical Cult of Personality" *Down Beat* (Jan. 13, 1966): 18-19.
31. Leroi Jones, *Black Music*, p. 18.
32. Jones called Smith a "thief" who stole from Albert Ayler and others and "will get rich from Albert's sound." Leroi Jones, *Black Music*, p. 143.
33. John Balleras, "Burton Greene: Jazzing the European Heritage," *Down Beat* (June 1980): 28.
34. This incident began with Kofsky's "State of Jazz Criticism," *Jazz* (May 1965): 22. See letters to the editor in subsequent issues.
35. Frank Kofsky, *Black Nationalism and the Revolution in Music*, p. 88.
36. H. Wiley Hitchcock, *Music in the United States: A Historical Introduction*, 2nd ed. (Englewood Cliffs, New Jersey: Prentice-Hall, 1974), p. 51.

A Ted Curson Discography

Robert Kenselaar

Ted Curson is probably best known for the recordings he made with Charles Mingus in the year 1960, when the regular Mingus lineup included Eric Dolphy and Booker Ervin. The experience was a dramatic one for Curson—it helped give him a direction to follow in his career. Prior to 1960, Curson had been drawn to the more radical avant-garde, playing in bands with Cecil Taylor in New York and Hasaan Ibn Ali in Philadelphia. After his stint with Mingus, Curson's direction was more along the lines of Mingus's own: a kind of mixture of the jazz traditions of Ellington, Parker, and Monk with the so-called "free jazz" that was emerging at that time. Even as late as 1976, Curson's strongest influence still seemed to be Mingus. He states in the liner notes of his Inner City recording *Jubilant Power:* "My aim is to make this a very modern Mingus-like band, but with even more activity in the background, a very flexible sense of time, and more freedom for the guys in their solos."

Born in Philadelphia in 1935, Curson counts among his early influences three brothers who lived in his neighborhood, Jimmy, Percy, and Albert Heath. Another Philadelphian who had a great effect on young Curson was trumpeter Clifford Brown. Among Curson's earliest professional experiences were tours with carnival bands and record dates with singers Dionne Warwick and Lloyd Price. Miles Davis heard the young trumpeter and encouraged him to move to New York. There Curson continued to work in a variety of contexts, including Latin music, rock, and jazz. He soon started playing regularly with Cecil Taylor, which was a very rewarding experience for him musically, if not economically.

After Mingus, Curson co-led a quintet with fellow Philadelphian Bill Barron off and on during the early 1960s. The pair made a trip to Europe together in 1964. Curson became one of the many American jazz musicians who found it easier to make a living in Europe than at home. Starting in 1965, he began to spend about six months of every year abroad. He continued to remain active in the United States, but also did a wide variety of work in Europe. In addition to recording dates and major festival appearances, he has appeared frequently on European television, did the music for Pier Paolo Pasolini's film *Teorama,* and played trumpet and acted in German productions of *Marat/Sade* and *Threepenny Opera.*

Robert Kenselaar is Assistant Chief, the Rodgers and Hammerstein Archives of Recorded Sound, New York Public Library.

Note on the Discography

Ted Curson's habit of continent-hopping makes him an interesting subject for a discography. A great deal of the information included here comes from an examination of Curson's own record collection, and I would like to thank him for his kind cooperation. In addition to this source and such standard jazz discographical references as the *Schwann Catalog,* Jorgen G. Jepsen's *Jazz Records 1942-* (Denmark: K.E. Knudsen, 1965-70), and Walter Bruyninckx's *60 Years of Recorded Jazz, 1917-1977* (Belgium: 1978-1982), I have also relied heavily on Vladimir Simosko's *Eric Dolphy: A Musical Biography and Discography* (Washington, D.C.: Smithsonian Institution Press, 1974), *Swing Journal* (Japan), and the German *Bielefelder Katalog,* an annual publication.

I have attempted to include all of Curson's commercially released jazz recordings, though there are bound to be some omissions, particularly among European and Japanese issues. The country of issue is given after each record label name unless it is a U.S. issue. In a few cases I was only able to determine that the issue was European.

The format of the discography basically follows the standard jazz form, with one major change. The record label and issue number, along with the record album title, appears after each group of song titles of a particular LP issue. Discographers seem to have a problem with listing album titles. Although the LP title is used as an important identification of recordings by collectors, most discographies disregard it entirely. Others omit listing LP titles in the main body of the discography, but do list them in an appendix, which creates some inconvenience for the user. The format employed here is one way to solve this problem, though it may be impractical for artists whose recording careers are longer, or more varied in terms of types of recordings issued.

Abbreviations

arr	arranger		p	piano
as	alto sax		perc	percussion
b	bass		ptp	piccolo trumpet
bars	baritone sax		s	sax
bcl	bass clarinet		ss	soprano sax
cl	clarinet		tb	trombone
dr	drums		tp	trumpet
fl	flute		ts	tenor sax
flh	flugelhorn		tu	tuba

Titles followed by the notation (TC) indicate Ted Curson compositions.

DISCOGRAPHY

CECIL·TAYLOR QUINTET   **NEW YORK, APRIL 15, 1959**

Ted Curson, tp; Bill Barron, ts; Cecil Taylor, p; Buell Neidlinger,
b; Rudy Collins, dr.

    Little Lees
    Matystrophe
  *Carol/Three Points

Love For Sale: United Artists UAL 4046, UAS 5046, (Japan) LAX 3117, Blue
    Note (Europe) 84488
In Transition: Blue Note BN-LA458-H2

*appears on In Transition only

CHARLES MINGUS   **NEW YORK, MAY 24, 1960**

Marcus Belgrave, Hobart Dotson, Clark Terry, Ted Curson, Richard
Williams, tp; Slide Hampton, Charles Greenlee, Eddie Bert, Jimmy
Knepper, tb; Don Butterfield, tu; Robert DiDomenica, fl; Eric
Dolphy, as, bcl, fl; John LaPorta, cl, as; Yusef Lateef, ts, fl; Bill
Barron, Joe Farrell, ts; Danny Bank, bars; Harry Shulman, oboe;
Roland Hanna, p; Charles McCracken, cello; Charles Mingus, b, arr;
Dannie Richmond, dr; "Sticks" Evans, George Scott, Max Roach, perc.

    Half-Mast Inhibition (Gunther Schuller, conductor)
    Mingus Fingus Number Two
    Bemoanable Lady
    Yusef Isef Too (unissued)

                        NEW YORK, MAY 25, 1960

Ted Curson, tp; Jimmy Knepper, tb; Eric Dolphy, as, bcl, fl; Yusef
Lateef, ts, fl; Booker Ervin, Joe Farrell, ts; Roland Hanna or Paul
Bley, p; Charles Mingus, b, arr; Dannie Richmond, dr; Lorraine
Cousins, vocal. (Hanna and Bley alternate where not specified)

    Weird Nightmare vLC
    Prayer For Passive Resistance
    Eclipse pRH, vLC (other vocals also present)
    Do Nothin' Till You Hear From Me/I Let a Song Go Out of My Heart
    Take the "A" Train/Exactly Like You pPB

Prebird: Mercury MG-20627, SR-60627, (Japan) SFX 10545, (Europe)
    633632, Limelight EXPR-1015
Mingus Revisited: Limelight LM82015, LS86015, Limelight (UK)
    SLML 4009; Mercury-International (UK) SMWL21056; Mercury
    (Eur)mce 126016 (except Half-Mast... and Bemoanable Lady),
    (UK) 10021 mce (contains only Prayer..., Mingus Fingus...,
    Do Nothin'..., and Weird Nightmare); Bemoanable Lady also on
    Fontana (UK) FJL115, (Eur.) JCL683265, JCY883265

CHARLES MINGUS   **ANTIBES JAZZ FESTIVAL, JUAN-LES-PINS, FRANCE,**
                                                    JULY 13, 1960

Antibes Jazz Festival, Juan-Les-Pins, France, July 13, 1960

Ted Curson, tp; Eric Dolphy, as, bcl; Booker Ervin, ts; Charles
Mingus, b, p; Dannie Richmond, dr.

    Folk Forms, No. 2
    Better Get It In Your Soul CM p,b
    Wednesday Night Prayer Meeting CM p,b
   *I'll Remember April (Bud Powell, p,added)

Charles Mingus Live With Eric Dolphy: Vogue (Japan) YX-7009
Charles Mingus Live: Affinity 19
Mingus at Antibes: Atlantic SD 2-3001 (Better Get... appears as
    Better Get Hit In Your Soul; Folk Forms, No. 2 appears as
    Folk Forms, No. 1)

*appears on Atlantic issue only

CHARLES MINGUS

Ted Curson, tp; Eric Dolphy, as, bcl; Charles Mingus, b, vocal;
Dannie Richmond, dr, vocal.

    Folk Forms, No. 1
    Original Faubus Fables vCM, DR
    What Love bclED
    All the Things You Could Be By Now If Sigmund Freud's Wife
        Was Your Mother

Charles Mingus Presents Charles Mingus: Candid CJM8005, CJS9005,
    SJM 6178, Barnaby/Candid Jazz 190-5012, Barnaby Z30561,
    America (French) 30AM6082
Folk Forms, No. 1 and Original Faubus Fables also on Candid 45-601
    in edited versions.

CHARLES MINGUS   **NEW YORK, OCTOBER 20, 1960**

personnel same as above (Dolphy plays alto only)

    Stormy Weather

Ted Curson, Lonnie Hillyer, tp; Jimmy Knepper, Britt Woodman, tb;
Eric Dolphy, as, bcl; Charles McPherson, as; Booker Ervin, ts;
Nico Bunick, p; Charles Mingus, b; Dannie Richmond, dr.

    MDM

CHARLES MINGUS   **NEW YORK, NOVEMBER 11, 1960**

personnel same as Oct. 20 except trombones out; piano is either
    Bunick or Paul Bley

    Vassarlean
    Lock 'em Up pPB

Mingus: Candid CJM8021, CJS9021 (except Vassarlean), Jazz Man JAZ 5002
Stormy Weather: Barnaby/Candid 190-6015
The Candid Recordings: Barnaby KZ31034
also on CBS (Eur.) S64675
Vassarlean also appears on The Jazz Life: Candid CJM8019, CJS9019,
    SJM 6195, Barnaby/Candid 190-5021
An excerpt of MDM also appears on The Jazz Life: Jazz Man JAZ 5050

BILL BARRON   **NEWARK, N.J., FEBRUARY 21, 1961**

Ted Curson, tp; Bill Barron, ts; Kenny Barron, p; Jimmy Garrison,
b; Frankie Dunlop, dr.

    Blast Off
    Ode to an Earth Girl
    Fox Hunt
    Oriental Impressions
    Back Lash
    Nebulae

The Tenor Stylings of Bill Barron: Savoy MG 12160

TED CURSON   **NEW YORK, APRIL 1961**

Ted Curson, tp, ptp; Bill Barron, ts; Kenny Drew, p; Jimmy Garrison,
b; Roy Haynes, dr.

    Caravan
    Flatted Fifth (TC)

Dannie Richmond, dr, replaces Haynes
    Nosruc (TC)
    Dem's Blues (TC)
    Mr. Teddy (TC)

Pete LaRoca, dr, replaces Richmond

    Ahma (See Ya) (TC)
    Antibes (TC)

Eric Dolphy, fl, replaces Barron

    Bali-Hai (TC)

Haynes, dr, replaces LaRoca

    The Things We Did Last Summer

Plenty of Horn: Old Town OTLP 2003, (Japan) YQ-7501AX, YW-7577

BILL BARRON   **NEWARK, N.J., JUNE 5, 1961**

Ted Curson, tp; Bill Barron, ts; Jay Cameron, bars; Kenny Barron,
p; Eddie Kohn, b; Pete LaRoca, dr.

    Men At Work
    Tone Colors
    Dedication to Wanda
    Keystone
    Noodlin'
    Duality
    Self Portrait
    Persian Street Scene
    Light Fantastic (unissued)

Modern Windows: A Jazz Suite From the New "Soul": Savoy MG 12163

THE CECIL TAYLOR UNIT   **NEW YORK, OCTOBER 10, 1961**

Ted Curson, tp; Roswell Rudd, tb; Jimmy Lyons, as; Archie Shepp,
ts; Cecil Taylor, p; Henry Grimes, b; Sunny Murray, dr.

    Mixed

Into the Hot--The Gil Evans Orchestra: Impulse A-9, AS-9, World
    Record Club (UK) T 748, ST 748
Taylor, Tolliver, Moncur, Shepp--The New Breed: ABC Impulse IA9339/2

TED CURSON QUINTET   **MONTREAL, SEPTEMBER 15, 1962**

  Ted Curson, tp, ptp; Al Doctor, as; Maury Kaye, p; Charles Biddes,
b; Charles Duncan, dr.

    Cracklin' Bread (TC)
    Ted's Tempo (TC)
    Playhouse March (TC)
    Straight Ice (TC)
    Quicksand (TC)

Live at la'Tete de l'Art: Trans World TWJ 7000

TED CURSON   **NEW YORK, DECEMBER 10, 1962**

Ted Curson, tp; Gildo Mahones, p; George Tucker, b; Roy Haynes,
b; Montego Joe, congas.

    *Fire Down Below
    *The Very Young
    Baby Has Gone Bye Bye
  **Show Me
    Falling In Love With Love
    Only Forever

Fire Down Below: Prestige LP 7263

*also on Prestige 45-241
**also on The Broadway Scene Played by America's Greatest Jazzmen:
    Prestige-Moodsville 38, and My Fair Lady:Status 8315

BILL BARRON, TED CURSON & ORCHESTRA   **NEW YORK, DECEMBER 5, 1963**

Ted Curson, tp; Bill Barron, ts; Kenny Barron, p; Ronnie Boykins,
b; Dick Berk, dr.

    Around the World
    Big Bill
    The Leopard   (TC)
    Hurdy Gurdy
    Dwackdi Mun Fudalik   (TC)
    Jes Swingin'
    In a Monastery Garden
    You Are Too Beautiful

Now Hear This!:Audio Fidelity AFLP 2123, AFSD 6123
The Leopard: (under Ted Curson, Bill Barron & Orchestra)
    Chiaroscuro CR2010

ARCHIE SHEPP AND THE NEW YORK CONTEMPORARY 5   **NEWARK, N.J.,
FEBRUARY 5, 1964**

Ted Curson, tp; John Tchicai, as; Archie Shepp, ts; Ronnie Boykins,
b; Sunny Murray, dr.

    Where Poppies Bloom
    Like a Blessed Lamb

Bill Dixon 7-tette/Archie Shepp and the New York Contemporary 5:
    Savoy MG 12184, CBS Realm (UK) RM 52422
Bley, Dixon, Pozar, Shepp, Watts: New Music: Second Wave:
    Savoy SJL 2235

TED CURSON QUARTET   **PARIS, AUGUST 1, 1964**

Ted Curson, tp, ptp; Bill Barron, cl, ts; Herb Bushler, b; Dick Berk, dr.

    Kassim (TC)
    East Sixth Street
    7/4 Time
    Tears For Dolphy (TC)
    Quicksand (TC)
    Reava's Waltz (TC)

Tears For Dolphy: Fontana (UK) 688-310ZL, Arista Freedom AL 1021,
    Freedom (Japan) PA-9711

TED CURSON QUARTET   **PARIS, AUGUST 1, 1964**

personnel same as above

    Searchin' For the Blues (TC)
    Desolation
    Light Blue

Flip Top: Arista Freedom AL 1030, Freedom (Japan) PA-7187
(for other selections on this LP,see August, 1966)

TED CURSON   **NEW YORK, FALL 1964**

Ted Curson, tp; Bill Barron, ts; George Arvanitas, p; Herb Bushler,
b; Dick Berk, dr.

    Straight Ice (TC)
    Star Eyes (TC)
    Ted's Tempo (TC)
    Nublu (TC & BB)
    Reava's Waltz (TC) (omit piano)
    Elephant Walk (TC)
    Kaleidoscope (TC) (unissued)

The New Thing & The Blue Thing: Atlantic SD-1441, (Japan) P-4514

ARCHIE SHEPP   **ENGLEWOOD CLIFFS, N.J., FEBRUARY 16, 1965**

Ted Curson, tp; Joseph Orange, tb; Marion Brown, as; Archie Shepp,
ts; Reggie Johnson, b; Joe Chambers, dr.

    Hambone
    Los Olvidados
    Prelude to a Kiss
    The Girl From Ipanema

Fire Music: Impulse A 86, AS 86, (Japan) YP8604AI

G. GARANAN SE SVOU SKUPINOU   PRAGUE, OCTOBER 1965

Ted Curson, tp; G. Garanan, as; N. Gromin, g; A. Jegorov, b;
V. Bulanov, dr.

    Armensky Bounce
    Corrida

Jan Hammer, p; Miroslav Vitous, b; Alan Vitous, dr, replace Gromin,
Jegorov, and Bulanov

    Caravan
    Marjo (TC)

Ozveny Jazzoveho Festivalu Praha 1965 : Supraphon DV 10195

GUSTAV BROM SE SVYM ORCHESTREM   PRAGUE, OCTOBER 1965

Ted Curson, tp; J. Milian, vbs; j. Blaha, p; M. Rezbek, b;
V. Skala, dr. Other personnel unidentified.

    Blues Pod Povrchem (Blues Beneath the Surface)
    Cleb Nas Vezdejsi Dejz Nam Jazz
    Blues pro Gustava
    Proklaty Sen (Darn That Dream)

Ozveny Jazzoveho Festivalu Praha 1965: Supraphon (Czech.) DV 10195

THE ANDRZEJ TRZASKOWSKI SEXTET   WARSAW, DECEMBER 1965

Ted Curson, tp; Janusz Muniak, ss; Wlodzimierz Nahorny, as; Andrzej
Trzaskowski, p; Jacek Ostaszewski, b; Adam Jedrzejowski, dr.

    Cosinusoida

Warsaw, early 1966

same personnel

    Seant
    Wariacja Natemat "Oj, Tam U Boru" (Variation on the Theme
        "Near the Forest")
    The Quibble

Seant: Muza (Poland) XL 0378 (Polish Jazz no. 11)

TED CURSON QUARTET   BAARN, NETHERLANDS, MAY 13, 1966

Ted Curson, tp; Booker Ervin, ts; Jimmy Woode, b; Edgar Bateman, dr.

    Roy's Boys (TC)
    You Don't Know What Love Is
    Cinq Quatre (TC)
    Music Sacrum (TC)
    The Leopard (TC)
    Latino (TC)

Urge: Fontana (Dutch) 883-910JCY, Fontana (English) FJL 910

TED CURSON   LJUBLJANA, YUGOSLAVIA, AUGUST, 1966

Ted Curson, tp; Zita Carno, arr; Miljenko Prohaska, conductor,
and the Zagreb Radio Orchestra (personnel unknown)

    Quicksand (TC)
    Straight Ice (TC)
    Flip Top (TC)
    Tears For Dolphy (TC) (unissued)

Flip Top: Arista Freedom AL 1030, Freedom (Japan) PA-7187

DIE JAZZ WERKSTATT '66   HAMBURG, AUGUST 5, 1966

Ted Curson, Bosse Broberg, Dusko Goyvich, Carmell Jones, Ronnie
Simmonds, tp, flh; Kurt Jarnberg, Albert Mangelsdorff, Ake Persson,
Emile Vilain, tb; Helmut Brandt, Dominique Chanson, Herb Geller,
Danny Moss, Ray Pitts, s, fl, cl; Jan Johansson, p; Spike Heatley,
b; Pierre Favre, dr; Bill Smith, cl, leader.

    The Band
    Tears for Dolphy (TC)

Die Jazz Werkstatt '66: Norddeutscher Rundfunk NDR (German)

TED CURSON QUARTET   COLOGNE, GERMANY, SEPTEMBER 16 OR 17, 1967

Ted Curson, tp, ptp; Nick Brignola, saxello, bars; Helmut Kandlberger,
b; Peter Schmidt, dr.

    The Leopard (TC)

Jazz am Rhein: Columbia (German) SMC 74334

KARIN KROG   OSLO, NORWAY, AUGUST 4, 1969

Ted Curson, tp; Elisabeth Sonstevold, harp; Berndt Egerbladh, organ;
Arild Andersen, b; Jon Christensen, dr; Karin Krog, vocal.

 Break of Day in Molde

omit drums, harp

 Blue Eyes

Break of Day in Molde: Sonet (Norway) T 9541 (7" 45rpm)

TED CURSON & CO.   FINLAND, SEPTEMBER 3, 1970

Ted Curson, tp, ptp, Eero Koivistoinen, ss, as, ts; Pentti Hietanen,
p; Pekka Sarmanto, b; Reino Laine, dr.

 Ode to Booker Ervin (TC)
 LSD Takes a Holiday (TC)
 Airi's Tune (TC)
 Montreux
 Festival Blue
 Typical Ted (TC)
 The Leopard (TC)

Ode to Booker Ervin: Columbia EMI (Finland) 5 E 062-34201

TED CURSON   PARIS, JUNE 18, 1971

Ted Curson, tp; George Arvanitas, p; Jacky Samson, b; Charles
Saudrais, dr.

 Pop Wine (TC)
 LSD Takes a Holiday (TC)
 Song of the Lonely One (TC)
 Quartier Latin (TC)
 Flip Top (TC)

Pop Wine: Futura (French) GER-26

TED CURSON   PARIS, OCTOBER 26, 1973

Ted Curson, tp, ptp, bugle; Chris Woods, as, fl; George Arvanitas,
p; Jacky Samson, b; Charles Saudrais, dr.

 Flatted Fifth (TC)
 Marjo (TC)
 Airi's Tune (TC)
 Searchin' for the Blues (TC)
 Typical Ted (Cattin' Curson) (TC)

Cattin' Curson: Marge (French) 01
(Typical Ted): Trident TRS-503   ("Typical Ted (Cattin' Curson)"
     appears as "Typical Ted")

LEE SCHIPPER   STOCKHOLM, AUGUST 31, 1973

Ted Curson, tp; Bjorn Jason Lindh, fl; Christer Eklund, ts; Jan
Schaffer, g; Art Lande, p; Stefan Brolund, b; Lee Schipper, vbs;
Ola Brunkert, dr.

     Phunky Physicist
     Transmogrification
     Still Life
     For Jackie
     Piccolo Blues (TC)
     Harvest Machine

Phunky Physicist: Europa Films (Sweden) CAM CMLP 5907
Jazz Meeting 1: Four Leaf FLC 5019   (released under Curson's name)

TED CURSON   NEW YORK, MAY 13, 1974

Ted Curson, tp, ptp; Robin Kenyatta, ss, as; Nick Brignola, bars,
ts, saxello; Kenny Barron, p, ep; Herb Bushler, b; Butch Curson,
dr; Lawrence Killian, conga, bell tree; Chicky Johnson, bongos,
timbales.

     Spiderlegs (TC)

Albert "Tootie" Heath, dr, replaces B. Curson

     Typical Ted (TC)
     Greasy as a Porkchop (TC)
     Sugar 'n' Spice (TC)

                                        NEW YORK, MAY 16, 1974

same personnel as above

     Tears for Dolphy (TC)
     Quicksand (TC)

Quicksand: Atlantic (Japan) P-7532

PORI BIG BAND   **PORI, FINLAND, JULY 1974**

Jaakko Satomaa, Jorma Kohijoki, Reijo Widbom, Juhani Terara, Ted
Curson, tp; Juhani Aalto, Tauno Koskinin, Martti Kojo, tb; Juhani
Bihanto, coro; Jukka Berg, tu; Ilkka Karumo, Matti Osterlund, as;
Kari Sarpila, Erkki Elo, Jarmo Laine, ts; Harri Kangas, bars; Pekka
Tyni, p; Seppo Tyni, g; Markku Kokko, b; Tapani Ikonen, dr; Kaj
Heinonen, congas; Kaj Backlund, conductor.

     Back to Pori

Live at Pori Jazz Festival: Pori Jazz Productions (Finland) PJPLP 1

ANDREW HILL   **NEW YORK, DECEMBER 20, 1974**

Ted Curson, tp, ptp, flh; Lee Konitz, ss, as, ts; Andrew Hill, p;
Cecil McBee, b; Art Lewis, dr.

     Spiral
     Laverne
     The Message

Spiral: Arista Freedom Al 1007, Freedom (Japan) PA-7104

TED CURSON   **NEW YORK, JULY 1, 1976**

Ted Curson, tp, ptp; Jim McNeely, p; Cecil McBee, b; Steve McCall, dr.

     All the Things You Are
     Blue Piccolo (TC)
     Playhouse March (TC)
     Song of the Lonely (TC)
     Dwackdi Mun Fudalick (Open the Door) (TC)

Blue Piccolo: Whynot (Japan) PA-7153
Ted Curson & Co.: India Navigation IN 1054

TED CURSON & COMPANY   **PHILADELPHIA, OCTOBER 16, 1976**

Ted Curson, tp, ptp, flh, cowbell; Chris Woods, as; Nick Brignola,
ss, bars; Andy LaVerne, p; David Freisen, b; Steve McCall, dr; Sam
Jacobs, congas.

     Reava's Waltz (TC)
     Ted's Tempo (TC)

NEW YORK, OCTOBER 17, 1976

same personnel as above except Jim McNeely, p, replaces LaVerne;
Bob Merigliano, dr, replaces McCall.

    Song of the Lonely (TC)
    Airi's Tune (TC)
    Searchin' for the Blues (TC)
    Marjo (TC)

Jubilant Power: Inner City 1017, (Japan) RJ-7311

THE NICK BRIGNOLA SEXTET   NEW YORK, DECEMBER 22, 1977

Ted Curson, tp; Nick Brignola, Pepper Adams, bars; Derek Smith, p;
Dave Holland, b; Roy Haynes, dr.

    Billie's Bounce

same personnel as above except Curson plays flh

    Marmaduke

Baritone Madness: Bee Hive BH 7000

DIZZY REECE AND TED CURSON   NEW YORK, JUNE 9, 1978

Dizzy Reece, tp; Ted Curson, tp, flh; Claude Williamson, p; Sam
Jones, b; Roy Haynes, dr.

    All the Things You Are (Reece out)
    Bass Conclave
    Marjo (TC)
    Walkin'

Blowin' Away: Interplay IP 7716
Moose the Mooche: Discovery 839 (released under "Dizzy Reece Quintet")

SAL NISTICO   NEW YORK, NOVEMBER 3, 1978

Ted Curson, flh; Sal Nistico, ts; Nick Brignola, bars; Ronnie
Mathews, p; Sam Jones, b; Roy Haynes, dr.

    Anthropology
    Fee-Fi-Fo-Fum

same personnel as above except Curson plays tp

    Blues for K.D.

Bambu

<u>Neo</u>-<u>Nistico</u>: Bee Hive BH 7006

TED CURSON   **NEW YORK, JANUARY 3, 1979**

Ted Curson, tp, ptp, flh, perc; Ray Drummond, b; Roy Haynes, dr.

    Snake Johnson (TC)
    Pent Up House
    Quicksand (TC)
    Straight Ice (TC)
    'Round About Midnight

<u>The</u> <u>Trio</u>: Interplay IP-7722

TED CURSON   **NEW YORK, JANUARY 5, 1980**

Ted Curson, tp, ptp, flh, perc; Ryo Kawasaki, g; Mike Richmond, b;
Adam Nussbaum, dr.

    I Heard Mingus (TC)

add Jim McNeely, p.

    Lost Her (TC)

add Bill Saxton, ts; Mike Morgenstern, bars; Montego Joe, perc.

    Please Please Please Don't Put the Pigsfoot in the Kreplach Soup (TC)
    Lin's Garden   (Collier/TC)

<u>I</u> <u>Heard</u> <u>Mingus</u>: Interplay IP-7729

TED CURSON   **NEW YORK, FEBRUARY 16 AND 17, 1980**

Ted Curson, tp, ptp, flh; Charlie Williams, as; Bill Barron, ts; Nick
Brignola, bars, ss; Jim McNeely, p; David Friesen, b; Steve McCall, dr;
Lawrence Killian, perc.

    Snake Johnson (TC)
    Searching for the Blues (TC)
    Blue Piccolo (TC)
    Dwackdi Mun Fudalik (TC)
    Marjo (TC)
    LSD Takes a Holiday (TC)

<u>Snake</u> <u>Johnson</u>: Chiaroscuro CR-2028

Bebop Melodic Lines: Tonal Characteristics

Steven Strunk

I. Introduction

What are the main characteristics of bebop melodic lines as they relate to their supporting harmonies? What sort of motivic organization unifies bebop melodic lines?

In an earlier article,[1] I discussed those characteristics which are unique to bebop harmonic progressions. In the present article, I hope to demonstrate the similarly unique tonal characteristics of bebop melodic lines. This purpose requires formulation of concepts, analysis of examples, and, at one point, a digression into the subject of chord voicings. Although there are many new examples, some of the compositions discussed in my earlier article are reexamined from the melodic standpoint.

II. Tensions

A. Introduction to and Definition of Tensions

A reference by Charlie Parker to one of the most important characteristics of bebop melodies has been quoted widely:

> I found that by using the higher intervals of the chord as a melody line and backing them with appropriately related changes, I could play the thing I'd been hearing. I came alive.[2]

By the "higher intervals of a chord," Parker very likely meant major sevenths, ninths, elevenths, and thirteenths—embellishing notes that have been in use for centuries but which play a special role in bebop melodies. The terms "chordal extension" and "superimposition" have been used along with numerical designations for these tones when they are explained as arising from superimposed thirds over the chord root (Example 1). This explanation is probably not the best way to understand the phenomenon, as these notes generally behave as melodic, not harmonic, events. I have maintained the numerical designations in the following discussion because of their firmly established general use.

Steven Strunk is a composer and associate professor of music at the Benjamin T. Rome School of Music at the Catholic University of America, Washington, D. C.

Ex. 1.

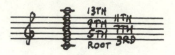

However, in order to separate these pitches from the vertical concept of chordal extension, these and certain other notes will be referred to collectively as *tensions*,[3] defined as follows: In a tonal diatonic setting, a tension is a pitch related to a structurally superior pitch (usually a chord tone) by step, such that the tension represents and substitutes for the structurally superior pitch, called its resolution, in the register in which it occurs. Most tensions are located a step above their resolutions. The concept of tension is broader than that of suspension, appoggiatura, passing tone, or neighbor tone, as there is no requirement of manner of approach, manner of leaving, or rhythmic position in its definition.

Use of tensions is one of the strongest characteristics of bebop melodic lines and chord voicings. Within the style, however, there are contextual limitations of their use. An examination of various harmonic contexts will reveal some of these limitations.

B. Tensions in Context

1. *General considerations.* Tensions take their names from the interval they make above the root of the chord (major seventh, ninth, eleventh, or thirteenth). Apart from the contextual limitations to be discussed, any chord potentially may support any diatonic major seventh, ninth, eleventh, or thirteenth as a tension above its root. The sense of dissonance of a tension derives, usually, from a potential seventh interval between the tension and a chord tone below it. For example. $\hat{3}$/V7[4] (a thirteenth) is not dissonant with the root, but does form a dissonant major seventh with the seventh of the V7. That dissonant relationship is often stressed, both in chord voicings and in melodic lines. Tensions are usually sounded above basic chord tones, in order that the dissonant seventh may be emphasized. As with a suspension, the resolution of the tension resolves the dissonance. Because mode mixture is common in tonal music, tensions may be derived from major or minor scale sources. Although the major-derived $\hat{3}$ is not used in a minor context, minor-derived tensions ($b\hat{3}$, $b\hat{6}$, $b\hat{7}$) are often used in major contexts. Sometimes the #$\hat{4}$ of Lydian or the $b\hat{2}$ of Phrygian are used as well. One constraint upon tension formation in chord voicings is the restriction of the minor ninth interval to only one location: between the root and minor ninth of a dominant seventh chord. Other minor ninths are avoided.

Tensions are ordinarily diatonic, with one important exception: chords having major thirds frequently support a tension one-half step below the (perfect) fifth as a substitute for the fifth. This tension is often referred to as a "flat" fifth, to distinguish it from the enharmonically equivalent augmented eleventh; however, I will refer to it by the less ambiguous term *diminished fifth*. The diminished fifth takes its dissonant quality from the major second it makes with the third of the chord, and resolves upward to the perfect fifth. For this reason, it is usually spelled as a leading tone to the perfect fifth (Example 2a). In contrast, the augmented eleventh takes its dissonant quality in the more usual way, from the seventh it makes with the fifth below, and resolves stepwise downward (Example 2b).

Ex. 2.

Other chromatic tensions such as #$\hat{4}$/III7 in major (Example 3) are rare, as they tend to weaken the tonality.

Ex. 3.

A potential tension will be avoided if it might obscure the local harmonic progression. For example, $\hat{7}$/II7 (a thirteenth) in a II7-V7 progression would interfere with one of the essential lines of the progression, $\hat{8}$/II7—$\hat{7}$/V7, so it is avoided (Example 4a). However, when II7 is a passing chord between I and III, the $\hat{7}$ tension is usable (Example 4b).

Ex. 4.

In two cases it appears that a tension may find resolution in a pitch other than a chord tone. The minor-derived $b\hat{7}$/V7 (an augmented ninth), receiving its dissonance from the chord tone $\hat{7}$ a major seventh below, can resolve that dissonance by progressing to $b\hat{6}$, itself a minor ninth tension, dissonant with the root (Example 5). The other case involves $\hat{6}$/I, the function of which in jazz is unique. $\hat{6}$/I is not dissonant with the root; nor does it form a seventh interval with a lower basic chord tone; yet it is not a triad member. It can behave as a tension standing for, and resolving to $\hat{5}$/I (Example 6a)—see also Irving Berlin's "Cheek to Cheek," m. 1). But its consonant character enables it to serve as the resolution of $\hat{7}$/I, the major seventh tension (Example 6b), and this is its most usual role: an unresolved addition to I, not standing for $\hat{5}$ (which is often voiced a step away from it), but also not a chord tone. IV and bVI also support major seventh and sixth tensions, which behave similarly to those of I (Example 6c). A sixth usually is distinguished from a

Ex. 5.

thirteenth. The term *sixth* is used for a pitch that is able, in the given context, to be the resolution of a diatonic major seventh; the term *thirteenth* is used when the associated seventh is not major. The thirteenth is not the resolution of a seventh. The minor sixth tension is very rare (for example, see m. 1 of Cole Porter's "So in Love"), and does not serve to resolve any seventh.

Ex. 6.

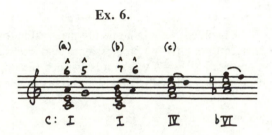

2. *Possibilities grouped by harmonic function.* Bebop performance practice groups chords by linear and harmonic function into five *substitution sets* headed by I, IV, IVm, V, and #IIø7.[5] Any chord of a set may be replaced in practice by any other chord of the same set without destroying the essential lines of the progression in which it is involved. The I set contains I, III7, VI7, and sometimes #IVø7 (e.g., in C: C, Em7, Am7, and F#ø7); the IV set contains IV and II7 (F and Dm7); and IVm set contains IVm, IIø7, and *b*VIIdom7 (Fm, Dø7, and B*b*7); the V set contains V7, VIIø7, VIIo7, and *b*IIom7 (G7, Bø7, Bo7, and D*b*7); the #IIo7 set contains #IIo7, VIIdom7, and sometimes IIdom7, IVdom7, and *b*VIdom7 (D#o7, B7, D7, F7, and A*b*7). Each substitution set represents a different harmonic function. The substitution sets can aid in an economical representation of available tensions.

Examples 7-11 show the possible tensions on the various substitution sets. The tension (black notehead) is slurred to its resolution (white notehead) above the lower chord tone (white notehead) with which it interacts most strongly. Tension numbers (ninth, eleventh, etc.) are not given because at times they would vary depending on which chord of the set were chosen as a reference. For example, in Example 9, the black notehead el is a major seventh on IVm, a ninth on IIø7, and an augmented eleventh on *b*VIIdom7.

Another type of harmonic function is the linear prefix,[6] which involves chords the roots of which serve as passing tones, neighbor tones, or incomplete neighbor tones in the context of surrounding chord roots. Tensions on linear chords are those diatonic major

Ex. 7. Tensions on the I set

Ex. 8. Tensions on the IV set

Ex. 9. Tensions on the IVm set

Ex. 10. Tensions on the V set

Ex. 11. Tensions on the #IIo7 set

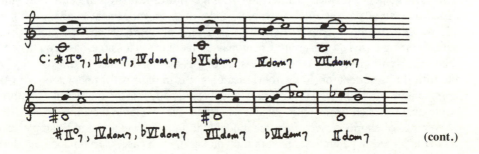

(cont.)

sevenths, ninths, elevenths, and thirteenths which do not raise any of the problems discussed in B(1) above. A chromatic embellishing chord (neighbor or incomplete neighbor) of the same structure as the chord embellished takes the same tensions as the main chord.

III. Tensions in Chord Voicings

A. General Considerations

In bebop a low bass root is always assumed to be provided by the bass player, although it may or may not be included in the voicing, and although the bass player may or may not actually play it. Because intervals smaller than a fifth can sound muddy if placed too low, the most usual interval above that root is a fifth or larger. (Voicings in general follow the structure of the overtone series: larger intervals below smaller.) The third and the seventh (if it is not major) are essential for aural determination of the function of the chord and are not normally omitted. The fifth, if perfect, is sometimes omitted. Any number of possible tensions may be used in any voicing. Because the tension represents its resolution in the register in which it occurs, resolution and tension do not ideally exist as adjacent voices in the same register. (Seeming exceptions are discussed in III(D) below.) Most voicings of chords in bebop may be understood as subsets of model arrangements of chord tones and tensions: a model built in thirds and a model built in fourths.

B. The Model Built in Thirds

The most "natural" arrangement of chord tones and tensions is in ascending thirds. This arrangement provides each tension with a chord tone a seventh below, bringing its dissonance aurally to the fore. A general model of this arrangement is given in Example 12, which lists chord tones and tensions in ascending thirds when read clockwise. An actual voicing based on this arrangement may omit either (1) tensions based on the considerations given in B(1) above or for the sake of greater convenience in the voicing, or (2) the fifth if it is perfect, or (3) the root, assuming it is in the bass or understood, or (4) any combination of (1) through (3). As previously explained, it is the intervallic structure and contextual function of the chord which determine the available tensions.

Voicings of chords derived from the model built in thirds are given in Example 13. The model is placed in parentheses next to the voicing in each case. Certain apparent discrep-

Ex. 12. The model built in thirds

ROOT

13TH   3RD

11TH   5TH

9TH   7TH

ancies may need explanation. In order to spread the voicings into the lower register, and in order to follow the pattern of the overtone series, occasionally one or more pitches in the model have been displaced by an octave in the actual voicing (e.g., the root and seventh of the Cm7 in Example 13a). In cases of mode mixture, the model is shown in the major mode. For example, in Example 13a, the model for the F7 chord contains g1, whereas the voicing contains gb1. The ninth, gb1, is derived from the minor mode of Bb; the concurrent thirteenth, d2, is derived from the major mode. The line $\hat{6}$-$b\hat{6}$-$\hat{5}$ (here g1-gb1-f1) helps to drive the progression toward its resolution, the tonic. Also, in the E half-diminished seventh chord of Example 13b, the f1 in the model would create a minor ninth with the root, E; therefore, the chord tone e1 which it represents is used instead in the voicing.

Ex. 13. Voicings in thirds

(cont.)

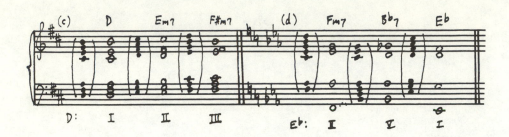

C. The Model Built in Fourths

Voicings stressing fourths have been popular in bebop because they maintain the dissonant seventh interval—a seventh is the sum of each pair of adjacent fourths—while eliminating the "sweetness" of thirds that characterizes the model built in thirds. The model built in fourths is given in Example 14, which lists chord tones and tensions in ascending fourths when read clockwise.

Ex. 14. The model built in fourths

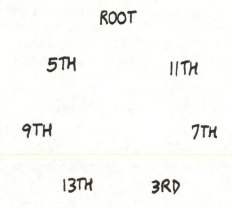

ROOT

5TH   11TH

9TH   7TH

13TH   3RD

Voicings which make use of subsets of this model are shown in Example 15. Again, the model is given in parentheses next to each voicing. In Example 15a, the G7 omits the $\hat{1}$ (eleventh) on V7 for two reasons: the arrangement in fourths places the chord tone B a major seventh above the tension C, making the B sound as if it were the tension; and because, on V7, $\hat{1}$ and $\hat{7}$ have long been mutually exclusive members of the most common type of 4-3 suspension. Example 15a also illustrates "modal intensification" on the dominant, in which the "modal" scale degrees ($\hat{2}$, $\hat{3}$, and $\hat{6}$) are first presented in their major mode forms (e1, a1, and d2 on G7), then lowered to their "altered" minor/Phrygian mode forms (eb1, ab1, and db2 on G7). This progression from major to altered modal degrees on the same chord provides a sense of intensified motion toward the tonic resolu-

Ex. 15. Voicings in fourths

tion of the progression[7] (cf. Example 13a above). The tonic chord includes #$\hat{4}$, a Lydian derivative which also might be heard as enharmonically equivalent to a "blue" note. This scale degree, having the potential to weaken the key, is prevented from doing so here by being placed in a high register at the top of the voicing, where, following the model of the overtone series, the ear expects to find the most distant, dissonant tensions. Consider the tonic chord of Example 15b. Following the model built in fourths, its lowest note might have been #$\hat{4}$ (B). (Bb is impossible for the same reasons C was impossible on the G7 of Example 15a). In this register, the #$\hat{4}$ would attenuate the tonality to too great an extent. Also, the voicing would surely sound like a G chord. Hence, a chord tone is used instead of the #$\hat{4}$. In Examples 15b and c, the bass line has been indicated by black noteheads, as it is important to the identity of each tonic chord. The eb of the F7 voiceleads to the d of the G chord rather than to the f# because of the need to resolve the seventh of F7 stepwise downward and to avoid the augmented second eb-f#. The f#2 is placed in the top voice. Without the bass, g2 would have been a better choice. Fourths are not generally used in voicing the #IIo7. They are not nearly as prominent in the D#o7 voicing of Example 15d as in the other voicings. The C chord contains some doublings for the sake of voiceleading.

D. Mid-range Voicings Involving Register Shifts[8]

In homophonic textures, accompanying chords of three to five voices are often limited to the tenor range. Whereas, in the "spread" voicings, the interval of a seventh provides dissonance, in voicings of more limited range, it is the second that serves this function.

The dissonant second may be seen in the most simple case in Example 16a, which shows tenor-range voicings derived from the model built in thirds. Again, the models are given in parentheses. Arrows indicate tones which are shifted in register in the voicing.

Ex. 16. Mid-range voicings

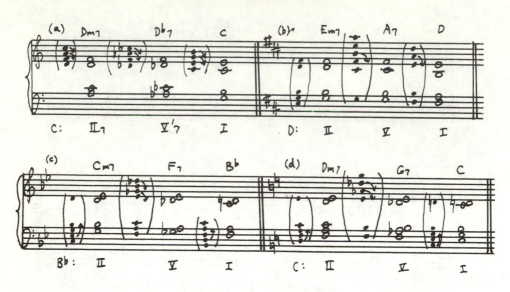

Example 16b is arranged so that one of the sevenths of the model is maintained in each chord, but another of the sevenths becomes a second by register shift. The last two chords are derived from the model built in fourths. The choice of thirds or fourths as a model for voicings is mainly dependent on contextual considerations, especially voiceleading. In Example 16c all the sevenths have become seconds. Example 16d is a five-voice example, which begins to give a "cluster" effect. The addition of a sixth voice within the same range would clarify the cluster effect but would obscure the relation of the voicings to the models.

E. Polychordal Voicings

There remains one other type of voicing, that which is partitioned by register into two units of three or four voices each. Because the units usually are separately identifiable as triads or seventh chords, this type of voicing is called a polychord. The two units are composed of chord tones and tensions. The lower of the two is interpreted by the ear as representing the chord being expressed by the voicing; therefore, the upper unit usually contains more tensions than the lower. There may be doublings between the two units.

Example 17 presents examples of polychordal voicings. In Example 17a, the upper unit of the Em7 contains the seventh, ninth, and eleventh; on the Dmaj7, it doubles the fifth and includes the major seventh and ninth; both lower units present the basic triad. In Example 17b, the tensions are again included in the upper unit: g2 is a minor thirteenth on Bϕ7, becoming an augmented ninth on E7, which also has a diminished fifth, bb2. The basic requirement of the lower unit is not that it be triadic, but that it clearly express the chord. To this end, the segment of the model built in fourths containing the seventh, third, and thirteenth of a dominant seventh chord serves well, as is illustrated by Example 17c. Example 17d, the lower unit consists only of the tritone made of the third and seventh of

Ex. 17. Polychordal voicings

the dominant seventh chord, and the bass roots are indicated below the voicings to avoid ambiguity: for example, the F7 voicing would work equally well as a B7. Example 17e, which uses the same lower unit as the A7 in (c), could easily be understood as a segment of the model built in fourths. However, it has a polychordal aspect in that the upper unit is an exact transposition of the lower. Example 17f shows dominant seventh chords as both units. The upper unit contains the ninth, augmented eleventh, and thirteenth.

Although the possibilities are polychordal voicings are very great, these few examples introduce the basic principles of their formation: (1) registral separation of the units, (2) inclusion in the lower unit of enough basic chord tones to express the chord, and (3) inclusion in the upper unit of most of the tensions used in the voicing.

IV. Melodic Organization

A. Arpeggiations of Chord Voicings

The voicings discussed above are often expressed melodically by arpeggiation in bebop melodic lines. "Donna Lee" by Charlie Parker (Example 18) contains numerous examples of arpeggiated voicings based on the model built in thirds. Among these, in m. 3, Bb7 is arpeggiated in thirds from its third (d1) through its ninth (c2). In m. 5, Bbm7 is horizontalized as root (bb), third, (db1), fifth (f1), seventh (ab1), ninth (c2), and eleventh (eb2). In m. 28, Bo7 supports the line ab1-b1-g2, drawing attention to the seventh interval ab1-g2. Dizzy Gillespie's "A Night in Tunisia" (Example 19) begins with a similar ascending arpeggiation of Eb7: bb (fifth), db1 (seventh), f1 (ninth), and c2 (thirteenth). Frequently the dissonant seventh between chord tone and tension is stated directly: see, for example, Sonny Rollins's "Airegin," m. 2 (Example 20) and Cole Porter's "I Love You," m. 1 (Example 21).

Ex. 18. "Donna Lee" by Charlie Parker (Atlantic Music Corp.)

Arpeggiations within the model built in thirds are more common in bebop melodies than arpeggiations within the model built in fourths. However, a clear example of the latter occurs in mm. 17-18 of Thelonious Monk's "I Mean You" (Example 22). Here Eb7 is expressed as the descending series f2 (ninth), c2 (thirteenth), g1 (third), and db1 (seventh). Other examples of arpeggiation within the model built in fourths include m. 9 of John Carisi's "Israel," (Example 23) in which Bbmaj7 is expressed as ascending d1 (third), g1 (sixth), and c2 (ninth); and mm. 21-22 of Thelonious Monk's "Epistrophy," (Example 24) in which B7 is expressed as ascending c#1 (ninth), f#1 (fifth), and b1 (root)—the d#1 and g#1 have been transferred up an octave from their position in the model.

Ex. 19. "A Night in Tunisia" by Dizzy Gillespie (M.C.A. Music, Inc.)

Ex. 20. "Airegin" by Sonny Rollins (Prestige Music Co., Inc.)

Ex. 21. "I Love You" by Cole Porter (Chappell and Co.)

Ex. 22. "I Mean You" by Thelonious Monk (Music Sales Corp.)

Ex. 23. "Israel" by John Carisi (Beechwood Music Corp.)

Ex. 24. "Epistrophy" by Thelonious Monk (Music Sales Corp.)

Arpeggiation of polychordal voicings developed most fully in the jazz of the sixties and seventies. However, André Hodier, writing in the late forties, described polychordal arpeggiation in the improvisations of Charlie Parker:

> His [Parker's] phrase frequently approaches polytonality. By that I mean that the notes he sometimes plays over certain basses are in a polytonal relation with them. This is notably the case in "Moose the Mooche," in which Parker grafts a major chord based on the sixth degree of the scale onto a dominant seventh, thus forming an altered thirteenth that suggests two different keys. . . .[9]

An early compositional example of arpeggiation of polychordal voicings may be seen in mm. 5-7 of Charlie Mingus's "Goodbye Pork Pie Hat" (Example 25). In m. 5 the melody arpeggiates Fm7 as fifth, seventh, ninth and eleventh of Bbm; in m. 6, an Ab triad is arpeggiated as augmented ninth, root, and minor thirteenth of C7; and in m. 7 an F diminished triad is arpeggiated as augmented eleventh, thirteenth, and augmented ninth of D7, followed by an E diminished triad arpeggiated as thirteenth, augmented ninth, and root of G7.

Ex. 25. "Goodbye Pork Pie Hat" by Charles Mingus (Jazz Workshop)

B. Types of Resolutions of Tensions

The resolution of a tension sometimes occurs immediately on the surface of the composition, before the chord supporting the tension changes. For example, in "Donna Lee," m. 4 (Example 18), g1 (a thirteenth) resolves to f1 (the fifth) on Bb7. Similarly in m. 7, on Ab, bb1 (a ninth) resolves to ab1 (the root). Only slightly more elaborate than immediate resolution is the case of a resolution which is delayed by melodic ornament, but not delayed so long as to allow the chord to change before the resolution appears. For example, in "Donna Lee," m. 5, on Bbm7, eb1 (an eleventh) is delayed in its resolution to db1 (the third) by the interpolation of two notes, a and bb. Such immediate and relatively immediate resolutions of tensions are extremely common in bebop melodies.

Another level of elaboration is reached when the movement in the direction of resolution of a tension is delayed until or after the chord has changed. In "Donna Lee," mm. 14-15, e1, a diminished fifth on Bb7, resolves (after interpolation) to f1, as expected, but the chord has changed to Bb7 by the time of resolution. In Vernon Duke's "I Can't Get Started," (Example 26) m. 18, f#1, a ninth on Em7, sustains to become a thirteenth on A7, after which it resolves to e1, a consonance, the fifth of A7.

Ex. 26. "I Can't Get Started" by Vernon Duke (Chappell and Co.)

Furthermore, elaboration results when the "resolution" is itself a tension because the chord has changed upon its arrival. "Chains" of stepwise tensions are possible when the progression is sequential, a common pattern being the alternation of melodic ninths and thirteenths. A clear example of the latter may be seen in Jerome Kern's "Yesterdays" (Example 27a), in which f2, a thirteenth on A7, "resolves" to e2, a ninth on D7; the e2 remains, becoming another thirteenth on G7, which in turn resolves to d2, a ninth on C7. The motion downward continues sequentially until c2, the ninth of Bbmaj7, resolves directly to bb1 on the way to the half cadence, a1/V. This chain of tensions is derived by contraction (or elision) from a standard linear intervallic pattern of fourth species counter-point: Example 27b shows the chain of dissonant sevenths between the tensions and the lower chord tones; Example 27c shows the fourth species pattern the contraction of which yields the sevenths.

Ex. 27. "Yesterdays" by Jerome Kern (T. B. Harms Co.)

Dizzy Gillespie's reharmonization of mm. 3-4 of "I Can't Get Started" (Example 28) produces a short chain of tensions, again, ninths becoming thirteenths. The resolution of the b1 of m. 4 is unusually delayed: it appears first as a ninth on Am7, then as a thirteenth on D7, continuing as a major seventh on C, finally resolving to a1 as root of Am7—a 7-6 resolution with change of bass.

Ex. 28. "I Can't Get Started" by Vernon Duke (Chappell and Co.)

Example 29 shows one last example of a chain of tensions: the bridge of Jimmy Heath's "C. T. A.," which consists of a chromatically descending series of thirteenths. The last of these, $\hat{3}$/V7, is unresolved—that is, by moving to $\hat{1}$/I the melody denies the possibility of a resolution ($\hat{2}$) in the register occupied by the tension.

Ex. 29. "C.T.A." by Jimmy Heath (Asa Music Co.)

Unresolved tensions of this sort are relatively rare in bebop melodies. "C. T. A." also exhibits, in mm. 3-4, the pattern of resolution moving to tension (Example 30). Here, although each tension is heard in association with its resolution, the tension is left unresolved. Sometimes a tension sustains through a chord change to become a consonance, thereby losing its "need" to resolve. For example, this effect is produced whenever $\hat{5}$/V7 is reharmonized as II7-V7. In Duke Ellington's "In a Mellow Tone" (Example 31), mm. 5-6, ab1, an eleventh on Ebm7 (II7), sustains to become the root of Ab7 (V7), and does not resolve stepwise downward. The V being the structurally superior of the two chords, the relation of the Ab to it as root is also structurally superior to its relation to the Ebm7 (II7).

Ex. 30. "C.T.A." by Jimmy Heath (Asa Music Co.)

Ex. 31. "In a Mellow Tone" by Duke Ellington (Robbins Music Corp.)

The more common sort of melodic "unresolved" tension actually finds its resolution in an accompanying voice in the same register as the tension. For example, in George Shearing's "Conception" (Example 32), the e1 of m. 1, a minor thirteenth on Ab7, in performance would resolve to eb1 as an inner accompanying voice either during the Ab7 or as a ninth on Dbmaj7.

Ex. 32. "Conception" by George Shearing (E.M.I. Music Publishing, Ltd.)

C. Levels of Structure in "Donna Lee"

Although in layered analyses style characteristics usually lie at or near the foreground, a thorough understanding of the melodic-harmonic structure of a piece necessitates consideration of the middleground and background as well. The following is a melodic-contrapuntal analysis of Charlie Parker's "Donna Lee," serving as an illustration in a larger context of the concepts presented above.

Graph A (Example 33) is a background graph for "Donna Lee." After two skips to an inner voice in mm. 7 and 17, $\hat{5}$ is prolonged by an upper neighbor at m. 23 which is supported by an embellishing chord (VI). The descent to $\hat{1}$ is accomplished in the last three measures.

Ex. 33. Graph A. "Donna Lee," background

Graph B (Example 34) shows the two skips filled in with chromatic passing tones supported by circle-of-fifths dominant prefixes: V/V-V-I. An implied inner voice (ab1 at m. 7) connects through stepwise motion and the first of many register transfers to the eb2 of m. 11. The main harmonic support for this line is a IV prefix. The neighbor $\hat{6}$/VI at m. 23 is prolonged by a prefix progression, IV-V. After m. 23, e2 acts first as a neighbor tone to f2, then as a passing tone to the structural eb2 of m. 29. There is a skip to an inner-voice leading tone just before the final cadence.

Ex. 34. Graph B. "Donna Lee," middleground

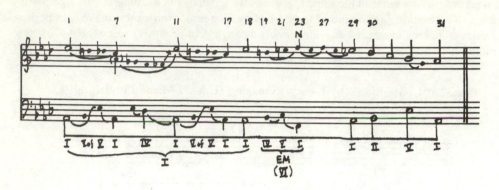

Ex. 35. Graph C. "Donna Lee," middleground

In Graph C (Example 35), one begins to find examples of tensions and their resolutions as well as more of the register transfers that are so characteristic of this wide-ranging melody. The temporal displacement of the first structural $\hat{5}$ allows it to serve as the melodic goal of a major seventh and its resolution, a major sixth. (An fb2 passing tone connects the f2 to the eb2.) The series of circle-of-fifths dominants that supports the passing tone line in mm. 1-7 is extended by one, the F7 in m. 2. An understanding of the prolongation of the eb2 which this F7 harmonizes is facilitated by an examination of the prolongation of the eb2 at mm. 11-12. Examples 36a-e show the development of the motivic pattern at m. 12. Example 36a shows the basic harmonic structure: a 7-6 suspension with change of bass; in (b), f2 is added as a consonant neighbor tone; in (c), this f2 becomes the resolution of a minor ninth tension, gb2; similarly, in (d), the minor ninth becomes the resolution of an augmented ninth neighbor tone; finally, in (e), a passing tone f2 connects the structural eb2 with the minor ninth. Mm. 15-17 have the same voiceleading in sequence with mm. 11-13.

Example 36f shows the voiceleading of the same motivic figure prolonging eb1 in mm. 2-3. Melodically the two voices are identical to those of mm. 11-13 in (e); however, they are shifted rhythmically in relation to each other: either the bass Bb enters early or the upper voice prolongation is delayed. This shifting redefines the gb1 as a thirteenth on Bb7, and the ab1 is no longer a tension. The d1 of this Bb7 leads to db1 in m. 5. Twice this Db is made the resolution of an eleventh tension: first as db1, then as db2 in a register transfer. A return to the lower register leads the db1 (as the seventh of Eb7) to c1 in m. 7. At this point a "reaching-over" begins, containing many tension-resolution pairs, which leads the melody up a tenth to the structural eb2 at m. 11. The ab1 of m. 7, skipped to

Ex. 36. "Donna Lee," middleground detail

from cl, becomes the resolution of a ninth, b*b*1. Similarly, the d*b*2 of m. 9, the root of the IV prefix, resolves the ninth e*b*2 at the beginning of that measure. This e*b*2 is itself the delayed resolution of a ninth, f2, imposed on the secondary II7 (E*b*m7) in m. 8. The f2 finds partial resolution by moving to the passing tone f*b*2, which is also the ninth of the substitute dominant of IV, but the chain of tensions does not come to rest until the arrival of the d*b*2/D*b* in m. 9. In this middleground graph, the g*b*2 of m. 10 is a tension (eleventh) resolving to f*b*2 on the minor IV chord. However, in the foreground, the IVm is replaced by *b*VIIdom7, changing the melodic-harmonic relationship. Mm. 18-20 repeat mm. 1-3. However, the B*b*7 of m. 19 serves as a IV chord in the IV-V progression tonicizing the embellishing chord of m. 23. (The line d1-e1-f1 is derived from the ascending F melodic minor scale.) Graph C also shows the transfer up an octave of the neighbor tone e2 at m. 26, its return to the lower register f1, and the transfer of that f1 to the upper register as f2. This f2 is part of a three-note approach to the structural $\hat{5}$, an approach melodically identical to that of m. 1, but with different harmonization. At m. 28 the g2 is a ninth resolving to f2; at the foreground it remains a tension on #IIo7. The last four measures contain further register changes and an arpeggiation of V at $\hat{2}$.

Graph D (Example 37) is a foreground graph containing all the notes of the melody. In mm. 1-6 dotted slurs show the retention of four voices arranged in thirds in the upper register. Although the e*b*2 of m. 2 has been transferred down an octave, and resolves to d*b*1 as an eleventh, the upward arpeggiation in m. 5 allows the e*b*2 also to resolve to d*b*2 at m. 6. Further dotted slurs connect notes of equivalent voice-leading function in the same or different registers throughout Graph D.

Ex. 37. Graph D. "Donna Lee," foreground

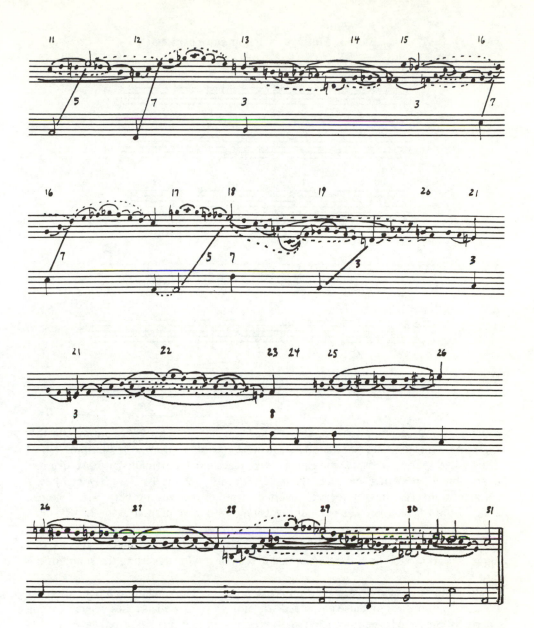

D. Motives in Bebop Melodic Lines

Motivic organization and development in bebop melodic lines does not seem to differ generally from that of any common-practice tonal music. Many of the usual processes can be seen in Examples 38a-f. Example 38a illustrates the direct repetition of a motive in mm. 1 of Dizzy Gillespie's "Groovin' High." In Example 38b, a descending perfect fourth, b♭1-f1, provides the framework for the real sequential repetition and elaboration

Ex. 38. Motives in bebop compositions

of two interior descending fourths, $ab1$-$eb1$ and $gb1$-$db1$, in mm. 1-2 of Jimmy Heath's "C. T. A." Example 38c shows tonal sequential repetition of a motive in mm. 7-8 of "Donna Lee." Tonal transposition can also take place at a temporal distance, so that it is not possible to speak of a sequence: Example 38d, mm. 1-2 and 16-17 of "Donna Lee." Retrograde, inverted, and retrograde inverted forms of motives are very rare. One can extract, from "Donna Lee," a contour inversion of a motive in m. 1 at m. 25 (Example 38e), as well as (because of symmetry) either a retrograde or inverted form of a motive from m. 11 at m. 14 (Example 38f). A bracket in Example 38a, b, c, and f marks the one unique aspect of these motives; a truncated descending skip suggesting the sound of the word *bebop*.

If the concept of motivic organization is extended to include relations among not only ordered sets of pitches, but also unordered sets of pitches, as well as cases where ordering is partially preserved, then inversion and retrogression gain increased relevance to melodic structure. Ordered inversion and retrograde inversion have a subtle influence on the organization of mm. 3-4 of Dizzy Gillespie's "Groovin High." Example 39a presents the original melody; 39b shows how the first four notes form the basis for the continuation by (slightly reordered) retrograde inversion; 39c and d indicate further inversional relationships in that excerpt. Example 40a shows mm. 1-8 of Jimmy Heath's "C. T. A."; Example 40b indicates by beams an ordered inversional relationship between subsets of mm. 1-2 and mm. 5-6. The transpositional level may be tonally significant, as it holds the first and last notes of the sets (tonic and dominant) invariant. (Recall the discussion of the fourth as a motive here with regard to Example 38b.) Example 40c compares the pitch-

Ex. 39. "Groovin' High" by Dizzy Gillespie (M. C. A. Music, Inc.)

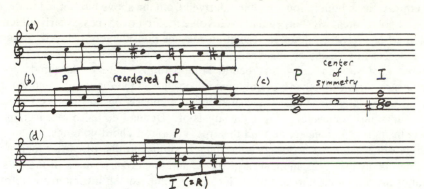

class content of mm. 1-2 arranged in descending order (as the general direction of mm. 1-2 is downward) with the pitch-class content of mm. 6-8 arranged in ascending order (as the general direction of mm. 6-8 is upward), to show the same inversional relationship, with the same tonic and dominant invariants.

These observations suggest material for further investigation. Inversion, retrograde inversion, and relations among ordered and unordered sets probably have more relevance to bebop melodic lines than has generally been recognized.

Ex. 40. "C.T.A." by Jimmy Heath (Asa Music Co.)

V. Summary

Bebop melodic lines are characterized primarily by surface emphasis on tensions—the major sevenths, ninths, elevenths, and thirteenths that are also contained in the chord voicings used to accompany the melodies. Because the melodies often arpeggiate the voicings, it is necessary to understand principles for the formation of voicings as a preliminary for understanding this aspect of melodic structure. Types of voicings include those built in thirds, those built in fourths, those derived from the above but limited to the tenor range, and polychords. Most arpeggiations involve the first two types. Nearly all tensions in melodic lines resolve, although resolution may be considerably delayed, sometimes forming descending chains of tensions.

Layered analysis can show that bebop compositions share background melodic-harmonic structures with other types of tonal music. It is in the foreground and to a lesser extent in the middleground that the characteristic emphasis on tensions as a means of elaboration is most noticeable. A layered analysis of "Donna Lee" also reveals numerous transfers to register in connection with the arpeggiation of chord voicings.

Motivic organization of bebop melodic lines is similar to that of earlier tonal music, exhibiting mainly direct restatement, sequences, and tonal transposition of motives. The renewal of interest on the part of twentieth century composers in inversion and retrogression as compositional techniques may have had some influence on the composers of bebop melodies. Further investigation of set relations in jazz melodies seems warranted.

Notes

1. Steven Strunk, "The Harmony of Early Bop: A Layered Approach," *Journal of Jazz Studies* 6 (1979): 4-53.
2. Nat Shapiro and Nat Hentoff, *Hear Me Talkin' to Ya* (New York: Rinehart and Co., 1955), p. 354.
3. The term *tension* was used in this way by the faculty of the Berklee School of Music in the 1960s. More recently, it has been used in a similar manner in Andrew Jaffe, *Jazz Theory* (Dubuque, Iowa: William C. Brown Co., 1983), pp. 25, 49, 72, and 128.
4. Explanation of notation: arabic numerals with carats indicate a melodic pitch as a scale degree. The slash (/) means "harmonized by." For example, in C major, $\hat{3}/V7$ indicates a melodic pitch-class E (third scale degree) harmonized by a G7 (dominant seventh chord). The E would be a thirteenth on the G7.
5. For discussion of "substitution sets," see Strunk, pp. 15-21.
6. The linear prefix is discussed in Strunk, pp. 8-13.
7. Subdominant modal intensification is discussed in Strunk, p. 13.
8. This type of voicing has little to do with melodic lines, but is included here so that the discussion of voicings may be complete. This type of voicing encompasses both the "block-style" and "open position" accompaniment voicings described in Joseph W. Rohm, "Jazz Harmony, Structure, Voicing, and Progression" (Ph.D. dissertation, Florida State University, 1974).
9. André Hodier, *Jazz, its Evolution and Essence* (New York: Grove Press, 1956), p. 104.

The Early Record Review:
Jazz Criticism's First-Born Child

Ronald G. Welburn

The record review, though a by-product of the sound recording industry, is the single most important genre of jazz criticism in America. By the early twentieth century, the recording of a wide spectrum of music and entertainment—available to consumers first on cylinders, then on flat disk records—and the creation of phonographs or "talking machines," through which these recordings could be heard, had become a viable business. While this equipment was not inexpensive, Americans supported the recording and phonograph business, spending from fifty cents to a dollar for each record and from $15 to nearly $400 for various Gramophone and Victrola models between 1902 and the early twenties.[1] The impressively high sales of such equipment and the enormous production of records in the early twenties was influenced by the appeal of jazz, which, during this decade, expanded its range beyond small improvising bands to embrace as well White-manesque concert orchestras.[2]

With the growth in record sales, the British music trade publication, *Talking Machine News and Journal of Events,* began to publish very brief descriptions of selected recent recordings. The first review, in March 1913, devoted just under 100 words, to a recording by a studio orchestra, the Peerless, of "Powder Rag March" and "I'm Going Back to Dixie." The unidentified writer described the first title's "bright and vivid brass opening" and the succeeding "shy interlude on the woodwind instruments." In closing the review, he assured the reader: "Well played and well recorded."[3]

The language of nearly all record reviews has remained remarkably consistent with this early example, though not all reviewers would cite a recording's outstanding attributes. Such early reviews were loosely a type of criticism, but, like later examples, they were also intended to serve a marketing purpose. The review or discussion of new records thus served both the consumer and the record company, the former by stating something about the quality of the product, the latter by advertising its existence. Performers and composers with some reputation received their just due, but contents and recording quality often took precedence over the performers. Titles were almost always listed first, followed by the artist or group.

In the same March 1913 issue of *Talking Machine News* (its popular abbreviated name),

This article is based on a chapter from Dr. Welburn's dissertation, *American Jazz Criticism, 1914-1940.*

two discs by the American Ragtime Octette were reviewed, and the syncopations of "The Syncopated Boogie Boo" were described as "a clever bit of work" by "these eight clever people."[4] In the August issue, a Gene Greene, described as a *"ragtimer . . .* known as the King of Ragtime . . . . is heard in that way which has won for him such distinction," singing "Ragtime Cowboy Joe" and one other song.[5]

The April issue contained a news item with all the characteristics of a favorable record review, not unlike many of the record reviews that jazz magazines and black newspapers printed in the 1930s. It is worth quoting:

> The latest ragtime number issued on Zonophone is No. 1042, which contains the ragtime that has been featured so strongly at the London Palladium and elsewhere, the "Ragtime Goblin Man." This infectious number by Harry Fay and Stanley Kirkby is sure to be eagerly welcomed by talking-machine enthusiasts just now when the ragtime craze is at its height."[6]

Later reviewers might be less likely to call attention to the reasons for a song's popularity or to its composer and lyricist, but the writing in this item was clearly intended to pique the reader's interest. This news item is important because it serves the same purpose as a record review, to which it bears a close generic relationship. Both are forms of journalism, the news item obviously an older one that functions as a brief sketch of an event, while the review functions as an announcement of a release and criticism of its contents.

Sources of Regular Jazz Criticism

The realization of a body of genuine jazz criticism may be defined as the point at which descriptive or analytical reviews of recordings began to appear in periodicals and newspapers on a regular basis. Jazz columnists in Europe took the lead in record criticisms during the twenties. The earliest issues of *Down Beat* contained only reportage and announcements, not reviews of any kind, but the establishment of a critical jazz press rested on there being sufficient recordings for review by self-styled critics, while regular publication of periodicals insured that recordings, issued with reasonable regularity, would have a forum for description and assessment.

A growing record business brought with it a rapid turnover of "old" records in favor of new releases, and the success of performers was often measured by how well their latest releases fared in the marketplace. Even in the Depression year of 1932, the lowest point in record sales between 1920 and 1940, the recording industry survived with sales of six million records.[7] Over time record reviews proved increasingly useful to consumers planning purchases and to serious listeners.

But record reviews did not achieve a large readership for some years, because they appeared primarily in music trade publications, some scholarly journals, and jazz magazines, with European periodicals publishing reviews at a comparatively early date. The first issue of *The Gramophone* appeared in London in April 1923 with a two-page "Review of April Records." The reviewer (possibly editor Compton Mackenzie) discussed several records, in about 200 words each, giving more attention to the experiences of Paderewski, for example, than the work being performed. At the end of this column appeared a subdivision, "Popular Records," and further on "A Note on Some Dance Records," written by James Caskett. There was an editor's note acknowledging records sent for review.[8] From the June issue on, the popular music column was listed as "New Dance Records."

The Rating System Appears

In the February 1924 *Gramophone* an asterisk rating system was introduced for popular records—two for a first-class record, one for second-class—but no such ratings were used for classical releases. The stated rationale for this rating system was "to give some idea of the output, and presumably of the varied demand for dances. They have been carefully tested and are marked [accordingly]."[9] Before 1940 this practice was adopted by American editors of popular music columns and magazines. Such ratings were not always appreciated by musicians, but they served as an indicator of perceived recording success, aimed at musicians, record companies, and consumers.

The practice of reviewing records was adopted over a period of years by both classical and popular music publications. The British *Music and Letters* began listing records and reviewing piano rolls in 1925. In the French *La Revue Musicale,* where jazz critic Hugues Panassié published his first writing, Henry Prunières began reviewing recordings in 1926. American journals were slower to publish reviews. As late as 1935, *Musical Quarterly* introduced a "Quarterly Record List," but with no substantive discussion of records. *Modern Music* did not begin reviewing recordings until 1936. *Chord and Discord,* published in New York by the Bruckner Society of America, reviewed recordings from its inception in 1932 because its editors realized that recorded music could benefit from such exposure, especially since commercialism in the marketplace adversely affected recordings of works by lesser-known composers. This publication, of course, was not interested in popular music or jazz records; nor was the short-lived *Recorded Music* of 1933-1934.[10] But in publishing record reviews at this time, their example is noteworthy.

While unstated, the attitude of classical music periodical editors and writers toward recordings probably involved two conflicting positions that had to be reconciled. To some, as Ernest Newman claimed in *A Musical Critic's Holiday* in 1925, the phonograph was a toy; such lovers of serious music keenly disliked recordings, if only because of the segmentation of classical works on 78 rpm disks. Further, the classical music publications initially shied away from reviewing records because the practice smacked of the song-plugging of Tin Pan Alley. Yet, as even Newman eventually realized, the phonograph deserved respect, if only because notices of new classical releases encouraged the appreciation of classical music—after all, wasn't that what pedagogues wanted instead of jazz or popular music?—and thus made discussion of these classical releases almost a necessity.[11]

Simultaneously, jazz publications and writers accepted the value of reviewing recordings, not only in reaction to the commercialism of the recording industry and its constant production of new releases but also from a desire to inform both established and potential listeners (and musicians) about good jazz. In both the classical and jazz fields, the concentrated critical focus afforded by a review of a single performance created a new branch of musical criticism.

The Impact of Recording Technology on Criticism

For centuries, the musical public had been simply a dancing, singing, or listening one, but the twentieth century introduced a new variable: the musical public as consumer of recordings and phonograph equipment. In this new spirit of technology, the modern music critic came to be a person who, in addition to other required talents, had to listen to as many recorded performances as live performances and to assess both.

The recording of a musical performance gives it a documentary significance. As often as a band or orchestra may perform a piece, recording it fixes it, making permanent the special characteristics present at that moment. For jazz, an improviser's art, the single recorded instance (and its potential alternate takes) fixes just that performance in history and thereby involves a danger that lasting assessments of a band's or instrumentalist's talents will thereafter be based on that performance. In addition, the recording, distribution, and sales of popular music and jazz records was well established before musicians fully understood their significance, and record reviews created a new forum in which negative comments could further fuel the antagonism traditionally prevailing between artists and critics.

R. D. Darrell and *Phonograph Monthly Review*

October 1926 marked an important point in the emergence of record reviewing in the United States—the first issue of *Phonograph Monthly Review,* published in Boston. Nine by twelve inches in format, it soon proved to be a major publication, for its content and shrewd critical judgments prefigured the sincere critical evaluations of such late-1930s magazines as *Jazz Information* and the *H.R.S. Society Rag.* It served the same purpose as London's *Gramophone* and the British music trade paper *Melody Maker,* also first published in 1926. *Phonograph Monthly Review,* recalled by its cofounder, R. D. Darrell, as "the first non-trade American record magazine,"[12] was a literary and musical phenomenon in catering to the sophisticated American record buyer. Darrell, in an article asking whether or not American homes were musical, conveyed the magazine's philosophy in stating that "the true phonograph enthusiast is first of all a music lover; his passion for collecting records, for experimenting [with equipment] is secondary."[13]

In the first issue, Moses Smith began a six-part series, "From Jazz to Symphony: Self-Education in Music by Means of the Phonograph."[14] Smith was not particularly concerned with jazz, but his essays reflected the appeal of recordings to American consumers at a time when popular music was at the peak of its appreciation for that decade. (According to Roland Gelatt's study, total record sales for 1927 came to 104 million units.[15]) Recordings, and the phonograph equipment and accessories profusely advertised in music and nonmusic periodicals and newspapers, came into their own at this time, and Darrell perceived that the pretensions of owning such equipment often had little to do with the enjoyment of recorded music.[16] Darrell's subsequent articles included a history of American music on record and a treatise on appreciating the best in music.[17]

Darrell resorted to pseudonymous bylines for his jazz record reviews: "The Jazz Editor," "Rufus," and "Rufe Harlem," the last two being marks of a self-styled hipster, a man supposedly familiar with the jazz doings of blacks. In the first issue of *Phonograph Monthly Review,* "the Jazz Editor" listed two-and-one-half pages of "Dance Records" by Louis Armstrong's Hot Five, Ted Weems, and Jean Goldkette. With the March 1927 issue, "Rufus" also took over reviewing recordings of popular and dance music, categorized by label. To keep abreast of the deluge of releases, he commented tersely on recorded performances as being either on or below the level of an artist's talent.

That Darrell was faced with so many recordings to review may account for the wilting enthusiasm of his commentary, but in July 1927, when he reviewed Duke Ellington's "Black and Tan Fantasy," his enthusiasm revived, establishing his significance as a jazz critic and influencing the course of jazz criticism. What contributed to the outstanding quality of Darrell's review was his understanding of Ellington's method of constructing his original compositions for jazz band from many elements and nuances, some of which would appeal, perhaps inadvertently, to classical music listeners. Even better was his review, as "Rufus," of Ellington's "Black Beauty" and "Take It Easy," in which he pointed to the "curiously twisted and wry" work of the trumpeter, and to the "nostalgia and bitterness" the latter work as a whole evokes. As in his first Ellington review, Darrell used words like "amazing" and "eccentric." "Eccentric" might justifiably mean singular and outstanding yet peculiar effects of expression; "amazing," however, may communicate wonder but is a cliché too easily relied upon by jazz writers and journalists.[18]

Still, this kind of descriptive critical writing for jazz recordings assisted reader-consumers in selecting records for purchase. And it also quickly lifted the language of jazz criticism above that of mundane reportage and the hue and cry of the debate over the music's social value. Calling attention to specific qualities in recorded versions of particular works was consistent with newspaper accounts of concerts.[19] Darrell, knowledgeable about classical music, found in Ellington a jazz composer who served the critic as a catalyst for erudite analysis. In short, Darrell successfully applied the craftmanship of classical music criticism to jazz recordings in *Phonograph Monthly Review,* even though this periodical, like others, treated jazz and popular music as a lesser entity, a musical stepchild, for example by failing to list jazz and popular performers in its index of artists.

Music Lovers Guide and *American Music Lover*

By the spring of 1930, Darrell had become managing editor of *Phonograph Monthly Review,* replacing cofounding editor Axel Johnson. In October 1931, Darrell resigned as managing editor but continued to contribute special articles. The last issue of *Phonograph Monthly Review* was published in March 1932.

Both Darrell and Johnson moved to New York, where they brought out *Music Lovers Guide* in September 1932. In a six-by-nine-inch size, *Music Lovers Guide* followed the format of its predecessor in giving individual classical composers their own review listings while all dance and "hot jazz" records were lumped together. Darrell continued to write these reviews as associate editor, consistently lavishing praise on Ellington and Louis Armstrong. In four 1933 installments, an anonymous group of writers contributed another "From Jazz to Symphony" feature, starting in the April issue and continuing through June, August, and September. Its subtitle was adjusted to the purposes and direction of the periodical: "The Phonograph as a Modern Medium for Self-Education in Music."

Darrell resigned effective with the June 1934 issue; Horace Van Norman replaced him as associate editor. While Darrell wrote the "Hot Jazz" column without a by-line, Van Norman, writing as "Van", wrote the "New Popular Records" column and rated records from "A" through "AAAA." Thus "Van" rated Ellington's "Ebony Rhapsody"/"I Met My Waterloo" AAAA and Glen Gray's "Dallas Blues" AA. While he liked Ellington's music, the proportions of records chosen for review indicates a general preference for white bands.[20]

Peter Hugh Reed took over the helm of *Music Lovers Guide,* and with the May 1935 issue it became *American Music Lover.* Darrell was not associated with this publication. "Van" wrote the "In the Popular Vein" column, and the general format adhered to what its two predecessors had established. In February 1936 Enzo Archetti contributed a "Swing Music Notes" column, presenting some engaging opinions about critical methodology along with jazz news coverage and mention of occasional club appearances, dances, and tours.

An editorial in the first issue explained that *American Music Lover* proposed to serve as "a handbook in the best in reproduced music in the home" at no music's expense over another and in the interests of no radio or record dealer or manufacturer. While it remained sympathetic to popular music, it continued the practice of putting all popular music under one heading, though it must be acknowledged that until 1938 there were subcategories within "In the Popular Vein" for "Vocal," "Ballroom Dance," and "Hot Jazz." No reason was given, but these records were rated whereas classical records were not, following the established precedent. Popular record reviews averaged between 100 to 160 words; classical records received from 200 to as many as 1,000 words each. The index to volume 3 listed no jazz reviews or jazz critics. Classical reviews were printed in a bolder typeface, contained more detail, and appear to the reader today to be less strained in style and more leisurely in arriving at their conclusions. The "Ballroom Dance" and "Hot Jazz" subcategories included some of the same artists' recordings, based on apparent differences in the editors' views of the "hot," "sweet," or ballad stylings of particular performances.

"Van" wrote both to please the informed listener-consumer of swing and to enlighten the mildly interested. He sought to win converts by avoiding jargon. His enthusiasms ranged from Ellington to Ray Noble (a visiting British dance band leader and composer) and Benny Goodman. Nearly every issue carried a review of a Goodman record. His review of Maxine Sullivan singing "It Was a Lover and His Lass" and "Dark Eyes" with the Claude Thornhill orchestra ran to 225 words—his longest—and, it so happened, appeared in the 1938 issue without the usual sub-categories for popular and jazz recordings.[21]

The Criticism of Enzo Archetti

Enzo Archetti apparently wrote about jazz only in *American Music Lover* and remains the most neglected jazz journalist-critic of the 1930s. Archetti put forth perceptive judgements in his relatively few articles, not being a record reviewer in the usual sense but rather a reporter and essayist whose articles ranged from 1000 to 1500 words.

Archetti's first article discussed improvements in recording technology but contained also his estimation of Ellington's recorded music as "the most significant *American* music being created today" which, had it not been for recordings, would have remained isolated in Harlem.[22] His "Defense of Ellington" is a pivotal piece in jazz writing. He points out that other critics, in their attacks on Ellington, had failed to analyze or comprehend the controversial "Reminiscing in Tempo," a suite covering four 10-inch sides. He accused the critics of either slavishly praising the work or dismissing it outright for its arhythmic character.

> To [these critics] it was something in which the rhythm could not be tapped out with a foot nor the melody whistled. . . . On the other hand, a few reviewers have hailed it as a great

work in empty words, like Van [Horace Van Norman] in his review in this magazine in the December 1935 issue, but this type of review also fails for the same reason—that is, it did not analyze or explain.

But the specific review Archetti questioned was both analytical and descriptive, for, according to Van Norman, the highlights of Ellington's music lay in its challenging harmonies and rhythms:

> Employing a harmonic idiom that at all times verges on the atonal, it is a hard nut for many of his admirers to crack, and there are several passages that will furrow the brows of the most ardent of them. There are, on the other hand, other passages which are too plainly more eloquent than anything he has yet written. A work of incalculable importance and one not to be judged in one or two hearings.

This did not satisfy Archetti, because he sought analysis in the strictest sense, not the apparent gloss Van Norman offered. The length of this review happened to be typical, however, of published record reviews of jazz and popular dance music records. Archetti wanted important recorded jazz works to receive the same kind of detailed descriptive analysis routinely bestowed on recordings of classical music, but editors typically felt that such serious musical analyses would create unacceptable space problems.

In his call for more analytical criticism, Archetti reprinted the bulk of British critic Leonard Hibbs's review of this recording from the London *Swing Music* of December 1935. Hibbs wrote a rambling discourse expressing his frustration with "Reminiscing in Tempo," and Archetti's enthusiasm for its prose analysis is a bit naive. Not to be overlooked, however, are Hibb's comments on the effect of record reviews.

> Readers of record reviews are roughly divided into two groups. Those who when they disagree with the critic think that he is nuts, and those who are so unwilling to think for themselves that they blindly follow his judgments without stopping to think whether the critic is right or wrong or why.

The second group, he claimed, obstinately maintained their opinions even when a critic had altered his "or the artist or band whom he once praised has deteriorated."

> For example, there are thousands who believe in the Divine right of the Duke, because his best work has been lauded to the skies in highbrow language, which the majority of them do not understand. . . . In spite of their childlike faith, the Duke *can* go wrong.

What Archetti liked was Hibbs's statement that "neither group appears to realize . . . that any review is only the opinion of one critic." Hibbs's method was to scrutinize the music section by section. "Reminiscing in Tempo" was the first lengthy work in the jazz idiom, *Rhapsody in Blue* notwithstanding, to inspire such blow-by-blow critical analysis.[23]

In his critique, Hibbs exhausted the possibilities he alleged Ellington had in mind. He declined to consider the work as an example of swing music, and, since he did not consider jazz a music proper, he reviewed the work as a example of pure music, contending that only its last section was true swing. In the final analysis, he viewed this composition as a work in progress that crystallized in the fourth section all the ideas the composer had stated in the first three.

Commenting on his reprint of Hibbs's article, Archetti advanced the idea that Ellington was influenced by Delius, Stravinsky, and Debussy, "all of whom can be traced [in] Ellington's orchestration."[24] Ironically and significantly, this association of Ellington's orchestration and compositions with masters of the classical tradition was made by critics favorable to jazz, in interpreting Ellington's music for their mixed readership of classical and popular music listeners, a gesture the jazz magazines and their writers refrained from making, at least at that date.

In other articles, Archetti wrote conversationally about the audio quality of records, mentioned where appropriate the inspiration or history of recorded tunes, and in his column on swing took note of the attendance and enthusiasm of listeners at specific performances. A minor symbol of the slowly increasing stature of critical jazz journalism was that by 1938 Archetti's column, initially relegated to the back pages of *American Music Lover* with the rest of the popular music coverage, began to appear in the middle of the magazine. A still more significant indication of the development of the criticism of jazz recordings was the subsequent publication by *American Music Lover* of Warren W. Scholl's lengthy and partially annotated discographies of Bix Beiderbecke and Benny Goodman. The emphasis on jazz recordings as such is even more striking when one considers that this periodical published no profiles of jazz musicians, concert reviews, or book reviews.

American Music Lover and its predecessors, with their jazz criticism by R. D. Darrell, Horace Van Norman, and Enzo Archetti, created high standards for the critical assessment of jazz music which were only partially equaled by the jazz magazines themselves until after 1940.

Notes

1. Roland Gelatt, *The Fabulous Phonograph* (Philadelphia: Lippincott, 1954), pp. 193, 212.
2. Gelatt, *Fabulous Phonograph*, p. 213.
3. *Talking Machine News and Journal of Events* 5 (March 1913): 225. Hereafter cited as *Talking Machine News*.
4. *Talking Machine News* 5 (March 1913): 229.
5. *Talking Machine News* 5 (August 1913): 475.
6. *Talking Machine News* 5 (April 1913): 242.
7. Gelatt, *Fabulous Phonograph*, p. 255.
8. *Gramophone* 1 (April 1923): 20-21.
9. *Gramophone* 2 (Feburary 1924): 187.
10. Henry Prunières, "La Musique par disques," *La Revue Musicale* 7 (August 1926): 181; "Phonograph-Recordings," *Chord and Discord* 1 (February 1932): 24; Aaron Copland, "Scores and Records," *Modern Music* (November-December 1936): 36; "Quarterly Records List," *Musical Quarterly* 21 (1935); *Music and Letters* 6 (1925).
11. Ernest Newman, "The World of Music: The New Recording," (London) *Sunday Times*, July 11, 1926, p. 7, quoted in Roland Gelatt, "Music on Records," *One Hundred Years of Music in America*, ed. Paul Henry Lang (New York: Schirmer's, 1961), p. 190.
12. R. D. Darrell, letter to the author, May 12, 1980.
13. Robert Donaldson Darrell, "Are American Homes Musical?", *Phonograph Monthly Review* 1 (November 1926): 14.
14. *Phonograph Monthly Review* (October 1926 through March 1927).
15. Gelatt, *Fabulous Phonograph*, p. 255.
16. Darrell, "American Homes," p. 13.

17. Robert Donaldson Darrell, "A Glance at Recorded American Music," *Phonograph Monthly Review* 2 (July 1927): 410-413; (August 1927): 450-453; (September 1927): 495-496; Robert Donaldson Darrell, "Does America Appreciate the Best in Music?", *Phonograph Monthly Review* 1 (October 1926): 8-11.
18. "Rufus," "Dance Records," *Phonograph Monthly Review* 2 (September 1928): 457.
19. Cf. Richard Aldrich, *Concert Life in New York, 1902-1923* (New York: G.P. Putnam's Sons, 1941); Nicholas Slonimsky, *Music Since 1900* (New York: Scribner's, 1971).
20. "Van," "The New Popular Records," *Music Lovers Guide* 3 (March 1935): 29; "From Jazz to Symphony: The Phonograph as a Modern Means for Self-Education in Music," *Music Lovers Guide* 1 (April 1933): 230-231; (June 1933): 295-298; (August 1933): 354-358; 2 (September 1933): 6-7, 18-19. The conclusion to this long serial article was never published.
21. Horace Van Norman, "In the Popular Vein," *American Music Lover* 4 (May 1938): 34.
22. Enzo Archetti, "The Record—As Spokesman," *American Music Lover* 1 (July 1935): 68-70, 78-79.
23. Leonard Hibbs, in *Swing Music,* December 1935; quoted by Enzo Archetti, "In Defense of Ellington," *American Music Lover* 2 (April 1936): 360, 364.
24. Enzo Archetti, "In Defense of Ellington," pp. 359-360, 364.

Slam Stewart Interview

James M. Doran

On May 20, 1984, Slam Stewart was honored by the State University of New York at Binghamton with the degree of Doctor of Music. The citation stated:

> *Your name is synonomous with jazz. Your unique style has infused the string bass with a vibrant life of its own. You have made it stand tall as a solo instrument, and audiences around the world applaud your inimitable talent. As one of music's greatest innovators, your genius has shaped the course of jazz as an art form. You have been generous in sharing your love of music and your exceptional talent with your community and with your students. You and your music have given great joy to all who have known and heard you. It is with pride and admiration that the State University of New York confers upon you the degree of Doctor of Music.*

Leroy Elliot "Slam" Stewart was born on September 21, 1914, in Englewood, New Jersey, to Elliot Edward and Mary Harris Stewart. Slam Stewart's half-century-plus as a professional musician began in 1934 at the Little Dixie Club in Boston with Dean Earl's Band. Stewart has received numerous honors and awards. He is an Ellington Fellow at Yale University and a Newing Fellow at the State University of New York at Binghamton. In 1976 he received a congratulatory message from President Gerald Ford: "You have enjoyed a remarkable career built on a talent which has brought pleasure and enjoyment to people throughout this country." In 1982 President Ronald Reagan wrote: "Over many years, through the universal language of jazz, you have been an ambassador of goodwill around the world. Here at home, you have brought many rich moments of musical enjoyment to fans everywhere."

With his wife, Claire, Stewart maintains an active schedule assisting school and community groups in the Binghamton area. Plans are being made for a 1985 summer festival in Binghamton to honor his fiftieth anniversary in music.

The following interview took place at the Picadilly Hotel in New York City on April 3, 1979.

James M. Doran is the author of *Erroll Garner: The Most Happy Piano* (Metuchen, New Jersey: Scarecrow 1985). His previous article, "Erroll Garner: A Discography Update," appeared in the *Journal of Jazz Studies*, vol. 6, no. 1 (Fall/Winter 1979). He is currently conducting research on jazz pianist Herman Chittison.

DORAN: How did your bowing, singing style come about?

STEWART: Well now, that goes back to my early days when I went to Boston to study my bass fiddle. I had been playing bass fiddle a few years before then, but I went to study at the Boston Conservatory of Music. At the same time, I was gigging and working my way through music school. I was working at a club with a group in Boston. We worked seven nights. We started at eight o'clock at night and didn't get out until two o'clock in the morning. During the day I was going to school. Do you know my first salary at that time was $12 a week? That was 1934, my first experience at earning a salary. Compared to now $12 went a long way; sugar at that time was five cents a pound.

DORAN: What was the name of the club in Boston?

STEWART: It was called Little Harlem, Massachusetts Avenue right off Columbus Avenue. I'll never forget I worked with the band leader, Everett Earl. We used to call him "Dean." He played beautiful, beautiful piano. That was my real start, you might say, at professional playing.

DORAN: Who were the other members of the group?

STEWART: Well, if I can remember, especially the fiddle player, his main instrument was alto sax and he doubled on the violin. His name was Ray Perry, one of the Perry Brothers. On trumpet was Jabbo Jenkins and on tenor and alto was Amer Graves. It was during that time that I started using my little gimmick of bowing and humming along with my solos on the bass fiddle. I'm proud to say the alto player [Ray Perry] that played a little jazz violin gave me the idea to hum along with my bass. Ray Perry used to hum his solos in the same register as his violin. I don't see how in the world he did it because you know how high the fiddle is. His voice was right up there with his violin. That's where I got the idea. After awhile I started to try it; it was very difficult for me because I had to strain my voice to get down as low as the bass fiddle. All of a sudden one day I said: Why don't I raise my voice one octave above the note that I'm playing? All of a sudden it came to me that it would be so much easier. From then on, you might say, I've been stuck with it. That's been my style with the bass fiddle, and it's been good to me ever since.

DORAN: Did the singing come before or after the humming?

STEWART: It was a simultaneous thing because whatever I did I would hum along with it or sing along with it. Same difference, it was a unison thing.

DORAN: When you were through with that group, is that when you came back to New York?

STEWART: Yes, which is nearer to home, Englewood, New Jersey. This is where I met Slim [Gaillard].

DORAN: What year?

STEWART: The latter part of 1935.

DORAN: How did you meet Slim?

STEWART: I met Slim at a jam session up in Harlem at a place called Jock's. We had jam sessions after hours at this particular club. I met Slim just passing through and getting in on one of those jam sessions. It was an immediate get-together. At that particular time Slim was on a program at radio station WNEW; that's how I came to meet Martin Block. When I met Slim this particular night, he asked me to come down to join him on this program that he had on the radio station. He had a few tunes lined up for me to play with him, and we got together and sort of clicked, you know.

DORAN: Is that when you gave yourself the nickname "Slam"?

STEWART: That happened after we had been together and we tried to find a name for me.

DORAN: Were you going by Leroy Stewart?

STEWART: Yes. Automatically within a week's time, Martin Block became our agent. That's when we tried to decide on a name for me to match "Slim." We thought and thought and finally came upon the name of "Slam" which was close to "Slim." Slam, slamming the bass around or slapping the bass around. "Slap" was close, but it wouldn't be too good, especially when I was bowing instead of slapping like a lot of the bass players did. So the team of Slim and Slam was born.

DORAN: What a team, too! When was it and how was it that "Flat Foot Floogie" came about?

STEWART: Slim had been hemming and hawing with this "Flat Foot Floogie." He asked me to think of a few things, lyrics that is, to enhance it musically. I took a couple of solos with my bass, and naturally we got together on it. It was a collaboration. As a matter of fact, we started working on it not too long after we'd gotten together, which was in 1935. We worked on it and before we knew it, we were recording it around '36. I think it was maybe '37 because it was very popular. I think the year we actually made this first recording was 1937.[1]

DORAN: Then it became an overnight success, didn't it?

STEWART: Yes indeed! In fact, after our recording, quite a few other groups made it. Louis Armstrong did it, Fats Waller did it in Europe, and I think Benny Goodman and his band did it. In 1939 Slim and I played the New York World's Fair, and we were honored to have our recording of "Flat Foot Floogie" buried in the time capsule, along with John Philip Sousa's famous march, "Stars and Stripes Forever." The time capsule is supposed to be dug up a hundred years from that date, which will be 2039.

DORAN: Tell me how you met Art Tatum.

STEWART: I met him out in California at a jam session in one of the local after-hours clubs. We'd go quite often to this spot and jam up until four or five in the morning, or later. Tiny Grimes was on the scene that night, too, and I had met Tiny before, and we all were jamming together. Tiny and I both sounded Art that we would like to play with him. He immediately said, "Yes, I'll look into it," and somehow within a couple of days he asked us to join him. He was working at a club out in Hollywood as a soloist and he took us on as part of his trio, and that was the beginning of a wonderful experience.

DORAN: Approximately what year was that?

STEWART: That was the latter part of 1941.

DORAN: You were with him for how long?

STEWART: I was with him on and off up until he passed away, I think November 1956.[2]

DORAN: One of the things about Art Tatum was his tremendous technique. Was it one of the most unusual styles you ever experienced?

STEWART: Very unusual, in fact, when I first went with him I was really frightened, I was wondering how I was going to turn out with him. He was amazing on the piano. I remember a lot of stories a lot of people used to mention about Art Tatum when he made his rounds in the after-hours places and what have you. I remember some folks used to tell me that when Art used to walk in on jam sessions where the cats were playing, all of a sudden somebody would shout out, "Uh oh, God is in the house." They just meant the greatest on the piano has just arrived. That was quite an experience for me. As I went along I learned quite a bit: progressions, chord changes, and what have you. That Art Tatum was something else, beautiful.

DORAN: What type of man was Art Tatum?

STEWART: He was very, very quiet. Of course, he was almost totally blind, except for one eye I think, where he could see visions, like slightly see forms which he probably couldn't hardly make out at all. I remember he was quite a card player, like pinochle. That was his favorite game. He used to have a habit while we played pinochle: he used to put his card hand up to that good eye and he could read the cards that way. He was quite a pinochle player.

DORAN: I've heard he used to take a little rubber ball and roll it between his fingers.

STEWART: Yes, exercises. He would use a peanut or a marble for exercise between his fingers, especially the thumb and forefinger.

DORAN: What other unique aspects of Art Tatum intrigued you or made you a better bass player?

STEWART: You might say I had and still have practically absolute pitch, and you know, as the old saying goes, I kept my ears open all the time. The things that I heard Art play I learned, like his bass lines were something else. I learned from Art Tatum just by listening. I was really a good listener.

DORAN: When you left California did you come back to New York as the Art Tatum Trio?

STEWART: Yes, for awhile, and after Tiny had left the group, we had another guitar player named Everett Barksdale. We went right into the Three Deuces, which became my home, more or less, after Art Tatum left the trio.

DORAN: So you just took over?

STEWART: After Art Tatum left I took over. Yes, and 52nd Street was really jumping. After Art Tatum had left, the manager of the Three Deuces approached me to see what I could do about staying on at his place, and asked if I could hire another pianist to fill Art Tatum's place. Well, immediately down the street, a couple of doors down, there was another young pianist who was doing a single. The name of this place was Tondelayo's, in which this young man by the name of Erroll Garner was playing. While working with Art I used to stop in at two or three of the clubs to dig the musicians, especially this place where Erroll was playing. I used to go in there quite a bit to listen to him play, so this was quite an opportunity for me to go up to Erroll and see how he felt about making it with me at the Three Deuces. Erroll sounded his boss, and it turned out so that Erroll was able, for a few days, to keep his own gig and at the same time double at the Three Deuces with my group. He played with Tiny and myself each night for about a week until it was time to go back to his place and play. You should have seen Erroll running and jumping back and forth to his gig and helping me out at the same time. Finally, it got to the point where his boss agreed to let him go so he could join me permanently down at the Three Deuces. In fact, Erroll told me himself, I was the cause, more or less, of him being in the big time.

DORAN: You discovered him?

STEWART: I discovered him, more or less. That [the Three Deuces engagement] lasted for a year or two and by that time Erroll had branched out on his own because he was getting pretty big. We had recorded, and Erroll was becoming very well known. After Erroll left me at the Three Deuces, I got hold of Billy Taylor. Billy stayed for a little while, and I got hold of Beryl Booker. Beryl Booker didn't join me until I had left Benny Goodman because I went with Benny Goodman in 1945. Working with Benny Goodman lasted from 1945 to the latter part of 1946. I would say about a year and a half. I was working on 52nd Street during 1945. I joined Benny at a theater on Sixth Avenue called the Ziegfeld Theater, and they had a musical going on there called *The Seven Lively Arts*.

And that's when I joined Benny Goodman and his group.' Finally, I left Benny about 1946. That's when Beryl was on the scene with John Collins and Sid Catlett. We all ventured out to Hollywood and that's about the time, around 1947, we had gotten together making this picture.[4]

DORAN: Going back to when you started musically, can you explain about yourself as a young boy and the violin?

STEWART: Oh yes, the little fiddle. I used to call it the squeak box. My parents bought me a little violin when I was around seven or eight years old. I had a teacher back home in Englewood, and it sort of interested me quite a bit. I can't imagine when I got to the point that I wanted to play the violin. There wasn't any music in my family. I was the only musical one. At least I used to listen to the radio and all of the jazz that they used to play. This was long before television ever came in. I used to listen when Duke Ellington's band used to broadcast from here and there and even Louis Armstrong. I guess that's the reason why I was very happy to get hold of this violin to see what I could do with it. So, fortunately my folks got me a fiddle, and I studied that for awhile. But somehow in listening to the different jazz bands on radio I became very interested in the sound of the bass fiddle plucking, and somehow I automatically thought that I would want to try out this bass fiddle. The sound really fascinated me, and the little squeak box didn't move me at all. It so happened in high school, in the music room, they had a couple of instruments locked up in there. One was a bass fiddle. No one was playing the bass, so I asked the music teacher, "Could I try out this bass fiddle?" She said, "Go ahead, help yourself."

So I got it out one day, and I didn't know one thing about tuning or anything, so fortunately one of the fiddle players knew how to tune the bass fiddle. He had some experience, not with playing the bass fiddle, but he knew how it was tuned. It was altogether reverse from the little violin, so he helped me out in tuning it. Then I started out practicing when the orchestra used to play their marches for assembly, you know, to bring in the kids. I rehearsed and practiced on that bass fiddle. You should have seen me. Come time for assembly, I was standing up back in the corner with my bass fiddle with all the rest of the orchestra, and I was going right along with them. I couldn't read a note. I was just going by my ear, and that was the start of my career as a bass fiddler.

DORAN: You started on the violin when you were seven?

STEWART: Yes. I had a violin teacher up until my latter years in high school. During my latter years in high school I was still playing a little bit of violin. I wasn't interested in it, you know.

DORAN: Prior to the age of seven you had no musical training at all?

STEWART: No.

DORAN: Were your parents or your brothers and sisters musically inclined?

STEWART: No, in fact I was the only one, no sisters or brothers. After my high school days I gigged a little bit. That's when I met Sonny Marshall.

DORAN: Was that in Newark?

STEWART: Yes, Newark. I met Sonny Marshall a little before I went to the Boston Conservatory. That was directly after I had gotten out of high school. He had heard about me, and he gave me a call to see if I could come over to play with him in his little band [Sonny Marshall's Royal Stompers], which consisted of five or six pieces: trombone, trumpet, and rhythm section, and he [Marshall] played alto. Anyway, after my little stint with Sonny—it didn't last long, a few months—I went to the Boston Conservatory.

DORAN: Now, when you went to the Boston Conservatory, you said you played by ear?

STEWART: When I went to the Boston Conservatory, I was taught how to read and what have you. I didn't know what I was doing as far as reading notes. I didn't know one note from another. I was just going by sounds. Anyway, I learned my notes; I didn't have to have too much help with the ear training, but I had a pretty good time of learning, especially how to hold my bow and what have you.

DORAN: I noticed that in the movie *Stormy Weather* you used a certain technique with your arm.

STEWART: Yes, what I was doing then, I was showing off, more or less. It wasn't exactly a technique, but a kind of gimmick.

DORAN: Going back to Erroll Garner, you once told me that while he was with you on 52nd Street he never grunted. Was this something he picked up later on?

STEWART: No, not while I was with him. He never did grunt or hum. When Erroll left me, I noticed that he started humming and grunting along with his playing, you know. I guess that was a form of concentrating on what he was doing. When he worked with me, I used to hum along and grunt with my bass fiddle, so maybe he got the idea, and maybe it helped him make his beautiful music the way he did. Well, through the years, even up until he passed, Erroll has always, whomever he talked with in interviews or a friendly chat, he has always given me that credit for putting him into the big time, which I appreciated. It was very nice of him. And of course together, we had some wonderful, swinging days.

Notes

1. "The Flat Foot Floogie" was recorded in New York on the Vocalion label on February 17, 1938. Brian Rust, *Jazz Records: 1897–1942*, volume 1 (New Rochelle, New York: Arlington House, 1978) p. 550.
2. Art Tatum died on November 4, 1956.
3. Stewart recorded with Benny Goodman for the first time in New York on February 4, 1945. D. Russell Connor, *The Record of a Legend* (New York: Let's Dance Corporation, 1984) p. 165.
4. The motion picture Stewart refers to is *Boy! What a Girl* (1947). David Meeker, *Jazz in the Movies* (New Rochelle, New York: Arlington House, 1977), reference number 267.

The Evolution of Bebop Compositional Style: "Whispering"/"Groovin' High"

Joan Wildman

The advent of bebop has left an indelible imprint on the jazz tradition. While much has been written about the performers and the sociological climate in which they worked, the analysis of the music itself has often been a secondary consideration. In addition, such elements of bebop which are immediately perceptible, such as its angular melodies or complex rhythms, are ordinarily associated with solo improvisations rather than written-out compositions. The jazz composition itself is a blueprint of style, however, and many bebop tunes remain an important part of today's jazz performance repertoire.

Most standard bebop compositions were derived from the 12-bar blues or from popular songs of the twenties and thirties. Indeed, these new stylistic layers were set squarely upon a pre-existing structure, thus maintaining elements of two distinct styles simultaneously. The interaction of the older layers with the new provides an illuminating view of style change in general and of bebop's evolution in particular. Therefore, an examination will be made of the stylistic transformation of a popular song from 1920, "Whispering," into the bebop composition, "Groovin' High," which was written in the mid-forties.

"Whispering"

One of the first hits of the recording industry, "Whispering" (music by John Schonberger, lyrics by Malvin Schonberger), as recorded in 1920 by Paul Whiteman and his Ambassador Orchestra, sold more than two million copies. Written in the key of Eb, "Whispering" consists of 32 measures of 2/2 meter (Example 1). Its melodic line begins with a four-measure phrase that is sequentially treated for two additional phrases. Next, a culminating phrase functions as a first ending at measure 16 and, after the repetition of the first three phrases, as a second ending at measure 32. The over-all form, therefore, consists of two 16-measure sections ending first with a half-cadence, then a full-cadence in the tonic key.

Joan Wildman teaches theory and jazz improvisation as an associate professor of music at the University of Wisconsin, Madison. She is the co-author (with Bruce Benward) of *Jazz Improvisation in Theory and Practice*.

Ex. 1. "Whispering"

The structural pitches of the melody comprise a descending E*b*-major scale within each section (shown in the circled notes of Example 1). Throughout the first three phrases these pitches furnish the rhythm pattern ♩ ♪ ♩ ♪ , with accents on the first and third whole notes (Example 2). Together, the structural melodic pitches and the characteristic rhythm and accents provide a consistent focus on the first beat of the measure, emphasizing the 2/2 meter.

Ex. 2. Structural Pitches and Accents of Phrases 1, 2, and 3

The accent pattern also outlines the duple metric scheme at a higher organizational level. During the first three phrases, for instance, the first beat of each phrase coupled with its accented third measure provides two larger metric units of 2/2 within each four-measure grouping. The rhythm in phrase 4, although different, maintains the same regularity through its repetition. Thus, the same accent organization remains constant throughout the composition.

The chord progression, while reinforcing the macro-accent structure, also creates a subtle balance between tension and relaxation. For example, although the E*b* tonic chord appears at the beginning of five of the eight phrases, the tension level increases within each succeeding phrase. In phrase one, the C dim chord of m. 3 provides the harmonic tension peak coinciding with the melodic peak D. Phrase 2 follows at a higher tension level with the stronger C7 chord (V/V), containing its corresponding melodic A*b*. Phrase 3 continues an ascending-fourth harmonic movement toward the dominant, B*b*7, bringing about the climactic tension point of the first three phrases.

It is interesting to note the orderly process of tension growth by which C dim, C7, and B*b*7 serve as harmonic goals: each occurs at the beginning of the third measure of the phrase, but the E*b*-G*b* of C dim moves chromatically higher, first to E-G in the C7 and finally to F-A*b* of the dominant B*b*7 chord.

After the continual tension growth of the first three phrases, phrase 4 begins with a tonic chord, followed by two measures of the dominant. However, the last measure includes the raised 5th of the V chord (B*b*+), lifting the F another half-step higher as a final thrust of tension before the beginning of the second section. The whole process is repeated in section two until the relaxation of the E*b* tonic occurs in m. 30, signaling the end of the composition.

"Groovin' High"

"Groovin' High" is a bebop adaptation of "Whispering" by Dizzy Gillespie (Example 3). The form and key of the original have been retained but the meter has been changed to 4/4.

Although the melodic line follows "Whispering's" 4-measure-phrase format, the manner of organization differs considerably. "Groovin' High," based on faster-moving note values, is constructed from a two-eighth-note motive, B*b*-G. Separated from its repetition by rests, the last half of the phrase (mm. 3-4) continues with an eighth-note development of the original material until the tied eighth-quarter "D" signals the highest point of tension in m. 4. The same rhythm pattern is repeated in phrases 2 and 3; each time the tension peak is delayed until the end of the phrase.

The pitches are assembled from separate layers (Example 4). The ascending contour of the outer voices (B*b* moves up to C and D while, after G, E moves up to F) is countered by the descending chromatic line, B*b*-F. Thus, both the line's chromaticism and the outer voices help determine its overall structure.

The relative importance of each pitch is ultimately determined, not so much by its harmonic implications or contour, but by the placement of its melodic accents. A fundamental characteristic of bebop composition/performance is the ability of the accent organization to function independently, a process brought about by the careful alternation between metric downbeats and upbeats. Thus, it will be shown that the accent structure of

Ex. 3. "Groovin' High"
(as performed by Charlie Parker on Everest FS-254)

"Groovin' High" can be traced from the formation of accent-motives into accent-phrases, much the same way as pitch/duration units are combined into melodic phrases (Example 5.)

Metric placement assures the importance of both B*b*'s as structural accents in the first two measures of phrase 1, setting up the most elementary level of accent organization, the accent-motive. The presence of the chromatically descending A-G-G-F would seem to indicate further significant accent formations: while only G appears at the beginning of a measure, all occur at the beginning of a beat.[1] Indeed, all beats throughout the phrase begin with one of the chromatically descending pitches, with a single exception—B-natural.

The presence of these chromatically descending pitches, alone, does not offer a coherent accent-phrase construction, however. After the accent-motive is set up in the first two measures, it appears again in m. 2, with accents on beats 2 and 3, the chromatically descending G (beat 4) replaced by B-natural. The strength of B as a primary accent arises

Ex. 4. Melodic Structure of Phrase 1, "Groovin' High"

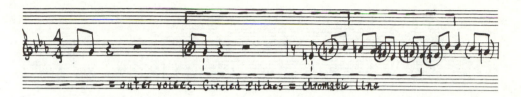

from its metric position, and from its chromatic ascent from Bb. It also appears as a chromatic descent from C, one of the outer, rising voices. Therefore, the second occurrence of the accent-motive is contracted, with attacks moving from a weak to a strong beat. This disruption of regularity provides a higher level of tension to make way for the climax in m. 4.

The accent-phrase becomes complete with the third appearance of the accent-motive. Although the chromatically descending G remains important, F follows too closely to produce a cohesive unit. Instead, the ear is drawn to D, the culmination of the higher, outer voices which occurs on the last half of beat 2. Thus, the accent-phrase ends with G and F, the arrangement of alternate downbeat/upbeat (attacks on beats 1 and 2$^1/_2$) accents holding together the entire structure.

The chord progression builds tension throughout the phrase by an emphasis on non-diatonic chords and a quicker harmonic rhythm in its last two measures. The added chords in phrase 1, for example, suggest a repeated ii-V progression in the key of G, while in phrase 2 a repeated ii-V of F occurs—the ii-V of the original Eb appearing only during the last half of phrases 3 and 4. To provide maximum tension toward the end of the section, phrase 4, after the initial Eb chord, consists of two different ii-V root relationships, altered both by tritone substitution and by chord quality (the root F substituted as the tritone replacement for C, with its quality changed to minor, and E7 derived from its tritone Bb) to construct a chromatically descending line.

Melodic Comparisons

As "Groovin' High's" melodic line is placed over the harmonic framework of "Whispering," there remains a close relationship between the original melody and its successor. Instead of similarities of melodic contour or rhythmic content, however, their association

Ex. 5. Accent Pattern of Phrase 1 of "Groovin' High"

Ex. 6. "Whispering/Groovin' High," Phrases 1-4

more closely resembles that of a countermelody ("Groovin' High") to be played along-side the original.[2]

The alternation between faster- versus slower-moving durations becomes apparent at the outset: "Whispering's" half note is countered by the eighth notes of "Groovin' High," while during the remainder of the first measure "Groovin' High" remains silent during "Whispering's" quarter notes. As m. 2 continues, a repetition of "Groovin' High's" two eighth notes is set against "Whispering's" four quarters. Still a greater contrast appears in mm. 3-4 as the whole notes of "Whispering" appear with the predominant eighth notes of the more recent melody (Example 6).

Because of the correspondence of faster-moving durations and longer rests, the melodic line of "Groovin' High" contains a higher tension level then does "Whispering." More-over, the increased tension is not restricted to durational relationships; the first pitch of "Whispering" begins on the tonic, Eb, while "Groovin' High" starts on Bb, the fifth of the tonic chord. "Groovin' High" also sustains a higher level of tension throughout the phrase—while both compositions retain D as the climactic point, in "Groovin' High" D occurs nearly a measure and a half later.

Further, despite the repetition of each melody's rhythm during its first three phrases, the pitch choices of "Groovin' High" reflect a shift in compositional style at the midpoint of each phrase. First, the number of different pitches in the first phrase varies from two in mm. 1-2 to nine in mm. 3-4. Secondly, the harmonic rhythm shifts from only one chord during the first two measures to a chord change every two beats in mm. 3-4. Thirdly, the two accents of mm. 1-2 occur only on beat 1, but are incorporated, in the latter half of the measure, into a complex structure which functions as an accent-phrase. Finally, the chord choices vary from the tonic only, in mm. 1-2, to the use of substitute chords, in mm. 3-4, which both enhance the basic harmonic structure and also lessen the influence of the E*b* tonic. Thus, the balance and regularity of the earlier popular song alternates with the unpredictability of the emerging bebop line—a model of style evolution within a single phrase!

Consequently, "Whispering" and "Groovin' High" relate to each other as countermelodies, although "Groovin' High" contains a higher level of tension, through the use of faster note values, pitch choices, and accent structure. At the same time, "Groovin' High" maintains distinct elements of the earlier style alongside its innovative bebop characteristics.

Rhythm and Accent Comparisons

"Whispering's" whole and half notes, emphasizing beat 1, contrasts with the richness of the eighth note downbeat-to-offbeat rhythms and accents of the newer melody (Example 7.) The accents of "Whispering" form a repeated rhythm which enhances the 2/2 meter but is unable to stand alone as a developmental rhythm pattern. "Groovin' High," on the other hand, after incorporating the downbeat emphasis of "Whispering" for its initial motive, expands the possibilities from offbeat/downbeat to downbeat/offbeat positions throughout the remainder of the phrase to form an independent accent-phrase.

Each occurrence of the accent motive in "Groovin' High" emphasizes its second accent, thus signaling a basic departure from its pop song origins.[3] Pushed further, this concept also illustrates the tendency to build tension until the end of the phrase rather than releasing it near its midpoint as occurs in "Whispering." Thus, each incidence of the accent-motive grows in intensity throughout the phrase.

Consequently, the maintenance of tension growth by the combination of shorter durations and rests into jazz accent-motives/phrases provides the basis for the transfer of style

Ex. 7. Comparison of Accents Between "Whispering" and "Groovin' High"

from the pop song into bebop. Where the regularity of downbeat accents in the first half of each of the first three phrases of "Groovin' High" suggests the accent structure of the earlier model, the last two measures introduce the fully developed bebop style of the late forties.

Harmonic Comparisons

The chord progression of "Groovin' High" follows the same tension outlines as its melodic and accent formations. After the two-measure Eb tonic chord, the dissonance level rises throughout the remainder of the first phrase—the C dim chord of "Whispering" is first substituted with Am, then added chords, E+, Am7, and D9 complete the harmonic pattern.

Compared to "Whispering," the tension levels of "Groovin' High" are both elevated and extended, although the basic progressions remain the same. Whereas "Whispering" maintains a "tension chord" in the third measure of each of its phrases, "Groovin' High" begins a repeated ii-V progression on each of its third measures which matches the "tension," i.e., dominant chord, of the original. As the C dim of "Whispering's" first phrase is considered to be a functioning dominant built on D (D7 b9), "Groovin' High" adds the ii chord (Am7) and first alters the dominant (E+ reflects D9+11) then extends it (from the original) to include the 9th (D9). Thus the G of E+ resolves to the A of D9. This process continues throughout the next two phrases as the key relationships move down by whole steps (G-F-Eb).

In phrase 4 the added ii-V progressions emerge from the original progression, as well: Gm7 consists of the Ebm9 chord, and functions as the ii, followed by the altered V of F. Finally, instead of two measures of the dominant (Bb7-Bb+), "Groovin' High" adds another ii-V (with a tritone substitution (E7 for Bb7), this time in the original key.

Consequently, although both compositions retain the same basic harmonic progressions, "Groovin' High" provides greater tension through the use of extended, added, and substitute chords. The tension shapes also differ: "Groovin' High" contains a faster harmonic rhythm, stretching the climactic point past that of the original, toward the end of the phrase.

Conclusions

The evolution from "Whispering" to "Groovin' High" not only provides an intriguing view of the processes which generated the emergence of bebop style, but also includes several factors which can suggest criteria applicable to stylistic changes on a broader scale: First, stylistic transformation does not require the eradication of the original material. What at first may seem a radical departure often retains many characteristics from the previous style, more or less intact. "Groovin' High," for instance, not only sustains the form[4] and basic harmonic progression of "Whispering," but its melodic construction functions as a countermelody to the original line. Thus, new elements can be superimposed over the old, allowing both styles to be recognizable as distinct entities.

Second, the evolution of a new style often develops from innovations within only one or two musical elements. The melodic alterations of "Groovin' High" contrast sharply with its traditional harmonic and formal construction. While the basic harmonies are reflected in the melodic line, both the pitch alterations and the rhythm and accent patterns are indicative of a basic change in stylistic concept.

Third, priorities must be established as to which elements will be "modernized." In the evolution of "Groovin' High" from "Whispering," as with most stylistic changes in the jazz tradition, the most predominant roles are played by rhythm and accent. In fact, the unity and independence of the accent-phrase (without pitch references) is truly unique to jazz composition (and performance.) In contrast to the circularity of African rhythm and accent patterns, and the regularity of accents in the American popular song, the Afro-American bebop innovators formed independent, *developmental* accent structures, usually focusing attention toward the end of the phrase.

Fourth, stylistic maturity is evidenced by the influence of the increased complexity of the innovative elements "spilling over" into those elements which were previously unaltered. The permeation of the innovative elements of "Groovin' High" are reflected in the added and substitute chords as well as in the alteration of tension shapes. (Interestingly enough, the latter part of each phrase more closely reflects the mature bebop style while the first half retains many characteristics of the earlier popular song.)

In conclusion, the transition from "Whispering" to "Groovin' High" is only one instance of the superimposition of the bebop style onto a popular song format, reflecting more than two decades of compositional and improvisational evolution. While the process of deriving a bebop composition from a popular song written some twenty years earlier probably required the intermediate influence of big band riff tunes from the thirties, contemporary jazz compositions continue to project both the careful preservation of many bebop characteristics as well as the superimposition of contemporary idioms. Thus, the jazz composition remains much more than a set of chord progressions from which to improvise; instead it provides an illumination of tradition and the processes by which that tradition can evolve.

SELECTED DISCOGRAPHY

"Whispering"

1. Paul Whiteman. *Paul Whiteman: An Experiment in Modern Music*, Smithsonian DMM 2-0518.
2. Jan Garber. *Jan Garber and his Orchestra: 1939-1941*, Hindsight HSR-130.
3. Gene Krupa. *The Exciting Gene Krupa*, RCA Victor, Giants of Jazz GOJ 1028.

"Groovin' High"

1. Dizzy Gillespie. *Echoes of an Era*, Roulette RE 105.
2. Dizzy Gillespie. *Dizzy Gillespie Quintet: Live at Carnegie Hall*, Limelight LM 82017.
3. Dizzy Gillespie. *Dizzy Gillespie/Charlie Parker*, Emus ES 12017.
4. Charlie Parker. *The Comprehensive Charlie Parker: Live Performances, Vol. 1*, ESP Bird 1.
5. Charlie Parker. *Charlie Parker Broadcast Performances, Vol. 2*, ESP Bird 2.
6. Charlie Parker. *Charlie Parker, Vol. 3*, Everest FS-254.

Notes

1. While both the highest and lowest of the ascending outer voices occur at the same metric position, neither layer appears on a downbeat. C and D, for example, occur on beat $2^1/_2$ in mm. 3 and 4, while E and F both occur on the last half of beat 1 of mm. 3 and 4.
2. See Frank Tirro, "The Silent Theme Tradition in Jazz," *The Musical Quarterly* 53, no. 3 (July 1967): 327. Gillespie affirms that he composed "Groovin' High" as a countermelody to "Whispering."
3. In contrast to pop song style, the commonly found bebop accents on beats 2 and 4 also apply to shorter durations. Thus it is the second of two consecutive eighth notes which receives the normal accent. It also follows that the jazz "accent motive" usually contains a stronger accent on the second attack rather than the first.
4. Recorded performances of "Groovin' High" by Charlie Parker usually contain a six-measure introduction before the melody is played in unison by the horns. In a recording of the 1947 Carnegie Hall concert (Emus E S-12017 with Dizzy Gillespie, trumpet; John Lewis, piano; Al McKibbon, bass; and Joe Harris, drums), another six-measure extension is added before the beginning of the solos.

Themes of Protest and Criminality in American Recorded Jazz, 1945-1975

Ronald L. Morris

Jazz music has often been made to assume the workhorse role of both contributor to and reflector of urban pathological values. In this role, jazz has a well-established link to crime, violence, deviant behavior, and social protest, although the link has not usually been stated directly. Consider the following two observations made nearly 50 years apart:

> In its sinister aspects, jazz is doing a vast amount of harm to young minds and bodies not yet developed to resist evil temptations. Perhaps this is the explanation of America's enormous crime rate at present [1925].[1]

> Jazz is social protest. It expresses ghetto urban tensions, alienation, anomic response. Its bold, lean, and shocking cacophony lends itself to this purpose [1972].[2]

How accurate are such statements when scrutinized for a specific time period? Can ghetto tensions find authentication through "bold, lean and shocking cacophony"? And during moments of high drama and revolutionary fervor, can jazz protest find its niche? Artists themselves are a useful focus for further analysis. To what extent do jazz musicians reinforce urban protest or crime-related values by transmitting socially conscious themes through their music?

This study assesses the frequency of crime- and protest-related themes found in American recorded jazz between 1945 and 1975. In the process I explore the extent to which streetwise artists have expressed in recorded jazz their attitudes to crime, deviance, the criminal justice system, and protest. I have not imposed my own judgments of these expressions, but I have attempted to study the sources of rebellious perspectives and of other resentments. I have also tried to imagine the variety of means at jazz artists' disposal for registering protest, made a few topographical remarks of my own on those who indeed left their calling cards, and appended a discography to conclusions I feel are appropriate to my findings.

Considered for review were recordings, made in America, that comment on violence, criminal life, police activity, rioting, street crime, and the like, regardless of the specific

Ronald L. Morris, assistant professor of sociology at Hunter College, City University of New York, is a historical sociologist and former musician who has written and lectured on jazz in the United States and abroad.

political views. I ignored "Prisoner of Love" and "Jailbait" titles for obvious reasons, as well as those with opaque drug or "Back to Africa" references. Also omitted are scores written exclusively for crime movies. Many jazz notables wrote or performed for the cinema, and an extensive list of such crime movies can surely be drawn up,[3] but significant differences may exist between studio musicians whose works must conform to a preexisting plot and those whose ideas more closely reflect their own community attitudes and values.

Let it not be said that by selecting a time period with readily available jazz records, I arbitrarily set blind forces in motion. There is ample reason to see this era as tremendously important, especially for black people prodded into scarred city anthills. It was a period which witnessed the rise of the freedom riders; the Muslim and Black Panther Party movements; urban-located assassinations of key political leaders with subsequent destructive fallouts; a depressed black economy that encouraged the invasion of drugs and crime into the black community; and widespread anti-war demonstrations—all of which culminated in extensive rioting and a massive extension of police activity. The upshot was a tremendous overloading of the criminal justice system. Millions of Americans, many of whom were black, faced imprisonment on a staggering array of charges, and musicians were hardly exempt from this trend. Black males, ages 18-26, while comprising approximately four percent of the national population, totaled nearly half the prison inmate society for these years.[4]

Having painted a picture of surging rage and confusion, one might well wonder what jazz musicians of the time were thinking. Jazz drummer Art Blakey claims saxophonist Charlie Parker "wanted to kick the drug habit so he could tell others" what he knew of the system.[5] The urban riots which began in Watts, California, in 1965 had a powerful impact on black consciousness. Pianist Hampton Hawes says, "They changed a lot of things," and saxophonist Sonny Criss adds that after Watts "blacks became more aggressive." He surely would know, having sat in the middle of 103rd Street and Central Avenue in black Los Angeles during the riots, watching the fires and looting swirl around him. It is even speculated that some jazzmen began using heroin at this time in an attempt to gain "a new sense of masculinity and revolt."[6]

Militant poet Leroi Jones (Amiri Baraka) included Parker in his list when he wrote of "bopsters who were outspoken about who they were and 1957 marks their musical takeover." In these years, jazz artists have been described or labeled by various observers and critics as "dirty radicals," "musical revolutionaries," "wild-eyed revolutionaries," "protesters against the narrowness of semi-feudal Southern life," "outlaws," and an "underground" element.[7] In the late 1960s pianist Cecil Taylor was convinced: "There is a growing trend for jazz artists to draw upon the ghetto environment for their material."[8]

Accepting these labels at face value, we may ask how much actual revolt there was within the jazz community, as evidenced by recordings. Nor need we exclude the jazz listenership. One report pinpointed a growing ethnic audience that "preferred songs which dealt with current Black social problems."[9] Evidence from other studies suggests that many of the young were highly attentive to music attacking social injustices, out of which their own views might be shaped and directed. This seems to have happened, at least partly, as the result of the social stridency blended into folk, blues, hard/acid rock, and soul music in the 1960s.[10] Again, we may ask whether jazz can be placed on an equal footing with these other musical forms and whether the critics are justified in describing jazz artists as revolutionary. If crime itself posits some elemental statement of conflict between perpetrator and society, this subject, when studied along musical lines, should allow us to observe wider sociological issues at work.

Two cautionary notes are in order: First, no direct relationship is implied between the jazz artists' strength of political conviction and their degree of originality, insight, or technical mastery. Second, musical boundaries are not rigid, and artists, even those with strong political commitments, often performed works devoid of ideological content.

Jazz Musicians as Revolutionaries

Historical "curators" of jazz have often sketched certain artists in relatively red and pink hues, seeing them as likably impatient social realists. A few have even gone off the deep end and branded jazzmen as musical Robin Hoods or Marcus Garveys striving to unite the Afro-American nation. Many writers, particularly Europeans, agree that these artists are social militants on the strength of their ideological alienation and their breezy bohemian style, which often lends itself to biting the patron's feeding hand.

What arguments have been advanced to support this view of social militancy, and how do they stand up to my survey of jazz protesters between 1945-1975? First, the presumed artistic, technical, and improvisational superiority of jazz artists over popular musicians seems to require the former to eschew materialism while forcefully challenging the crass music business. Jazz artists, having selected a style of life and art, must persevere, and even endure poverty, to assure their autonomy and self-respect. Marxists have been quick to argue that modern jazz springs from lower class origins, that it "is basically a protest against monopoly control of music." Merriam and Mack link jazz musicians to the "deviant community" on the basis of their natural bohemian tendencies and inherent nonconformism. On this last point, Boulding further widens our scope:

> It is in the non-conformist subcultures that images are most likely to be sensitive and subject to change. And since the subculture puts a high level on revolt against the orthodoxy of society, this also leaves it open to revolt against the orthodoxy of the present.[11]

My own examination reveals otherwise. While it is true that some of jazz's most socially conscious performers lived fairly arduous existences for at least part of their careers, there is no reason to believe they were generally mired in disrepute. Artistic—and sometimes financial—recognition was freely given to men such as Charles Mingus, Herbie Hancock, Donald Byrd, and Art Blakey—to name a few. That such musicians are generally of lower class origins is also suspect. The majority of my list went as far as college, often with generous support by supportive parents. There is implied here at least a lower middle class respect for education that saw many not only graduate, but advance to teach, sometimes in nonmusical fields. Indeed, such artists may well display middle class yearnings for recognition and respectability.

I must also take exception to Pollilo's findings that "these jazz militants were scarcely in their 20s . . . and from the Middle West. They were provincials, new to city ways, and keen to be heard."[12] Musicians in my survey were neither young, nor provincial, nor from the Middle West. The group was, in fact, relatively old at the time of Watts. Fully 73 percent were at or above the age of 30 in 1965, an age we rarely associate with social and political impetuosity, much less with criminal inclination or even sympathy (crime is usually associated heavily with the 16-22 age range). Also, 68 percent hailed from large cities which helped form their social consciousness. Eastern cities of New York, Philadelphia, and Boston accounted for 18, 12, and 3 percent, respectively, whereas rural settings, typical birthplaces for legendary bluesmen and those in Pollilo's study, contributed but 19 percent of the total. These figures require some juxtaposing, since migration brought many of these rural musicians and their families to large inner cities before they had reached their teens.

A second argument in support of the social militancy of jazz artists derives from their presumed aggressiveness toward commercial music entrepreneurs, untalented and imitative players, and middle class white audiences. This attack can be summed up in the phrase "bandstand bellicosity." According to one source, "Hard boppers used complex musical variations to scare away no-talent guys" (read: white imitators and Uncle Toms).[13]

Militant bandstand deportment assumed many guises. Miles Davis sometimes ignored his audiences by performing with his back to them, and others, including Charles Mingus, might upbraid their patrons. Perhaps the crowning, if indirect, impertinence to an audience with a bourgeois sense of punctuality was the artists' vying with one another to see who could arrive at a set latest or take the longest breaks during intermission. Ralph Ellison warns that even as some might view this behavior as militant or antiwhite, its original intentions would backfire:

> [The result was often] a grim comedy of manners with musicians employing calculated surliness and rudeness . . . and whites accepting such treatment as evidence of artists' temperament [and coming to] . . . expect it as part of the entertainment.[14]

Of course, this vein of militancy required someone to ridicule. Only one artist in my list (Mingus) attacked his audience, as it were, in a live recorded session, and this somewhat playfully.

The third alleged source of inherent militancy derives from a general conflict perspective. This means that jazzmen almost consciously reflect and register protest against the black condition in a racist society; in some cases a lifelong battle ensues. One observer noted: "White repression created a great demand for nonverbal channels of communication filled by the cry of jazz."[15]

Walton writes of this group: "They are against the social order by the very challenge of their music . . . and by the built-in hatred of racialism." This view is also expressed by Finkelstein and by Carles and Comolli, who, in equating jazz with the Black Power movement, "see political implications in everything the jazz artist did." Saxophonist Archie Shepp views jazz as a "reporter, an aesthetic journalist of America," and Jones defines jazzmen as "radicals within the context of the American mainstream."[16] All such claims appear excessive, and I found little foundation for them in my survey. Whatever their attitudes and the musical expression of those attitudes, few musicians were direct activists. (The most notable exception, Steve Reid, seriously challenged the establishment by his pacifist position on Viet Nam and was imprisoned for two years as a result.) My study indicates that jazz manifestations of the social ferment of these three decades—whether expressed in lyrics or titles about crime, rebellion, drug use, war, or the like—were the exception rather than the rule. Indeed, there is much to be said for Sun Ra's apparently opposite view: "Jazz songs were always about love. Very seldom did they branch over into anything else. . . . It was always about human emotions, and always a repeat thing."[17]

Access and Susceptibility to Leftist Attitudes

As roses affect otherwise docile bees, so, too, can musicians be influenced by their social surroundings. Doubtless some were deeply affected by the squalor, street crime, and unequal systems of justice they had encountered, as convincingly argued by Merriam, Mack, Boulding, and others. Popular attitude surveys taken as widely apart as 1948 and 1970 also suggest that the attitudes of the jazz audience must also be considered. These surveys reveal jazz as a magnet that attracted the educated, northern, urban listener under 30 whose social and worldly perspectives were correspondingly radical.[18] Newton believes cross-pollination, to pursue our bee metaphor, must have taken place: "I suspect the left-wing musician came mainly from contacts with strongly progressive bonds of jazz enthusiasts and critics."[19] We are thus faced with the insoluble problem of who is influencing whom.

Jazz fans, in contrast to patrons of more commercialized music, bring to their aesthetic pleasures a relatively high degree of intellectual curiosity, buttressed, according to Kofsky, by a parallel additive of alienation.[20] This accounts for the "political and philosophical implications within the music" that not only satisfy the listeners' auditory requirements but also further their desires to act out some of the music's basic messages. Racial integration, drug usage, or fighting for equal rights are some examples. The irony here is that the militant offspring of jazz are more likely to be white than black. Ellison recalls how jazz artists with the faintest tinge of lawbreaking notoriety were accorded a special heroic status by nonconformist whites bent on emulating these unique folk characters.[21]

My study supports Newton's hypothesis. The likelihood of contact and mutual understanding between jazzmen and leftists was probably very high during this period. How much radical thought was absorbed by any single artist is speculative. One does see influences at work, of course, as many jazzmen admit being affected by newly developing activism within the black community, most notably the Black Panthers and the Black Muslims, and their respective spokesmen (Huey Newton, George Jackson, and Malcolm X). European influences were also at work. Here personal relationships are harder to disentangle, and one might well view such relationships in cultural terms. Fully 60 percent of those in my survey had visited a turbulent, increasingly radical Europe, with its small cadre of revolutionary youth, during the mid-1960s. Perhaps from casual exposure and conversation, both the European radicals and the black jazzmen discovered a certain sense of shared grievance and impatience that caused foreign music critics to consider artists fleeing a racist society as naturally militant.

Involvement with Crime

Crime is often a matter of strict cultural definition—a definition which rests on how culture sets "normal" limits and imposes sanctions for actions beyond those limits. Perhaps due to its lower class and minority origins, jazz has often been seen as a plaything for the underworld, and ties between jazzmen and criminals, forged for mutually beneficial reasons, predate 1890.[22] Criminal sponsorship, developing concurrently with racist trends that severely restricted lower class pleasures, brought jazzmen into contact with the law itself. Arrested merely for being out after hours, for street corner gambling—or worse— musicians found themselves sharing vermin-infested cells or breaking rocks in road gangs with men whose volatile tempers bespoke dangerous dispositions. Such introduction into criminality, however unintended, could occur early in a musician's life, shaping his personality forever.

"Wrong time, wrong place" is axiomatic for many jazz artists. they have been alternately criminals, crime victims, and, by reason of segregated living patterns, witnesses to street disorder. In the 1950s and 1960s (commensurate with the new interest in hard drugs), the list of artists unable to avoid police detention was incalculable but high. "Many good people were busted between 1955-65," recalls Hampton Hawes, "that didn't even deserve it."[23]

Jazzmen were occasionally tempted into crime by virtue of their job sites. Areas around night clubs were often crime-ridden; anyone with the necessary motivation could turn instant predator. One musician confided that orchestra sidemen longed for hotel gigs since these placed them in an environment screaming to be manipulated—from confidence games to open theft or more discreet room burglaries.

After 1945, the law defined not only drug usage but even possession as a crime. Much covert experimentation with drugs took place in this era of beefed-up law enforcement. Horror stories abound among jazzmen. Many musicians were tempted by drugs— influenced perhaps by role models such as Charlie Parker, perhaps by that "new sense of masculinity and revolt"—and were arrested and detained for lengthy periods of time. Many new drug detention centers rose simply to accommodate remanded musicians. Leonard Feather believed he could create a top-flight jazz orchestra composed solely of inmates from Federal prison hospitals.[24] Some of the jazz artists caught in the net included Art Pepper, Jimmy Heath (five years in Leavenworth), Donald Garnett, Bud Powell, Miles Davis, Dexter Gordon, Tadd Dameron, Stan Getz, Parker, Frank Rehak, Wilbur Ware, Arnold Ross, Gerry Mulligan, Chet Baker, Jack Purvis (whose criminal career predates his first prison sentence in 1937 and who, as late as 1947, was still being sent up), Red Rodney, Fats Navarro, Gene Ammons (a seven-year sentence), Sonny Rollins, Anita O'Day, Billie Holiday (herself, like many other young women singers, introduced to crime as a night blue owner's rape victim), and Bill Crawford. Crawford, later a participant in the Synanon drug cure community at Santa Monica, California, described his not-unusual pattern as an aspiring drummer in 1950: "I spent 10 years after high school graduation smoking weed, shooting dope, going to jam sessions in Los Angeles and San Francisco, and in and out of jail while working at various music jobs."[25]

Owing to the circumstances in which artists found themselves, stealing was a great temptation to the musician of frail character. Years of scraping the bottom of the barrel and the hand-to-mouth existence of jazzmen encouraged criminal associations, and it comes as no great shock to see such abundant duplication in jargon between musician and crook.[26] Racial pressures also took their toll. Despite his proverbial kindness towards younger artists, men like Parker were quite ready, when circumstances demanded, "to pull a knife and pick a fight."[27] As a result, victimization occurred all too frequently, and street frays were too numerous to calculate.

Victimization by police may have been the greatest irritant in the life of the jazz artist. Billie Holiday, for self-protection, learned to "spot a cop fifty feet away in a night club through a haze of smoke." Mingus complained that police pestered any club owner who tolerated integration in his club. Added to this is a description of the Los Angeles police loitering outside Central Avenue clubs in the late 1940s, ready to pounce on would-be integrators. "There were more blinking red lights," one source tells us, "than on any other street in the city." New York's famed 52nd Street experienced similar intrusions after 1945.[28]

Planting evidence was another police device, aimed at arresting otherwise law-abiding nuisances. Three prominent artists, at least, appear to have been so entrapped: Charlie Parker and Billie Holiday were victimized by this tactic, as was Art Pepper, who provides a shattering account.[29] His autobiography recites further injustices and barbaric practices both he and other musicians experienced at the hands of the police. He discusses strip searches he underwent in his own apartment, alludes to other harrowing encounters, and vividly sketches his 1953 detention in the "Hole" at a county jail where "the depression you feel is indescribable." One may assume that what was bad for whites like Pepper was worse for blacks. Just such a victim was Hampton Hawes, who also spent time in jail and claims he was restrained with arm and leg shackles while left to sleep upon a cold cell floor.[30]

Jazz artists visiting the Deep South, no matter how briefly, were likely victims of waiting police. Dizzy Gillespie recounts the monotonous regularity with which jazzmen were arrested and detained, often on the slightest of pretexts, for having caught the eye of a local white belle; these were common problems in the 1950s, when black men seemed very attractive to rebellious (southern) white women.[31] Legal ties offered no immunity. Drummer Ed Blackwell and his new white wife spent their honeymoon in the New Orleans jail following their wedding there in 1958.[32]

Smoky night clubs and cabarets, together with the streets, rooming houses, and nefarious characters around them, guaranteed that jazz artists would be exposed to sordidness. Miller and Skipper, Morris, and Coles amply document this shabby scene. Working and living in the seamier urban pockets, musicians could hardly be unaffected by the illegalities they witnessed. Coles first heard saxophonist John Coltrane amidst the grime of a downtown Pittsburgh bar: ". . . (where) minors were drinking and drugs passed without comment, and there was prostitution and pickups of underage girls."[23] Hawes felt jazzmen, estranged from society and forced into dubious rooming houses on tour, encountered many disreputable types. In this way, younger artists were first introduced to drugs.[34]

Tragedies were common. Jazzmen went few months without some late night telephone caller reporting the wanton demise of a colleague. These years were awash with tragedy and violence. Death came to Lee Morgan (shot while performing on a New York City podium), Eddie Jefferson, Paul Cobbs (a mysterious hit-and-run affair), Denzil Best (who cracked his skull "falling" down subway stairs), Albert Ayler (rumored to have been killed by Brooklyn police in 1970), Joe Keyes (his body was found floating in the Harlem River in 1950), and Chano Pozo (Gillespie's frenetic bongo player, knifed to death in a Harlem bar). Untold numbers were maimed, assaulted, and wounded in scuffles. Trumpeter Chet Baker was luckier than some, surviving, as he did, a brutal, face-smashing beating by hoodlums who left him for dead in San Francisco in the late 1960s.

Musicians were not required to run with criminals, however, to experience the system.

Some became involved while working with public rehabilitation agencies. Curiously, I found a positive correlation between those who recorded protest music and those who assisted ex-offenders and thereby became aware of the system. A list would include Sonny Criss, Ken McIntyre, Jimmy Lyons, Jackie McLean, John Jackson, Steve Reid, Archie Shepp, Johnny Lytle, Ernie Wilkins, Major Holley, Grachan Moncur III, Kenny Dorham, Elvin Jones, Charlie Haden, Andrew Hill, and Buddy Montgomery. On the other hand, few artists with known criminal records chose to publicize this fact and to utilize their experiences didactically. I can think only of Art Pepper, Elmo Hope, Sunny Clark, Charles Mingus, and the crew at Synanon.

But we have now reached the crux of the matter and can examine my original questions. I have already provided many sources from which musicians might have chosen crime-related and protest material to record. Now I wish to discover how many artists distilled these experiences into their music.

Results of Study

This discussion has noted the potential sources, criminal and otherwise, for a musician's radical perspective on social issues. Jazzmen were certainly close to the scene, some occasionally dabbling in crime themselves, and the social tensions of this period were too worrisome for even the most ivory-tower-based musician to ignore. This said, how frequently did jazz artists respond to protest raised by the black communities, and what mannerisms and devices did they select for their response?

My examination of recordings from the 1945-1975 period concludes that most jazz musicians refused to challenge or portray a repressive, racist regime. This is best argued by making comparisons with other available studies. One survey of all blues music recorded from 1920 to 1950 determined that approximately 7 to 14 percent of the recorded blues dealt with crime-related themes, a figure somewhat higher than was found in a second compilation of material recorded between 1943 and 1966. Of the nearly 10,000 records in the latter study, I found almost 2 percent whose titles made explicit references to crime. Since I could refer only to titles which were explicit, the 2 percent may be too low by half.[35]

How do these figures compare to my survey of jazz recordings from 1945-1975? Like the blues list from 1943 to 1966, I had to survey a universe of approximately 10,000 recordings. On the basis of the blues studies, ranging widely from 2 to 14 percent in references to crime or protest, I initially expected to identify a minimum of 200 such references and a potential maximum well over 1,000. Certainly a finding on the low side of the range might have been anticipated, given the fact that blues is a predominantly vocal music with a long tradition of relating stories taken from lower class life. Jazz recordings, on the other hand, are predominantly instrumental and drawn from a broad range of sources, including the standard tunes of the mainstream popular repertory. Nevertheless, I was surprised to find only 64 recordings (just over 0.6 percent) which reflected crime, protest, or related social concerns, even though I included a number of titles with ambiguous meanings. Even allowing for the broad sources of the jazz repertory and the pressures on jazz musicians to appeal to a diverse audience, the small number of titles seemed starkly at odds with the life-experience of the black community (for example, the fact that there are 358 blacks in every 1,000 persons imprisoned).[36]

I then analyzed the contents of the 64 albums containing protest or crime-related material. Only one of the major big companies (Capitol) issued a recording of jazz protest, and this but once. Large recording companies have recently come under fire from jazz critics incensed at their conservatism. But the fact remains that whereas the companies were not issuing *jazz* protest, they were distributing militant music from hitherto commercial pop groups, indicating some willingness to assume risks. Failure to assume equivalent risks in jazz recordings may probably be apportioned equally between jazz recording impressarios, with their desire for "pure" music, and musicians who acquiesced, whatever their own views.

Kofsky provides us with an example of censorship, in which a recording firm, in this case Riverside Records, withdrew Sonny Rollins's "Freedom Suite," because of his bitter liner notes advocating struggle against repression. The album was then resold under the title "The Shadow Waltz," with its inoffensive liner notes supplied by a company publicist. I am also reminded that John Hammond of Columbia Records is said to have considered Billie Holiday's "Strange Fruit," her lament for a black lynching victim, to be "unbecoming" for a star of her importance.[37]

Artists were capable of rebelling against such restraints, even if few made the effort. I identified one pure act of artistic rebellion against record company dictation. In his liner notes, Nat Hentoff claims that Charles Mingus, when denied the right to include protest lyrics and to berate the audience in a performance about to be recorded, promptly switched to a firm which allowed his piquant style to remain untrammeled (see Mingus on Candid 8005).

My survey reflects music from 23 major labels, mostly jazz independents (e.g., Blue Note, Impulse, and Atlantic); 22 lesser labels known primarily to jazz devotees; and 19 obscure companies. The latter produced the fiercest, least compromising albums, most of which, because of the firms' meager size, found only a limited buying public. More music of a militant nature was recorded after 1965, but the number is still unimpressive (35 of 64) and casts further doubt on the impact of the urban riots on recorded black jazz.

Modes of Expressing Messages

Because messages relating to protest or crime can be advanced in a variety of interdependent ways, I examined the 64 albums for pertinent reflections of these themes in album-cover art, sound quality and volume, titles and thematic materials, use of live performances as the occasion for recording, liner notes, and verbalization (vocals, talking, and poetry).

Album covers offer a potential for protest, since leaders of record dates sometimes control all production charges, including album photos. To some extent, packaging may reflect their values. In my survey, blandness was almost universal. Visual packaging usually had nothing to do with the music itself. Of the 64 albums, only three portrayed crime or protest: Herbie Hancock's "Prisoner," which shows him surrounded by the bars of ghetto life; a gun-toting lawman in cartoon form for the Modern Jazz Quartet's album *Sheriff*; and a fiery Black Power motif of vivid red, black, and green insurrectionary flames. Facial and action photos of working musicians were common elements used in over half the albums, banal logos were found in 25 percent of the cases, and the reminder were aswirl in surreal art forms.

Studies suggest that sound in the form of *pitch, tone, intensity, volume, even harmony* can induce rebellious and emotional states in the listener. Furthermore, Kate Hevsner's analysis concludes that "tension-release" rhythms offer meaningful comment for socio-logical discussion. Of course, Alan Lomax, Jr., spent a lifetime proving these points on a global basis.[38] How well do these observations match up with the material found in my survey? Not very well, actually. To the ear of the listener, fast or slow meters, and intensities, are highly subjective, open to individual interpretation. Sound and tempo meant little here: 40 sides had uptempos that could be characterized either as surging, punching and fierce (if one is politically inclined) or as happy, funky, and with a campy groove. I found it hard to reach political conclusions based on tempo alone. There were 18 others (30 percent) that did seem to convey anger. One may question whether such a limited number justifies one critic's argument "that the cry is the quintessence of the new sound of protest in . . . jazz today [1968]."[39] Only six were of the slow, moody, sombre category, laden with a poisonous atmosphere I personally felt best suited to express long-standing grievances against the system. But, again, this is highly subjective.

Titles provide a third opportunity. Mingus believed titles should address social issues, and his outrage at a Southern prison execution prompted his ire in one of several of his charts included in the study.[40] Titles may be the easiest way a creator can insert social attitudes into a record with the minimum of external obstruction. Nevertheless, relatively few records in this survey match the deeply disturbing and emotional material found in the more explicit blues repertoire described by Leadbitter and Slaven. With the ratio 4:1 against, only 22 jazz titles struck me as politically thought-provoking. This contrasts baldly with the blues documents to injustice made by musicians Fred McDowell ("I'm in Jail Again"), Sidney Maiden ("San Quentin Blues"), Sippie Wallace ("Murder Gonna Be My Crime"), Junior Wells and his Eagle Rockers ("Prison Bars All Around Me"), or Jimmy Reed ("Shot My Baby" and "I'm Just Trying to Cop a Plea"). Set against these are such vaguer, if more assertive, contemporary jazz titles as "Backdrop for an Urban Revolution," "Suicide City," "Aggression," and "The White Man's Got a God Complex." The appended discography lists further jazz examples.

Themes offer another potential reference point for musical resentment, which usually occur on a broader scale. Again, my study found little use of themes, excluding those written for police-detective heroes and orchestrated for television. This group (i.e., "Baretta," "The Rockford Files," "The Mod Squad," "Kojak") was devoid of com-mentary, and one could infer only a modicum of political content from the usual sugges-tive chase sounds, percussive rock beats, and effects of sizzling tension.[41] Far more rele-vant was the Thornton chart, "Free Huey," that employed 26 musicians and a large chorus to berate the judicial system. Johnny Lytle, Sonny Rollins, and Archie Shepp each offered lengthy symphonic poems about urban violence, policy brutality, societal inequi-ties, and the barbarism of Attica prison. Pimps appear as a common figure of defiance, and this reference crops up in Horace Silver's "Filthy McNasty" (which Silver introduces to his audience as a "mythical young man of rather dubious character"); in Benny Golson's musical portrait of a street hustler, "Killer Joe," described as "impeccably dressed. . . . . and definitely against manual labor"; and in a remembered piece by Ar-chie Shepp for which I could find no reference. Other theme pieces include Art Blakey's "Freedom Rider" composition, and a similar freedom piece by Max Roach.

In comparing thematic jazz material with Leadbitter and Slaven's large blues sampling for roughly the same period prior to Watts, a shift in emphasis is revealed. Jazz themes focused less on the self-pitying, fatalistic, personal imprisonment woes and the abrupt violence found so often in the blues. Instead we find notions of depersonalized—almost faceless—street strife, institutionalized policy brutality, and the specter of drugs in the community. In short, we have moved from a highly individual reaction to protest against social injustice on a more global basis. Table 1 quantifies this contrast through percentages.

TABLE 1

Crime-Related Issues	Jazz Survey ($n=64$)	Leadbitter ($n=105$)
Prison Life	20%	51%
Riots/Street Crime	20	2
Deviant Behavior	19	18
Drugs	19	5
Police Injustice	13	3
Violence	9	21

Live Recordings and Protest

Since the 1930s, night clubs have been scenes for *live jazz recordings*. There is, in fact, general agreement that as a result of a certain chemical reaction with the patrons, musicians are enlivened and become highly charged, even demonstrative. This atmosphere certainly permits them to drive home any ideas they might wish to convey, and blues musicians, in similar surroundings, have often used this opportunity to good effect. My survey found 12 such examples (19 percent) who seemed to be playing to receptive audiences in clubs.

Why musicians felt comfortable in some clubs and not in others when playing protest music must await future research. I can only point to the examples, which include Charles Earland, Cannonball Adderley, Art Pepper, and Sonny Clark at the Lighthouse in Hermosa Beach, California (why so many here, I ask?); Art Blakey at Birdland, Horace Silver at the Village Gate, and Charles McPherson and Eric Dolphy at the Five Spot, all in New York; Charles Mingus before a specially assembled audience; and Milt Jackson at the Mannehole in Hollywood. Also before live and enthusiastic crowds are the Archie Shepp/John Coltrane performances of "Scag" and "Rufus" (vivid stories of Harlem drug addiction and a lynch victim) at the 1965 Newport Jazz Festival, and the tamer prison concerts given by Elmo Hope at Riker's Island and by Jimmy McGriff and Lucky Thompson at Chicago's Cook County Jail.

Colleges have also been jazz meccas. Despite the receptivity one would think these artists could expect for militant music, I found no examples of campus performances. Elvin Jones, Art Lewis, and Andrew Hill regularly perform for prison groups, but so far as I know, they, like the Archie Shepp concert at Attica shortly after the bloody massacre, have not been recorded. This seems unfathomable in light of comments made by country/ western singer Johnny Cash, whose two prison albums were highly successful releases of the conservative Columbia Record Company: "Prisoners are the greatest audiences that an entertainer can perform for. We bring them a ray of sunshine in their dungeon, and they're not ashamed to respond and show their appreciation".[42]

A significant source of information and protest within the black cultural tradition lies in its oral history. *Jazz vocals and poetry* thus seem to be appropriate avenues to investigate. Yet pertinent vocals were almost as rare as unicorns. The most effective of the three or four possible examples came from Nat Adderley's 15-year-old son, who gave melodic advice to a 1971 Lighthouse assemblage:

> I've been in this jail cell, O so long.
> How much time must I serve?
> Tell me, Mr. President,
> Are you gonna give me what I want and
> What I deserve?
> 'Cause if you not just tell me true,
> 'Cause I'm gonna fight until you do . . .

Black Panther advocate Elaine Brown produced some of the fiercest and most militant music on criminality and injustice. Using a slow, powerful beat, Brown exhorted her her 1971 listeners:

> Well, then, believe it, my friend,
> That this silence will end.
> We'll just have to get guns
> And be men.

Poetry has been a more commonly traveled byway, and much jazz poetry was rendered before live audiences in the 1950s and 1960s. Still, only a few speak of protest or crime, and even fewer have been recorded. In this area some of the younger artists have led the way in producing the most scorching materials, and this later in the period rather than earlier. Gil Scott-Heron/Brian Jackson offer many vituperative pieces, including Scott-Heron's introductory remark "How long do you think it's going to be before even our dreams ain't free" (on "King Arthur Plan"). Then there is Ishmael Reed's reading on the New Jazz Poets' views of urban revolution: "We will rush like crazed antelopes . . . into a scorching, burning lake"; the Leroi Jones (Amiri Baraka) discussion of injustice on a Sunny Murray recording; and the many explosive contributions from the Last Poets.

Oral language in jazz neatly illustrates the inevitable differences in racial viewpoints on crime. Sharp ethnic differences are best seen in two jazz poems spaced but six years and at least one urban revolt apart. The subject is the police. Bob Dorough, in the first case, recites the loping work from Lawrence Ferlinghetti, "Dog," a 1961 piece of quiet restraint and mild indifference toward police:

> He doesn't hate cops. He merely has
>   no use for them.
> He would rather eat a tender cow than
>   a tough policeman.
> But either might do.
> For he will not be muzzled.

In the second, the New Poets present us with a 1967 tale of rage:

> The rage of a helpless people . . .
>   to 10,000 rounds of ammunition.

> The only Messiah we will know this year
> is a bullet in the belly
> Of a Harlem youth shot by a coward
> crouched behind an outlaw's badge.

Liner notes represent the last of our potential sources. Here, too, we can observe how a relationship between an album's cover and theme can be verbally amplified. In the 1960s this single aspect appeared as the most viable, regularly used weapon for protest, and then not always by a musician but often from the pens of Nat Hentoff or Leroi Jones. By 1975 the use of liner notes had given way to a dramatic increase of photos, with less commentary, splashed across both sides of an album, extending still further the apolitical nature of the musical product. Several examples illustrate how liners might effectively promote themes of protest or crime:

> People say that I'm hollering. Man, I feel like hollering. . . . [This piece] is based on my struggle within myself to get free from prison chains, the invisible ones and the real ones. (Mingus, *Ecclusiastics*)

> The American system has killed and cheated both audience and creator. (Ornette Coleman, *Free Huey*)

> We imagined a sheriff shooting at someone trying to escape, but the other fellow winning. (John Lewis, *The Sheriff*)

> Dedicated to the 1000s of militant youths for freedom. (Herbie Hancock, *The Prisoner*)

The lengthiest and most informative diatribe against the apolitical jazz artist, foreshortened here, was penned by Detroit disc jockey Martin Grant, writing for the Wendell Harris album *Consciousness*:

> Jazz must reflect the environment that we live in if it is to be educational and beneficial to our culture. It must portray our way of life . . . Harris's music reflects more than ever before the stress, tension, and discrimination that is taking place within our community.

Conclusions

This essay has attempted to gauge the extent to which jazz has conveyed rebellious messages. I have tried to answer two questions in the process: whether jazz artists did incorporate shared experiences of oppressed peoples, particularly experiences with the criminal justice system, and whether indignation at racism could be expressed within the confines of a basically instrumental music. My answers turned out to be, in order, no (as a rule, at least) and yes.

My examination of American recorded jazz between 1945 and 1975 reveals that these musicians rarely challenged the system or flaunted rebellious views despite the direct experiences many of them had with oppression or crime, their opportunities to make recordings, and the high social awareness their listeners probably brought to the music during a time of tremendous black resistance to a repressive system. The vast majority of jazz artists did not conform to romantic publicity about their rebelliousness and inherent social militancy, short of taking out their rage on night club customers or quietly performing in an artists' colony.

Thus, this survey supports Newton's view that jazzmen are highly apolitical and that from them we can look for little moral or social message:

> It is easy to associate jazz with radical or revolutionary politics . . . but left to itself jazz protest is unique and ambiguous . . . and frequently misunderstood by the anarchist intellectuals who have taken jazz to their bosoms against policemen, judges and prisons . . . Very few American jazz musicians express hatred and resentment of an unjust society, and all this only privately.[43]

And contrary to leftist stereotypes, those who did put up a fight were neither very young, very lower class, nor untainted by urban cynicism.

But there were many musical and extramusical ways to convey and depict indignation about racism, even if some were used and some were not. Even since Scriabin's *Prometheé Symphony* (1915), opportunities have existed for light shows to complement and heighten ecstatic musical experience. With the lone exception of Sun Ra's 1967 Central Park concert fiasco, where fire eaters and extravagantly dressed dancers joined his orchestra and light show to extol the joys of space travel, no other use of this technique springs to mind, certainly not in clubs. Noises *(Geräusche)* might also have been employed. Musical forms built from noises were a regular feature of progressive music during the 1920s and later, yet I found no jazz representations which, in this context, might have included police whistles, explosions, screams, gun shots, or metallic prison sounds for effect. Parenthetically and for contrast, I might recommend Johnny Cash's *Folsom Prison Blues* for example. Here we can detect the background sounds of clanging metal security during the concert, feet shuffling at the close as inmates are herded back to their cellblocks, and the warden occasionally interrupting to announce that prisoners A39879 and A50632 have visitors awaiting them at reception.[44]

Leaflets, dance rituals, art displays and photos linked to jazz concerts, speakers, costume shows, and tape recorder overdubs are other approaches that might have been used. In reference to costumes I am reminded of one Kansas City night club in the 1930s, the Jail Club, where the musicians wore uniforms of grey with thin black stripes and numbers.

Whatever the musical merits, by 1973, with the trickle of jazz protest albums, jazz resembled opera in its divorce from social reality and its member exclusivity. Ellison believed jazz had grown "quite independent of the social environment," and, on the basis of this study, I am inclined to agree with him.[45] Facing the apparent disrespect of the corporate music establishment and supposedly frustrated by white competition, one obvious strategy for jazz artists would have been to forge a bond with discontented but enlightened "opinion leaders" of black youth. Reggae spokesmen like Bob Marley, Jimmy Cliff, and Linton Kwesi Johnson seem to have attracted a large cosmopolitan following on the basis of direct confrontation with society. Marley sings:

> Woman hold your head and cry,
> Cuz your son has been
> shot down in the street
> and dies from a stray bullet . . .
> just because of the system.[46]

I believe the signal failure on the part of relatively apolitical jazz artists to confront black issues through their music has redounded unfavorably on the music. Black youth, searching for answers and deeply discontented, have been rejected by musicians who had the power and insight to do more. And through this neglect of its root culture, jazz has been refashioned into an elitist art form, untouched by the reality of daily life. As in the case of opera, it may very well be challenged as a "fossilised anachronism which belongs in a museum."[47]

DISCOGRAPHY:
PROTEST AND CRIME-RELATED THEMES IN
AMERICAN RECORDED JAZZ, 1945-75

Indicates a direct reference with obvious, explicit thematic material as opposed to simple title or indirect allusion. Only one listing per song title.

YEAR	GROUP	TITLE	LABEL
1945	C.P. Johnson Orchestra*	The "G" Man Got the "T" Man (vocal)	Stash 100
	Walter Thomas All Stars	Black Maria's Blues	Prestige 7584
	Barney Bigard Sextet	Sweet Marijuana Brown	Stash 100
1947	Charlie Parker	Relaxin' at Camarillo	Dial 1030
1951	Coleman Hawkins	Disorder at the Border	Phone Jazz 22
1952	Art Pepper and the Sunny Clark Trio	Brown Gold	Savoy 2215
1958	Ornette Coleman Quartet	Chippie	Contemporary 3551
	Shelly Manne & His Men	The Floater/Dreamville	Contemporary 3560
	Sonny Rollins*	Freedom Suite (liner notes)	Riverside 258
1959	Horace Silver Quintet	The Outlaw	Blue Note 1589
1960	Donald Byrd/ Booker Little	Call to Arms	TCB 1004
	Art Blakey Jazz Messengers	Justice	Blue Note 4015
	Charles Mingus*	Fables of Faubus (comments)	Candid 8005
	Charles Mingus*	Lock 'em Up (liner notes, vocal)	Barnaby 31304
	Art Farmer/Benny Golson	Killer Joe (talk)	Argo 664
1961	Oliver Nelson Orchestra*	Emancipation Blues	Prestige 7225
	Eric Dolphy Quartet	Aggression	Prestige 7611

YEAR	GROUP	TITLE	LABEL
	Horace Silver Quintet	Filthy McNasty (prologue)	Blue Note 4076
	Max Roach*	Tender Warriors (liner notes)	Impulse A-8
	Bob Dorough/Chico Hamilton Quartet*	Night Song for the Sleepless Dog (poetry)	World Pacific 1409
1962	Cecil Payne/Kenny Drew Sextet*	It's Your Life (drug commentary)	Parker 806
	Arnold Ross Group*	Sounds of Synanon (liner notes)	Pacific Jazz 48
	Charles Mingus*	Ecclusiastics (liner notes)	Atlantic 1377
1963	Elmo Hope All Stars*	Hope from Riker's Island (liner)	Chiaroscuro 2009
	Art Blakey Jazz Messengers*	Petty Larceny/Freedom Rider (liner)	Blue Note 4156
	Lou Donaldson	Coppin' a Plea	Argo 724
	Gene Shaw	Thieves' Carnival	Argo 726
1964	Lucky Thompson Quartet	Prey Loot	Prestige 7365
	Modern Jazz Quartet*	Sheriff (liner notes, cover)	Atlantic 1414
1965	Archie Shepp/John Coltrane*	Scag/Rufus (liner notes, vocal)	Impulse A-94
	Horace Silver	The Natives are Restless Tonight	Blue Note 4185
	Lee Morgan	Peyote/Speedball	Blue Note 4212
1966	Andrew Hill Quartet*	Violence (liner notes)	Blue Note 4253
	Marzette Watts & Company*	Backdrop for an Urban Revolution	Esperanto 1044
1967	Clifford Thornton's New Art Ensemble*	Free Huey (comments, liner notes)	Third World 9636
	New Jazz Poets*	Jitterbuggin' in the Streets/To Jackie in Jail/Jackal-Headed Cowboy (poetry, liner notes)	Broadside 461
	Sunny Murray/LeRoi Jones*	Justice (poetry)	Jihad 663
	Charles McPherson Quintet	The Viper	Prestige 7480
1968	Lee Morgan Quintet	Suicide City	Blue Note 4289

YEAR	GROUP	TITLE	LABEL
	Buddy Rich/Art Pepper	Acid Truth	Pacific Jazz 20133
	Gene Norman Group	Blowin' in the Wind	GNP 52015
	Archie Shepp Quartet	Stick 'em Up	Impulse AS9188
	Herbie Hancock Quartet	Riot	Blue Note 4279
	Milt Jackson Quartet	Frankie & Johnny	Impulse AS9189
1969	David Newman	Chained No More	Atlantic 1524
	Herbie Hancock Quintet*	The Prisoner (cover, liner notes)	Blue Note 4321
1971	Cannonball & Nat Adderley Sextet*	The Price You Got to Pay to Be Free (vocal, talk)	Capitol 636
	Elaine Brown*	The End of Silence/Seize the Time (vocal, cover)	Vault 131
	Last Poets*	The White Man's Got a God Complex/ Related to What? (poetry, liner, cover)	Douglas 7
	Johnny Lytle Sextet	Soulful Rebel Suite (comments)	Milestone 9036
	Roland Kirk*	Raped Voices (liner notes)	Atlantic 1578
1972	Charles Earland plus Six	Black Gun	Prestige 10050
	Archie Shepp	Attica Blues/Blues for Brother George (comments, liner notes, vocal)	Impulse AS9222
	Lucky Thompson/ Jimmy McGriff*	Friday the 13th (jail on cover, photos)	Groove Merchant 515
	Wendell Harris & the Tribe*	Consciousness (liner notes)	RSD 2212
	Gil Scott-Heron & Brian Jackson	King Alfred Plan/No Knock/Free Will/Billy Green is Dead (vocal, liner, prologues)	Flying Dutchman 10153
1973	Bernard Purdie	Attica	Prestige 10038
	Leon Thomas*	It's My Life I'm Fighting For (vocal)	Flying Dutchman 10167
	Marion Brown	Malcolm--A Social Commentary	Arista 1904
1974	Art Ensemble of Chicago	Fanfare for the Warriors (background talk)	Atlantic 1651
	Blue Mitchell	Harmony of the Underworld	Mainstream 402

YEAR	GROUP	TITLE	LABEL
1975	Charles Mingus	Free Cell Block "F" (comments, liner notes)	Atlantic 1678
	Charles Mingus	Remember Rockefeller & Attica (liner, vocal)	Atlantic 1677

Notes

Material for this project was derived mainly from my access to the archives of the Rutgers University Institute of Jazz Studies. Particular gratitude goes to Ronald Welburn and Edward Berger, whose unflagging assistance, if not concurrent philosophical agreement, and spontaneous recall of titles from their archive of 10,000 relevant albums, formed the backbone of my discography.

1. Anonymous, "Is Jazz the Pilot of Disaster," *Etude,* no. 43 (1925), pp. 5-6.

2. R. Serge Denisoff and Richard A. Peterson, eds., *Sounds of Social Change* (New York: Rand McNally, 1972), p. 27.

3. Such a list would include such arrangers as Johnny Mandel, Quincy Jones, J.J. Johnson, Tom Scott, Shorty Rogers, Don Ellis, and Pete Rugolo.

4. L.H. Masotti and D.R. Bowen, *Riots and Rebellion* (New York: Russell Sage, 1968): R.M. Stephenson and F.R. Scarpitti, "Negro-White Differentials in Delinquency," *Journal of Research in Crime and Delinquency* 5 (1968), pp. 122-33; Scott Christianson and Richard DeHais, *The Black Incarceration Rate: A National Problem* (Ph.D. diss., SUNY, 1980), pp. 2-7.

5. Quoted in Ben Sidran, *Black Talk* (New York: Holt, Rinehart, Winston, 1971), p. 52.

6. Hampton Hawes and Don Asher, *Raise Up Off Me* (New York: Coward, McCann and Geoghegan, 1972), p. 141; Sidran, p. 121.

7. Leroi Jones, *Black Music* (New York: Morrow, 1967), p. 23; Charles Fox, *Jazz in Perspective* (London: BBC, 1957), p. 33; Marshall Stearns, *Story of Jazz* (New York: Oxford University Press, 1956), pp. 218,222-230; Richard Boyer, "Bop," *New Yorker,* no. 3, July 1949, pp. 28-9; Sidney Finkelstein, *Jazz, A People's Music* (New York: Citadel, 1948), p. 233; Ralph Ellison, *Shadow and Act* (New York: Signet, 1964), pp. xii, 27; and Valerie Wilmer, *As Serious as Your Life* (New York: Hill, 1980), p. 12.

8. Quoted in Frank Kofsky, *Black Nationalism and the Revolution in Music* (New York: Pathfinder, 1970), pp. 105 and 153.

9. Carl Belz, *The Story of Rock* (New York: Oxford University Press, 1969), p. iv; James E. Harmon, *The New Music and the American Youth Subculture,* (Ph.D. diss., U.S. International University, 1971), p. 214; Robert W. Lundin, *An Objective Psychology of Music* (New York: Ronald, 1967), p. 8.

10. John P. Robinson and Paul M. Hirsch, "It's the Sound That Does It: Protest Music and the American Teenage Audience," *Psychology Today,* October, 1969; pp. 42-5; Rochelle Larkin, *Soul Music* (New York: Lancer, 1970), p. 172; Nelson George, "Rick James's Ghetto Life," *Village Voice,* 24-30 June 1981, p. 70; and Robert A. Rosenstone, "The Times, They Are A-Changin': The Music of Protest" in *Annals of American Academy of Political and Social Sciences* (March 1969), pp. 133-36.

11. Alun Morgan and Ray Horricks, *Modern Jazz: A Survey of Development Since 1939* (London: Gollancz, 1956), p. 30; Arrigo Pollilo, *Jazz: A Guide to the History and Development of Jazz and Jazz Musicians* (London: Hamlyn, 1969), p. 60; Philippe Carles and Jean-Louis Comolli, *Free Jazz: Black Power* (Paris: Union Generale d'Edition, 1972); Rex Harris, *Enjoying Jazz* (Bristol: Jazz Blook Club, 1961), p. 107; André Hodeir, *Introduction à la Musique de Jazz* (Paris: Larousse, 1947), p. 14; Alan P. Merriam and R.W. Mack, "The Jazz Community," *Social Forces* 38 (1960), pp. 211-222; Finkelstein, p. 238; Richard L. Means, "Notes on Negro Jazz: 1920-50," *Sociologi-*

cal Quarterly 9 (1968), 332-42; and Kenneth Boulding, *The Image* (Ann Arbor: University of Michigan Press, 1956), p. 132.

12. Pollilo, p. 69; also Means.

13. Kofsky, p. 57; Ralph Ellison, "The Golden Age, Time Past," *Esquire* (January 1959), p. 33; W.B. Cameron, "Sociological Notes on the Jam Session," *Social Forces* 32 (1954), pp. 177-82; Howard Becker, "Professional Dance Musician and His Audience," *American Journal of Sociology* 57 (1951), pp. 136-40.

14. Ellison, *Shadow,* pp. 221-222.

15. Sidran, p. 99.

16. Ortiz Walton, *Music Black, White and Blue* (New York: Morrow, 1972), pp. 93,97 and 154; Arthur Crook, ed., *The British Imagination* (New York: Atheneum, 1961), p. 111; A.H. Esman, "A Study in Cultural Conflict," *American Imago* 51 (nd), p. viii; Jones, pp. 155, 209; and Wilmer, p. 251.

17. Wilmer, p. 87.

18. Francis Newton, *The Jazz Scene* (New York: Monthly Review Press, 1960), p. 235; Denisoff, p. 17; Belz, p. ix; and *Playboy,* September 1970.

19. Newton, p. 214; also see H.H. Stuckenschmidt, *Twentieth Century Music* (New York: World, 1969) for the link between jazz-oriented German composers and the leftist movement after 1918 (p. 135).

20. Alan P. Merriam, *Anthropology of Music* (Chicago: Northwestern University Press, 1964), pp. 5, 104-5; Elliot McGinnies, "Cognitive and Behavioral Approaches to Persuasion" in *Human Communications: Theoretical Explorations,* Albert Silverstein, ed. (New York: Wiley, 1974), pp. 193-4; and Kofsky, p. 105. Also see Newton, p. 233.

21. Ellison, *Shadow,* p, xiii.

22. Ronald L. Morris, *Wait Until Dark: Jazz and the Underworld, 1880-1940* (Bowling Green: Bowling Green University Press, 1980), p. 96; Charles Mingus, *Beneath the Underdog* (New York: Knopf, 1971), p. 189.

23. Hawes, p. 115; Morris, p. 77.

24. Quoted in Denisoff, p. 85.

25. Liner notes for *Sounds of Synanon* (see Discography).

26. R.S. Gold, *Jazz Lexicon* (New York: Knopf, 1964): Dan Burley, *Original Handbook of Harlem Jive* (New York: private printing, 1944); and "The Anonymous Verses of a Narcotic Addict," *Southern Folklore Quarterly* (September 1958).

27. Ellison, *Shadow,* p. 225.

28. Nat Hentoff and Nat Shapiro, *Hear Me Talkin' to Ya* (New York: Dover, 1955), p. 368; Mingus, p. 349; and Hawes, p. 25.

29. Flo Kennedy, *Color Me Flo: My Hard Life and Good Times* (New York: Prentice Hall, 1976), pp. 47-8; Ross Russell, *Bird Lives* (New York: Charterhouse, 1973), p. 219; and Art Pepper, *Straight Life* (New York: Schirmer, 1979).

30. Hawes, pp. 131 and 138.

31. Dizzie Gillespie and Al Fraser, *To Be or Not to Bop* (New York: Doubleday, 1979), pp. 384-85.

32. Wilmer, p. 195.

33. Bill Cole, *John Coltrane* (New York: Schirmer, 1976), p. 3; Hawes, pp. 32-3; and Lloyd Miller and J.K. Skipper, Jr., in Denisoff, p. 23.

34. Hawes, p. 33.

35. Leonard Goines, "The Blues as Black Therapy: A Thematic Study," *Black World,* September 1973, pp. 313, 324; Mike Ledbitter and Neil Slaven, *Blues Records: 1943-66;* (London: Hanover, 1969).

36. Christianson and DeHais, pp. 2-4.

37. Kofsky, pp. 50-2; John Hammond and Irving Townsend, *John Hammond on Record* (Baltimore: Penguin, 1981), p. 209.

38. Ekkehard Jost, *Free Jazz* (Hamburg: Graz, 1974), p. 191; also see his bibliography of the "oriental wave." His more critical views of Coltrane and Mingus can be found in "Eine Experimental Psychologische Untersuchung zu Hörgewohneiten von Jazz Musikern," *Jazz Forschung* 1 (1969), p. 182; D. Dees, *On a Theory of Art: A Structuralist Analysis with Examples from Contemporary Popular Music* (Ph.D. diss., Notre Dame, 1972), p. 62; Kate Hevsner, "Experimental Studies of the Elements of Expression in Music," *American Journal of Psychology* 48 (1936), pp. 259-64; and Alan P. Lomax, Jr., *Song as a Measure of Culture* (Princeton: Princeton University Press, 1968).

39. Denisoff, p. 29.

40. Nat Hentoff's liner notes for Mingus's "Free Cell Block F, 'Tis Nazi U.S.A.," *Changes Two*, Atlantic SD 1678 (see discography).

41. Henry Mancini, *Cop Themes*, RCA Victor, RLP 1896 (1975). Also see the albums by Purdie and Manne in the discography.

42. Liner notes on J. Cash's *Folsom Prison*, Columbia, CS 9639 (1972).

43. Newton, pp. 272-3; Harmon, p. 214.

44. Cash, op. cit.

45. Ellison, *Shadows*, p. 234.

46. Anonymous, "What Went Down When Reggae Hit the Ghetto," *Revolutionary Worker*, 7 August 1981, p. 6.

47. Peter Stieber, "Opera as Irrelevance," *Vorwärts*, 9 April 1981, p. 13; Newton, p. 153; Belz, pp. 6-7; and John Rockwell, "Jazz and Classical Music," *New York Times*, 21 June 1981, p. D19.

Mildred Bailey on Records:
Addenda and Corrections to Rust

Loren Schoenberg

Since the publication of a fourth edition of Brian Rust's *Jazz Records: 1897–1942*, new discographical information has come to light regarding singer Mildred Bailey's recordings made during the period covered by this work. It is listed here in chronological order.

December 6, 1935

An alternate take from this session (featuring Bunny Berigan, Johnny Hodges and Teddy Wilson) has been discovered on some issues of Parlophone R-2201 and Decca 18108. Rust's listing should be amended as follows:

60202-A	Honeysuckle Rose	Dec 18108, Par R-2201, A-6482, Od A-2330
60202-B	Honeysuckle Rose	Dec 18108, Par R-2201

Incidentally, while Rust commonly lists the original 78 issue first, he here apparently has failed to realize that this session was issued on Parlophone in England several years before the first U.S. issue on Decca.

November 9, 1936

Johnny Hodges is listed as present on the second title recorded at this session, "It's Love I'm After." Careful listening reveals that no alto saxophone is audible. Rust lists the tenor saxophonist as "Francis Lowe," while the labels of the original issues show "Francis Love"; this is a pseudonym for Ben Webster, whose middle name was Francis.

March 27, 1937

Bailey's theme song, "Rockin' Chair," was recorded at this session and issued on 78 in two takes. A further issue of the first take has been found, and is italicized below. Rust

---

Loren Schoenberg, a tenor saxophonist and pianist, has led his own big band in New York and on records, and has produced and hosted jazz radio programs on stations in the New York metropolitan area. He served as musicologist for the Benny Goodman archives from 1980 to 1982 and is a member of Record Research Associates.

lists LP issues only when an item was issued in this configuration for the first time, but since he gives many wrong listings concerning takes used on Columbia's three-LP Mildred Bailey set (C3L 22—Rust shows CL 1861, the designation of an individual disc within the set), I will list the correct take assignments as they occur.

| C-1859-1 | Rockin' Chair | Voc 3553, S-88, Col 35943, *50043*, 80-G |
| C-1859-2 | Rockin' Chair | Voc 3553, S-88, Col 35943, 80-G, CBS-CL 1861 |

June 29, 1937

The take of "Heaven Help This Heart of Mine" on the LP set is incorrectly identified as an alternate but is in fact the same (21334-2) as issued on 78. No alternate is known to exist.

March 14, 1938

Rust lists only one take for "Don't Be That Way," when indeed there are two, both issued on 78. The correct information is as follows:

| 22566-1 | Don't Be That Way | Voc 4016, S-157, Cq 9022 |
| 22566-3 | Don't Be That Way | Voc 4016, CBS CL-1861 |

September 29, 1938

Rust lists an alternate take of "St. Louis Blues" as having been issued on the Bailey LP set, but this is the same as the 78 issue. Meanwhile, a true alternate has been issued on LP, on a two-record album under John Kirby's name.

| 23516-3 | St. Louis Blues | CBS CL-1861, Voc 4801, all other 78 issues. |
| 23516-4 | St. Louis Blues | CBS CG 33557 |

In addition, the last title recorded at this session, "Have You Forgotten So Soon?," has accompaniment by Red Norvo's orchestra, not the John Kirby Sextet plus Norvo as on the other titles. Thus the following personnel should be inserted between "St. Louis Blues" and 23519-1, "Have You Forgotten So Soon?":

John Owens-Jack Palmer-Barney Zudecoff-t.Andy Russo-Al George-tb/Hank D'Amico-cl-as/Frank Simeone-as/George Berg-Maurice Kogan-ts/Bill Miller-p/Alan Hanlon-g/Pete Peterson-b/George Wettling-d/Red Norvo-x-leader.

April 24, 1939

Both personnel and take information for this session is incomplete in Rust. The correct take numbers and personnel details are listed in their entirety below:

Charlie Shavers-t/Buster Bailey-cl/Russell Procope-as/Billy Kyle-p/John Kirby-b/O'Neil Spencer-d/Red Norvo-x (on first and third titles only)/Eddie Sauter-a/Mildred Bailey-voc.

24427-A	That Sly Old Gentleman	Voc 4815
24428-A	Tit Willow	Voc 4845
24429-A	The Lamp Is Low	Voc 4845
24430-A	And the Angels Sing	Voc 4815

November 3 and November 30, 1939

Dates for these sessions have been transposed more than once. Since it was very rare for studios to record matrix numbers out of sequence, I would list them as Rust himself did in earlier editions (the 4th has them in reverse order). Accompaniment for the second session has been credited both to Alex Wilder and to John Kirby (as in Rust's 4th). The labels merely state "Accompanied by Orchestra." In my opinion, the group includes Ben Webster (tenor sax) and Teddy Wilson (piano), plus trumpet, one other reed, guitar, bass and drums. Webster's and Wilson's presence has been confirmed by experienced listeners. The others may well be members of Wilson's big band of the time, which included Webster. Thus, the date shown by Rust as November 30 for the Bailey session accompanied by the Alec Wilder Octet should be changed to November 3 (the information is otherwise accurate), while the session he shows under November 3 should be corrected as follows:

November 30, 1939:

Unknown-t/cl/Ben Webster-ts/Teddy Wilson-p/unk-g/b/d/Mildred Bailey-voc.

26258-A	Blue Rain	Voc 5277
26259-A	I've Gone Off the Deep End	Voc 5236
26260-A	I Shoulda Stood in Bed	Voc 5236

January 15, 1940

Bassist Pete Peterson was hired for this session, and his name was entered in the studio files. Peterson failed to show up, however, and Roy Eldridge enlisted his bassist (italicized below) as a last-minute substitute. Thus the personnel should read as follows:

Roy Eldridge-t/Robert Burns-Jimmy Carroll-cl/Carl Preager-bcl/Eddie Powell-f/Teddy Wilson-p/John Collins-g/*Ted Sturgis-b*/Bill Beason-d/Eddie Sauter-a/Mildred Bailey-voc.

January 25, 1940

Rust shows takes A and B of "Give Me Time" from this session as rejected, and identifies the 78 issues as having take C, from April 2, 1940. However, I have not been able to find any copies of Col 35626 that do *not* contain take B, and while it is possible that Col 80-G does contain take C, as Rust shows, it is likely that this tune should be omitted from the April 2 session. Further, all copies I have seen of Col 35921, "Don't Take Your Love From Me," have take B rather than the A take that Rust shows for this issue. He does show take B on Australian Columbia DO-2226, which I have not been able to examine; it is thus possible that he reversed the take designations, or that take A was never issued. Moreover, oboist Mitch Miller, whom Rust shows only for the April 2 and May 25, 1940 Bailey sessions, is definitely present on January 25 as well. Thus, personnel for that session, otherwise identical with those given for January 15 above, should include Miller and the following details should be added:

26460-B	Give Me Time	Col 35626
26464-B	Don't Take Your Love From Me	Col 35921

February 24 and March 14, 1941

The personnels listed in Rust for these Bailey sessions fail to include the audible clarinetist. *Jazz Directory* suggests that he is Jerry Jerome; other possibilities are Sal Franzella, Jimmy Lytell, or Sid Stoneburn, all of whom are present on Decca studio recordings of the time.

The Bolden Band Photo—One More Time

Alden Ashforth

In 1939 the first edition of *Jazzmen* reproduced a photo (Figure 1) of six black musicians, captioned "Kid Bolden's Band before 1895."[1] As the only known photo of Charles "Buddy" Bolden, the most intriguing and lionized figure of early jazz, it engendered enormous excitement. Over the years intrigue and excitement have persisted, joined by hitherto unresolved controversy. In the many times the picture has been reproduced it has been cropped in different ways, it has been reversed ("flopped"), it has been given different datings, and the personnel have been differently identified. It is the intent of this article to suggest and substantiate answers to some photographic and historical questions that have puzzled jazz scholars for four decades.

In addition to being an object of curiosity as a sui generis jazz artifact, the photo has revealed some important information to historians. It shows that, even though Bolden's was the first "hot" band, his harmonic and rhythmic support, like that of the "sweet" society orchestras of the period, came from a guitar and a normally bowed string bass, rather than from the banjo and plucked bass later associated with this sort of music. Similarly, "tailgate" trombone glissandi (often thought of as a sine qua non of the style) could not have existed within this band's make-up: William Cornish's instrument is a valve trombone, not a slide trombone. It is also evident that on at least some occasions Bolden employed both Bb-clarinetist Frank Lewis and C-clarinetist William Warner simultaneously rather than alternately. It is unfortunate that Bolden's regular drummer, Cornelius Tillman, is unaccountably missing from the picture, thus depriving us of valuable information about the percussion instruments used.

In many reproductions of the photo, cropping has obscured a large canvas backdrop which implies performance at a circus show or carnival event, or possibly a large picnic. Such cropping has also excluded a smallish, round object in the foreground at the bottom of the photo. The lack of edge details on this object precludes the possibility of its being a banjo or drum: the inner curved line identifies it instead as some sort of bass brass instrument. Samuel B. Charters plausibly surmises that the proximity of such an instrument in the photo implies the possibility of its being employed as an alternate bass in performance by the Bolden band.[2] His further assumption that the string bass player James Johnson

---

Alden Ashforth began jazz research, criticism, and recording in New Orleans in 1950. He is currently Professor of Music at the University of California at Los Angeles in composition and ethnomusicology.

Kid Bolden's Band before 1895
Standing, Jimmie Johnson, Buddy Bolden, Willy Cornish (valve trombone), Willy Warner
Seated, Brock Mumford, Frank Lewis   *photo from Willy Cornish*

Fig. 1. The Bolden Band as it Appeared in the First Edition of *Jazzmen*.

played both instruments is conjectural, however. In the history of New Orleans jazz there are relatively few instances where a musician learned both string technique and brass embouchure, and such instances were sufficiently exceptional to have caused comment and to have been noted.

Charters's further assertion that the brass instrument in question is a saxhorn must be treated as speculation. The saxhorn, after its invention by Adolphe Sax, underwent so many changes in construction that its bell shape cannot be pinpointed. And further, the bell shapes of a host of bass brass instruments equally available in this period (e.g., the higher tubas and euphoniums, even flugelhorns), are similar. The photo does not permit accurate assessment of the bell diameter, and in any event the musicians used bass brass instruments on an availability basis and to this day refer to each and all, irrespective of type, as ''bass horn.''[3]

The mode of dress exhibited in the photo is, although not uniform, comparable in formality to that of the more polite ''society'' orchestras of the period, such as that of Bolden's chief rival, John Robichaux.[4] Bolden's appearance confirms reports of light skin and good looks; further, his cool half-smile and cavalier posture, cornet nonchalantly balanced on his palm, suggest a man of confidence and insouciance. In contrast, the other men pose stiffly.

Fig. 2. The Bolden Band. Photo (originally from Willie Cornish) probably taken between 1899 and 1903.

Standing, left to right: Frank Lewis, B*b* clarinet; William Cornish, valve trombone; Charles "Buddy" Bolden, cornet; James Johnson, string bass. Seated, left to right: William Warner, clarinet; Jeff "Brock" Mumford, guitar.

A Left-Handed Photograph

The credit "photo from Willy Cornish" appears in *Jazzmen* (Figure 1). Sometime after Cornish's death in 1940, Al Rose and Edmond Souchon borrowed the original from Mrs. Bella Cornish; in their invaluable photo album the acknowledgement is to her.[5] She later loaned the photo to Dr. Leonard Bechet (older brother of Sidney Bechet), a dentist, former trombonist, and indefatigable collector of jazz memorabilia; when Bechet died the original could not be found.[6]

The *Jazzmen* editors noted an apparent incongruity in the picture: the guitar and double bass players were shown as if playing their instruments left-handed. As it seemed improbable that two members of the band should play in such an unorthodox manner, and as no one interviewed recalled Jeff Mumford and James Johnson as left-handed, the photo was flopped when reprinted, to correct what seemed to be an error in the original printing.

Rose and Souchon did not reverse the photo in reprinting, however, and stated of it: "It has been published twice before, but printed backwards each time, because the photogra-

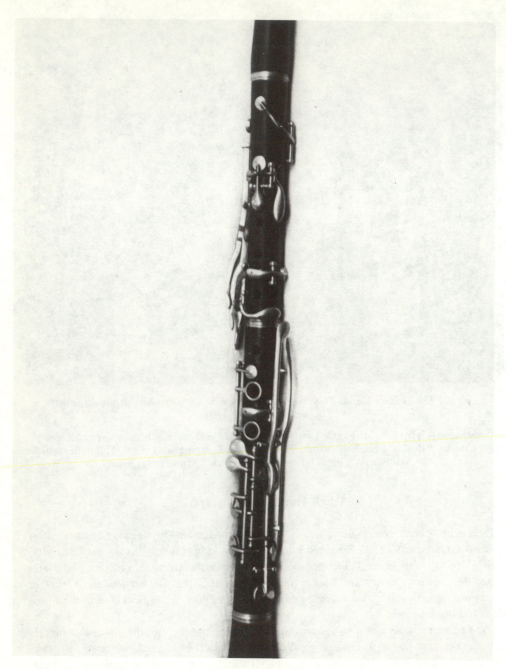

Fig. 3. Typical Albert System Clarinet (key detail); (collection of the author).

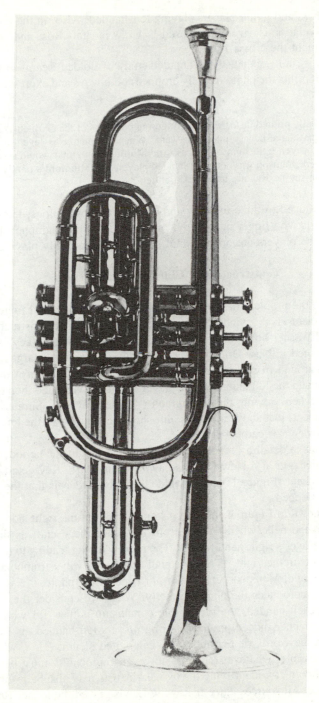

Fig. 4. Typical Cornet Construction.

pher posed the bass and guitar players playing left-handed. Also, in the present uses, the names of the two clarinetists were transposed.''[7] Unfortunately Rose and Souchon did not explain or document these assertions.

Donald Marquis, in his exhaustively detailed study of Bolden, seems to favor the *Jazzmen* reversal, but prints the photo (closely cropped) both ways and expresses some puzzlement:

> As originally printed in *Jazzmen* the fingering positions of the clarinetists indicate that the picture may have been printed backward. When the picture is reversed to correct these poses, however, both Johnson on bass and Mumford on guitar would seem to be playing left-handed. Johnson was not a left-handed player, and Mumford's family and others who knew him say he was not left-handed either.[8]

Thus we are reduced to three unlikely and disquieting possibilities: left-handed string players, clarinetists who finger incorrectly, or a capricious photographer. It is worth remembering that the players are only posing, however, not actually playing.

Construction of Clarinets and Cornets

The solution to the problem lies not in speculation about poses and fingering but with the instruments themselves: wind and brass instruments are not constructed symmetrically. Lewis and Warner both played the nineteenth-century, fifteen-key, Albert system clarinet, long favored in New Orleans. These instruments feature a large "pipe key" at the top, hooking around from the back and upward to the front center of the instrument. This key curls around the left side from the player's point of view and therefore should be seen to the right when viewing the photograph ("camera right"). Similarly, the lowest key on the instrument, just above the ball joint, should extend down the left side from the player's point of view, or camera right.

Figure 3 presents in detail a French Albert system clarinet of the period, in possession of the author, purchased at a New Orleans pawnshop in 1951. Key detail of the seated clarinetist's instrument (Figure 1) is clear, and comparison reveals that the photo should never have been flopped.

A cornet, as shown in Figure 4, has the pistons placed on the right side of the flaring tubing leading to the bell (when viewed from the mouthpiece end) as they are to be depressed by the player's right-hand fingers. The narrow tubing leading to the mouthpiece is on the player's extreme right. (This is equally true of a valve trombone.) Therefore Bolden should be holding his cornet on his right hand in the photo.

Figure 2, then, reproduces the photo correctly. When we consider the testimony that Mumford was not left-handed, the ineluctable conclusion is that, for whatever fanciful reason, the photographer indeed posed the string players left-handed, as Rose and Souchon propose. In the words of fiction's most celebrated sleuth, ". . . when you have excluded the impossible, whatever remains, however improbable, must be the truth."[9]

The problem of correctly identifying the two clarinetists may also be resolved by internal visual evidence. All sources agree that while Lewis played the longer Bb instrument, Warner played the shorter clarinet in C. Examination of Figure 2, where the uncropped bottom allows appreciation of more perspective, makes it clear that the seated clarinetist holds an instrument that is shorter than that of the standing clarinetist. It is shorter even by surface measurement, although the standing clarinetist is further from the camera. Thus Lewis stands; Warner sits. Once again Rose and Souchon rectified matters; it is unfortunate that Marquis did not follow their example.

Bunk Johnson's Testimony

The remaining problem of dating the photo is more complex and less susceptible of precise solution. The dating in *Jazzmen* is based on statements by ''Bunk'' Johnson, who consistently gave his name as Willie Geary Johnson. In a letter to the editors Johnson stated:

> Now that was all you could hear in New Orleans, that King Bolden's Band, and I was with him and that was between 1895 and 1896. . . .

In an extended statement made after seeing the Bolden Band photo, Bunk is quoted as saying:

> So I told Mr. Olivier that I think I could do better with King Bolden so he told me to suit myself and so I did and went on with King Bolden in the year of 1895. When I started playing with him Bolden was a married man and two children. He must of been between 25 or 30 years old at that time. Now here are the men in the band when I went in to it: Cornelius Tilman, drummer, Willy Cornish, trombone, Bolden, cornet, Bunk, cornet, Willie Warner, clarinet, Mumford, guitar, and Jimmie Johnson, bass. That was the old Bolden band when I went in to it. They were all men; I was the only young one in the Band, in short pants.
>
> The picture you have of Bolden's first band was taken just before I started playing with his large band. In those days he only carried a five piece band. In the late years Bolden's five piece band became so great in the city of New Orleans that he had to make his band bigger by putting in drums and cornet which made it a seven piece band.
>
> I stayed with Bolden until 1898 and then I left and started to playing with Bob Russell Band. I did not stay very long with it because they could not play very much. I went back to Bolden and when I started playing the second time he had taken Frank Duson in the band in place of Willy Cornish. I stayed about seven months and then I left and went on the road for two years with P.G. Loral and then I came in and started playing with one band and then another. That was the year 1900.[10]

The editors of *Jazzmen* reasoned that if Bunk joined the band in 1895, and if the photo was taken just before that, a reasonable dating would be ''before 1895.'' Almost all reprintings of the photo have retained this phrase, although Rose and Souchon refine it to a simplistic ''1894.''[11]

Marquis challenges this dating on the grounds of demonstrable birthdates, citing marriage certificates showing William Warner to be born in 1877 and James Johnson in 1884. And indeed it is obvious that in the photo Warner appears older than eighteen and Johnson is surely not eleven. Thus a photo dating of before 1895 is clearly disputable. He further cites Bolden's baptismal document as evidence that Bolden was born in 1877 (rather than the oft-quoted date of 1868), and reproduces the birth certificate of Bolden's first child, born in 1897.[12] Obviously Bolden does not look eighteen in the photo.

Marquis then hypothesizes that Bunk Johnson deliberately lied about his age, claiming to have been born on December 27, 1879 in order to falsely claim to have played with

Bolden. Referring to a photograph of the Original Superior Orchestra (reproduced in *Jazz-men,* undated[13]), in which Bunk Johnson is shown standing behind the violinist Peter Bocage, Marquis comments that the two men "look much the same age in this picture." Bocage, demonstrably born in 1887, said the photo was taken in 1908 or 1909.[14]

Persuasive hard evidence of a later Bunk Johnson birthdate has been evinced by Lawrence Gushee's scrutiny of an enumerator's schedule (door-to-door listings) from the 1900 federal census. A ten-year-old Johnson with a first name written as a semilegible "Gerry" (no "Willie") is listed, along with information covering relatives and an address which seems consistent with Bunk's own testimony. Unfortunately the age "10" has been written over, and while the birth datings of "Dec" and "1899" are clearly legible, only the month is graphologically consistent; the year was apparently added at a later time, although probably by the same hand. Gushee, a cautious and shrewd investigator with an excellent track record, notes these problems, and, with characteristic objectivity, adds caveats concerning census evidence. Nonetheless, he jocularly offers four-to-one odds in favor of the entry being that of Bunk Johnson.[15]

Ultimately Marquis decides to update the Bolden photo date to 1905, stating: "There are several reasons to believe that the date was actually closer to 1905, one reason being that Bunk Johnson's other information concerning Bolden is off by almost exactly ten years." The reasons are not several, however, nor is the exactness documented. Nonetheless, his dating is specific: "photograph from 1905."[16]

Certainty still seems unwarranted. Marquis's observation that Bunk Johnson appears to be too young for his averred age in an early photo is counterbalanced by photos taken in 1944 in which Bunk looks well into his sixties, hardly fifty-five. Marquis's assertion that Johnson's testimony is backdated by a decade "almost exactly" implies a precise and deliberate prevarication. Examination of Bunk Johnson's statement shows it to be nothing of the sort; despite an astonishing musical memory, his historical recollection is fraught with inaccuracies and internal inconsistencies.

Bunk refers to Bolden's early band as "five-piece" yet the photo shows a six-piece band with a second clarinetist whom Johnson does not mention in listing the personnel. In the same statement he says that he remained with Bolden until 1898, contradicting his earlier letter stating he was with Bolden "between 1895 and 1896." He then speaks of returning to Bolden's band for seven months and finally leaving in 1900, adding that Frank Duson had replaced trombonist Willie Cornish.

Willie Cornish and Frank Duson

Cornish did in fact leave the band temporarily to serve in the Spanish-American War of 1898, returning after demobilization.[17] The war lasted from April 21 through the armistice of August 12 to the treaty of December 10, 1898. Marquis is then probably correct in stating that Cornish rejoined the band in 1899.[18] Cornish was not finally replaced by Frank Duson (or Dusen) until somewhat later. Marquis dates that event 1906 (without documentation).[19] Yet, Marquis includes the lyrics of "Buddy Bolden's Blues" which refer to Dusen's arrests for loitering; with documentation he dates those arrests between September 1904 and April 1905. This implies that Dusen was already a member of Bolden's band by that period. Charters says that Dusen replaced Cornish "about 1903"; Rose and Souchon also cite 1903.[20]

The question of Bunk Johnson's alleged membership in the band is not, in fact, germane. In dating the photograph it is immaterial whether Bunk played regularly with Bolden (as he claimed), whether he could never have played with Bolden (as Marquis conjectures), or whether he played with Bolden, but only occasionally (as Charters suggests).[21] Rather, the key people in dating the photograph are Cornish and the bass player James Johnson.

Marquis successfully demonstrates that a date in the mid-nineties is impossible, due to James Johnson's age. Due to the presence of Cornish in the photo it then must have been taken after his return from the war: 1899 is the earliest possible date. As the weight of evidence points to Cornish leaving the band in 1903, that is most likely the latest possible date. A proper way to date the photograph would be as in Figure 2: "probably taken between 1899 and 1903."

A publishing curiosity remains to be mentioned. When the 1939 edition of *Jazzmen* was "republished" in 1972 (by Scholarly Press, Inc., St. Clair Shores, Michigan), it was identical to the original and is still identified as "first edition." The original errors in presenting the photo were of course duplicated. But the Harvest/HBJ paperback edition of 1959 quietly rectified matters in two respects, although nowhere is the edition identified as having been revised. The photo has been properly re-flopped, and the clarinetists are correctly identified. The date has been discreetly omitted.

Notes

1. Frederic Ramsey, Jr., and Charles E. Smith (eds.), *Jazzmen* (New York: Harcourt, Brace, 1939), facing p. 32.
2. Samuel B. Charters, "The Birth of Jazz" (descriptive notes), *The Music of New Orleans, Vol. IV* (New York: Folkways Records Album FA 2464, 1959), p. 3 (unnumbered).
3. William B. Schafer, *Brass Bands and New Orleans Jazz* (Baton Rouge and London: Louisiana State University Press, 1977), p. 97.
4. Donald M. Marquis, *In Search of Buddy Bolden, First Man of Jazz* (Baton Rouge and London: Louisiana State University Press, 1978), third unnumbered page of photos following p. 78.
5. Al Rose and Edmond Souchon, *New Orleans Jazz: A Family Album* (Baton Rouge and London: Louisiana State University Press, 1967), p. 160.
6. Richard B. Allen and William Russell, interview with Bella Cornish, January 13, 1959, in William Ransom Hogan Jazz Archive, Tulane University, New Orleans, cited in Marquis, *Buddy Bolden*, p. 76.
7. Rose and Souchon, *Family Album*, p. 160.
8. Marquis, *Buddy Bolden*, p. 77.
9. Sir Arthur Conan Doyle, "The Adventure of the Beryl Coronet," *The Complete Sherlock Holmes* (Garden City, N.Y.: Doubleday, 1905), p. 315.
10. Ramsey and Smith, *Jazzmen*, pp. v (unnumbered), 24-25.
11. Rose and Souchon, *Family Album*, p. 160.
12. Marquis, *Buddy Bolden*, p. 5.
13. Ramsey and Smith, *Jazzmen*, fifth unnumbered page of photos following p. 32..
14. Richard B. Allen and William Russell, interview with Peter Bocage, January 29, 1959, in Hogan Jazz Archive, cited in Marquis, *Buddy Bolden*, p. 6.
15. Lawrence Gushee, "Would you believe Ferman Mouton?", *Storyville* (June/July 1981): 164-168.
16. Marquis, *Buddy Bolden*, p. 77 and photo facing p. 78.
17. Samuel B. Charters, *Jazz: New Orleans 1885-1963, An Index to the Negro Musicians of New Orleans* (New York: Oak Publications, rev. 1963), p. 12; Rose and Souchon, *Family Album*, p. 30; Marquis, *Buddy Bolden*, p. 43.

18. Marquis, *Buddy Bolden*, p. 43.
19. Marquis, *Buddy Bolden*, pp. 78, 114.
20. Marquis, *Buddy Bolden*, p. 110; Charters, *Jazz: New Orleans*, p. 12; Rose and Souchon, *Family Album*, p. 30.
21. Ramsey and Smith, *Jazzmen*, pp. 24-25; Marquis, *Buddy Bolden*, pp. 3-6; Charters, *Jazz: New Orleans*, p. 34.

The Jazz Composition/Arrangement

Lawrence O. Koch

"Jazz composition/arrangement" seems a contradiction in terms; therefore it is necessary to attempt a definition. The examples that are used in this article, for instance, all meet the following criteria: the composed (and arranged) portion of the music is at least equal in importance to the improvisation, and/or the improvisation is presented in such a fashion so as to make it an integral part of the arrangement. To be sure, *some* improvisation is a necessary ingredient or else the term would be "jazz-*influenced*" composition/arrangement. One might say, however, that the improvisation is subservient to the whole rather than being the dominant attraction. In this respect, those themes which are merely attractive settings for a string of solos do not fit the definition for this article.

The Small Groups

An early example of the composition/arrangement for the small group is Jelly Roll Morton's "Original Jelly Roll Blues" (RCA Jazz Tribune [France] PM42405) done on December 16, 1926, as part of his famed Victor series of recordings (from September 1926 to June 1928). The twelve-bar blues is the germ of the form, and the complete piece uses the march form: ABA in the tonic key, moving to the subdominant for the trio (C section). Furthermore, each letter designation has a different blues harmonization with the A section being the simplest.

Morton shows his genius immediately in the piano introduction: It is based on the flat-submediant chord (Gb^7 in Bb, the key of the piece) for three measures and resolves to the dominant. No definite tonality is yet stated; the listener is kept waiting. Then the A strain begins, but the listener is *still* unaware that this has taken place, for the solo phrases over a Bb chord (banjo—two measures; trumpet and trombone—one measure apiece) sound like an extension of the introduction. It is not until the ensemble takes over at measure 5 (subdominant measure of the blues form) and finishes the form in New Orleans polyphony that the listener realizes he has heard the blues form.

Lawrence O. Koch is director of the Braun School in Pottsville, Pennsylvania, and a member of the jazz studies faculty at Moravian College, Bethlehem, Pennsylvania. He has combined a teaching career with jazz performing, composing, and arranging.

The second section (B) is another blues strain with a different harmonization in the first four measures: $Bb|D^7|Gm\ Dm|Bb^7$. Its opening features a trilling clarinet. Sometimes it is difficult to tell from the recording which parts are written and which are improvised, especially in the polyphonic style (this is a merit, not a liability), but the trill was definitely written, for Morton uses it on his 1924 piano roll recording of this piece (Everest FS-267). There is also a clarinet break at measures 7-8.

The A strain returns, with the piano playing breaks over the tonic harmony of the first four measures and the ensemble playing the last eight measures, before moving to a four-measure (written) modulatory section leading to the subdominant key for the trio. The ternary form of the first part of the piece (ABA) is now complete, but it is interesting to compare it with the piano roll version. On the latter, Morton plays AABBAA—repeats of each section with some variation (most surely conceived as 24-measure strains). This tends to make the form much clearer (especially with the deceptive beginning), but on the Hot Peppers recording he was faced with the time limit of the 78 rpm disc, and it is evidence of his genius that he was able to solve it and still maintain a balanced composition.

At the trio (C), there is another slight harmonic alteration (although related to B): $Eb|G^7|Eb^7$. This trio is the solo section, each solo being a half-chorus long with some special feature (breaks, stop-time, etc.) and the ensemble finishing the chorus. The features are:

1. Trumpet solo (theme, others behind, no true polyphony).
2. Low register clarinet solo (piano plays rhythmic background figures)—ensemble.
3. Clarinet (rhythm on beats 2 and 3)—ensemble.
4. Trumpet solo (improvisation)—ensemble.
5. Piano (breaks)—ensemble.
6. Ensemble (polyphony)—improvisation.

In "Original Jelly Roll Blues," Morton demonstrates his skill in using the two necessary elements for every composition: repetition and variety. These elements must be used in perfect balance, for too much repetition means listening monotony and too much variety means listening confusion. Balance was no problem for Morton, however; it was the root of his genius as a composer/arranger.

Kyle's "From A♭ to C"

Pianist Billy Kyle's erudite piece "From A♭ to C" for John Kirby's combo (October 28, 1938, Smithsonian Collection P2 14584) is a logical follow-up to the Morton piece. It too has a familiar base ("I Got Rhythm"), altered and used with variety. The beginning A section for instance, goes through the cycle of fifths from A♭ to C (hence the title) for the first half and then rolls through the standard "Rhythm" harmony. Two simultaneous themes are stated in the first half before culminating in a passage over the "Rhythm" chords. The one theme (trumpet) is a rhythmic statement of the roots of the cycle, while the other is a legato, eighth-note theme (alto and clarinet); only the legato theme is used on the repeat. The bridge, played in unison for half, then to trumpet with others behind, culminates in a two-bar chromatic sequence (ascending) that moves the tonality back to A♭.

The second chorus begins the improvised section with a piano solo on the "Rhythm" chords in the key of C for a half-chorus; the horns riff behind at two-measure intervals. At the bridge, a band phrase (2) alternates with clarinet improvisations (2); on the final clarinet solo a different sequence of ascending chromatic chords leads to the key of Bb. The clarinet has the final A section in the new key.

The alto sax solo begins the third chorus in Eb and is followed by the trumpet at the bridge (standard "Rhythm" chords). The trumpet continues through the final A section with riffs behind him until the final two measures, when the bass prepares the way for the theme restatement.

The "fifths" theme comes first; then the legato theme; then a final A section with the bass stating the "fifths" theme before the closing riff. A tag puts on the period.

Both the Morton and Kyle pieces use tonality changes as a means of variety. In the Morton piece, however, the tonality change was part of an existing form, a product of the status quo, whereas Kyle's composition uses tonality changes *within* the form in smaller but more frequent doses. In military terms, Morton's usage comes under strategy (the whole plan) and Kyle's under tactics (ways of achieving the whole plan). It is interesting that Kyle conceived the improvised portions in cyclical changes of tonality so that the restatement could start again on Ab (the solo section could be called "From C to Ab"); this is an excellent example of presenting the improvisation as an integral part of the arrangement.

Carisi's "Israel" for Miles Davis

With the recordings of the Miles Davis "Birth of the Cool" group in 1949, the small group took on a new aspect—that of the expanded combo with added "color" instruments such as the French horn and tuba. John Carisi's "Israel" (April 22, 1949, Capitol M-11026), done for the Davis group, is a stellar example of composing for this type of ensemble. The form is the blues, and Carisi flirts with both major and minor tonalities throughout the arrangement—that is, within each single twelve-measure form as well as a tonality change in the improvisation section.

After an eight-measure introduction that features rhythmic displacement and wild accents, the blues form begins in C minor with the basic sound being unison on the theme between trumpet and alto and baritone saxes, the other instruments adding color and backing phrases. The harmonic sequence in the first four measures is: Cm|Cm^{+5}|Cm G^{7+9} | Gm^7 C^7. At bar 7 (Example 1) there is an ingenious example of harmonic promiscuity that begins major and then goes in another direction with echoes of the minor. The parallel chord sequence is often misquoted in fake books.

In the second chorus, the trumpet states the theme, while the ensemble blurts out a low register counter-theme. At the second measure, the presence of an A natural in the second-

Ex. 1. "Israel," beginning bar 7

ary theme over a Dm^7 chord starts a momentary feeling of major. The sequence is: Cm Cm^{+5}|Dm^7 G^7|C G^{7+9}|Gm^7 C^7. Near the end of the chorus, the converging lines are dizzying.

Now comes the improvisation section. Davis has the third chorus with just rhythm and uses a variant of the chord sequence just described in the first four measures. Furthermore, the final two bars of the chorus are major, whereas they had been minor in the theme statements. Davis continues through another chorus, with ensemble backing added, and uses the chord sequence from the opening chorus for the first four measures.

Chorus 5 opens with a written four-measure ensemble passage that moves the tonality to G major. Lee Konitz's alto then solos for the remainder of the chorus. Konitz continues in chorus six with the band backing him in parallel scalar chords. His solo is completely in the major tonality.

The final ensemble chorus (back in C minor) uses elements of both the theme and counter-theme, starting with a direct statement of the latter; the approach is antiphonal between low and high instruments. The piece culminates with a wild condensation of the final phrase.

The shifting tonalities of the Carisi piece tend to blur the familiar form just as the cycle-of-fifths device did in the Kyle piece. Both pieces, however, give the listener a taste of the unadulterated form during the improvisation—the Kyle piece during the Shavers trumpet solo, and "Israel" during the Konitz alto solo, which is completely faithful to a G-major blues (even here the alto starts at the fifth bar of his first chorus, and the listener must wait until the next chorus to establish a tonality).

In both pieces the unadulterated form occurs just before the recapitulation and in a key other than the tonic. Moreover, the "Original Jelly Roll Blues," remember, had the deceptive introduction and beginning—also tending to blur the familiar form (much like the phrase which leads to the Konitz solo in "Israel"). There seems to be a definite impulse, then, to use one's originality to blur a familiar form—in effect to surprise the listener when he discovers what he is hearing. In this respect, this writer has always felt that the enjoyment of listening analytically to a great jazz composition/arrangement is somewhat akin to the enjoyment of solving a puzzle. Indeed, "Israel" can provide much enjoyment of this type.

"Vendome" by John Lewis and the MJQ

Some of the most interesting small group compositions of the 1950s were done by John Lewis for the Modern Jazz Quartet, and one of the earliest pieces, "Vendome" (Dec. 2, 1952, Prestige 7059), provides a healthy example. This fugal piece in C minor has a theme based on single phrase (Example 2). The phrase is seemingly out of J.S. Bach, but the second bar, with its blues scale implications, comes directly from jazz.

The first theme statement is 12 measures long: vibes (3) on tonic (continues); piano (3) on dominant (minor); then a repeat of this procedure. The final cadence leads to the minor

Ex. 2. "Vendome" phrase

dominant key (G minor), where Milt Jackson's vibes begin an improvisation section based on the chord sequence of ''All the Things You Are.'' This is a 16-measure section like the first half of the Jerome Kern ballad, but with a different relationship between the eight-measure sections. In other words, if one were playing the Kern piece beginning on a Gm^7 and ending in D at the first eight (as the ''Vendome'' sequence does), the next chord (beginning the second eight) would be Dm; here, however, Lewis uses secondary domi-nants at the end of the first eight and starts the next eight on a Fm chord. One sees here another example of an original approach to a familiar form. Jackson continues his im-provisation until the ending chord (C) leads to the second theme statement.

The second section statement (in Fm) is seven measures long (piano for three); vibes on V minor for four), and Lewis's improvisation on a Bachian progression follows for eleven measures (ending in A).

The third section (in D) has the vibes stating the theme for four measures and the piano answering. This section is extended with a written fugal development for the vibes and piano.

The vibes also begin the fourth section (in E minor) and the piano answers. Then there is an improvisation based, for four measures each, on E minor and B minor (piano and vibes simultaneously), followed by Jackson's improvisation on the ''All the Things You Are'' chords, beginning on a Bm^7 and ending in F#.

A four-measure pattern (D|D^7|G|G) repeats itself three times in ascending half-steps, after which Jackson moves to a section based on the dominant (G), before the final stretto in the tonic key (Cm). The piece ends in major.

It is the strength of Lewis's theme that holds the piece together; the references to the ''All the Things You Are'' pattern in an improvisational setting merely give the listener a familiar frame of reference. One does, however, want to hear more of it. This writer, for instance, has always wanted to hear an improvised fugue on the Kern chord pattern rather than the written fugal development in the third section.

As a pioneer effort, however, ''Vendome'' is an excellent jazz composition/ arrangement. It predates Lewis's masterpiece of this genre, ''Versailles,'' by four years, and although not as jazz-oriented as the latter piece, it paved the way for what was to come. ''Versailles'' is worth mentioning here, for in it Lewis uses the ''I Got Rhythm'' form and a touch of the blues to combine riffs and improvisation in a fugal manner never before attempted in jazz.[1]

Chick Corea's ''Spain''

For an example of the ''modern'' approach to jazz composition/arrangement we can look to Chick Corea's ''Spain'' done with the Return to Forever band (October 1972, Polydor 5525).

The basic form of the piece, as diagrammed in Figure 1, owes a debt to the ABA minuet form of Mozart and Haydn's era.

The form is *large* ternary (the opening portion returns making the *large* form ABA— regardless of repeats).[2] In terms of the minuet, ''ab'' would be the minuet proper and ''c'' would be the trio (usually with a key change). Here, however, ''c'' does not change keys but functions as the improvisation section. It also echoes the ''a'' section harmonically (going from G to B minor) but with each chord change being double the original value. After each improvised solo, the ''c'' theme is stated, and then the ''a'' (last eight bars only) and ''b'' themes return. This gives a constant ternary feeling.

Figure 1

```
Rubato Introduction

Introductory Riff (6)

     a (12) ─────────┐
     b (12) Unison line     │ A
     Repeat ──────────┘

     c (24)──────────── B

     a (last 8) ──────┐ A
     b ───────────────┘
```

Corea's rubato introduction is based on Joaquin Rodrigo's "Concierto de Aranjuez," and the introductory riff to the theme proper is six measures long. The theme to "a" is 12 measures long, as is the one for "b". This latter melody is a clipped, exciting riff stated by flute and bass that serves to "set up" the solos.

At the very end of the piece (after the final solo), the introductory riff replaces the "b" section at the return and then the "a" and "b" sections are repeated in their entirety, as shown in Figure 2.

Figure 2

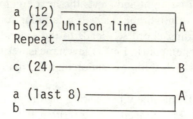

```
                          ┐Large
     c (solo and theme)__ │ B

     a (partial - 8 bars ─┐
     intro. riff (6 bars) │Final
     a (entire)           │Large
                          │  A
     b ───────────────────┘
```

In summary, the five small-group pieces demonstrate the following principles to some degree:

1. Originality applied to the overall form of the composition/arrangement.
2. Originality used to "blur" a familiar form (in the Corea piece the "blurring" is the use of double-value chord changes from the main theme in the improvisation section).
3. A debt to "legitimate" composition, either in the structural or technical aspects, or both (the Lewis piece is the most conscious example—a baroque rondo).
4. Improvisation used as an integral part of the form.

The Big Bands

It is common knowledge that big band jazz composition/arrangement techniques were pioneered by Don Redman with the Fletcher Henderson Orchestra; Henderson, in fact, learned from Redman. But during the late twenties, Duke Ellington's contributions seem more meaningful and original in a pure *jazz* sense. Furthermore, his efforts seem to exemplify the transition (really an expansion) of the small group to the big band. Our earliest example, therefore, is Ellington's composition/arrangement, "The Mooche" (October 1, 1928, CBS 67264 [France]).

The main theme is eight measures (repeated) with a unique extension that also serves as a modulation; the theme (stated by woodwinds with a muted trumpet growling the answers) is in C minor, and the extension leads to the relative major (E*b*). Here the ensemble performs the infectious second theme—a blues; then another secondary blues theme is freely stated (in the parallel minor—E*b* minor) by low-register clarinet and answered by guitar. An improvisation section (24 measures, two twelve-bar sections) follows with a "rasp throat" vocal backed by improvising guitar in major and muted trombone and alto sax alternating in minor. The final statement is the same as the beginning (back to C minor) with a short coda (actually the material from the extension/modulation).

Basically, the group is a "small big band" with three reeds (saxes doubling on clarinets—with the basic sound on "The Mooche" being clarinet), three brass (two trumpets and a trombone), and five rhythm (piano, drums, string bass, banjo, guitar); and, interestingly, Ellington uses the full ensemble only at the appearance of the second theme.

In comparison with the Morton small group piece of the same general period, "The Mooche" is less formal; Ellington creates an original form, but still maintains the blues as important (but not the main strain) material. There is also less improvisational material, however, and, less use of the polyphonic sound (the voice and guitar chorus being the only use); Duke was thinking more in terms of "question and answer" and block ensemble voicings than "many voices." Although both composer/arrangers used the individual sound to great effect, Ellington was certainly more concerned with texture than Morton. Both composition/arrangements, however, make use of the blues form and "blur" it at some point (the minor form of the blues was at least rare enough to be called uncommon except for Ellington's innovations and therefore can be considered his "blurring" technique).

Henderson's "Down South Camp Meetin' "

Fletcher Henderson's "Down South Camp Meetin' " as played by the Goodman band of 1937-38 (Columbia CL818) exemplifies the true "swing" approach to the big band composition/arrangement. This piece does not use a "blurring" technique, but rather uses short riffs in a developmental fashion. Before examining the riffs, individually, however, a look at the complete form is necessary.

The piece is in three sections, each in a different key (C-A*b*-D*b*), separated by modulatory sections. We can call the *over-all* form ABC, therefore, but each section is a song form of its own.

The opening section (Key of C) is ABA (eight bars apiece) and begins with the saxes stating a four-bar riff (repeated) over familiar chords (Example 3).

Ex. 3. "Down South," opening riff

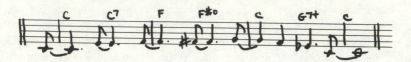

The bridge section (another four-bar riff repeated) of the opening portion (Example 4) moves to A minor through a diminished chord and is based on the end of the first riff.

All the improvisation is done in this opening section by Goodman's clarinet over sustained saxes. Then an eight-bar modulatory section moves through four different keys (C-F-Bb-Eb) for two measures apiece with a riff (Example 5) stated in each key by alto and trumpet alternating.

Ex. 4. "Down South," bridge section of opening

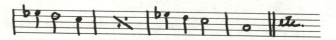

Ex. 5. Modulatory riff

Next is the *Ab* section (AABA—eight for A; four for B), which has an A section based on two riffs (Examples 6 and 7). The saxes state the riffs but the brass echo the final one in the last two measures.

Ex. 6. Riff for first four measures

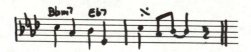

Ex. 7. Answering riff

The B section, also stated by the saxes, is a linear four-bar phrase that cannot be considered a riff but rather serves to add variety. This is true also of the end of the closing A section.

The whole A*b* portion is repeated with the brass playing the leading role and adding a new "answering" riff (Example 8). The saxes again have the bridge.

Ex. 8. New answering riff

A modulatory section makes use of the "boogie-woogie" break riff to move the tune into D*b* (Example 9).

Ex. 9. Boogie woogie break riff

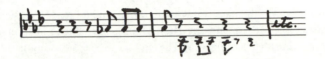

The final sixteen-measure section is the climax; it has the effect of a march trio and expands from a short riff (Example 10).

Ex. 10. Short riff

The woodwinds state the theme with muted brass behind, but on the repeat the woodwinds move to the higher octave with brass becoming open.

In total, Henderson uses eight riffs (not including simple variants) and mixes them creatively to form an interesting jazz composition/arrangement. The improvisation section is perhaps a bit short for this writer's taste, but the composition seems balanced in its entirety and contains a "building" quality that excites the listener. Further, Henderson's approach would become a fixture in big band writing and has remained valid up to the present.

The Evans-Davis "Blues for Pablo"

Gil Evans's "Blues for Pablo," which was recorded in May 1957 with Miles Davis as flugelhorn soloist and a supporting band of 19 (Columbia 1041), however, is this writer's selection as a prime example of the jazz composition/arrangement in a large setting for several reasons. It expands the big band setting in both size and texture by adding French horns and a variety of woodwinds. It uses a "blurring" of the blues form as its major device. Moreover, it is both "Spanish-tinged" and "bluesy" in different places and sometimes at the same time (shades of Jelly Roll Morton); this conveys a marvelously dualistic effect of the listener.

The rubato opening (in Gm) by the flugelhorn over a sustained chord, for instance, is definitely in the Spanish vein; it ends in major—after a Neopolitan chord—and continues into a section (minor) which alternates flugelhorn (4) and ensemble (4). But then comes a section which is a distortion of a minor blues—the fourth bar seems to be in $2/4$ and the end dissolves into a nebulous rhythm which leads to Bb (Example 11).

Ex. 11. "Blues for Pablo," blues theme

At the end of this section, the bass states a tango rhythm and leads to a section featuring flugelhorn improvisation. This begins by alternating a "double-time" version of the Bb theme with the flugelhorn (Example 12). The end of the section (eight measures) is all improvisation.

Ex. 12. Double-time version

A Spanish tinge returns, in minor, as the main theme of the next blues section (Example 13). The flugelhorn continues with the rest of the blues in *major* (improvisation). The "double-time" theme returns, alternating with Davis, who again continues to the end. He completes the piece with an incantation of the introductory Spanish theme (in minor).

Ex. 13. Spanish theme

In reviewing the composition, the beginning (Gm) section can be seen as the "Spanish" portion, introducing the piece. The real blues (in Bb), however, is a combination of blues and Spanish elements and can be viewed as AABA:

A^1(12)—ensemble exposition (major).
A^2(12)—"double-time"—alternating with improvisation—last half improvisation.
B(12) —"Spanish" theme (minor)—last half improvisation (major).
A^3(12)—as A^1, but ending in minor with opening "Spanish" theme.

These three representative big band examples echo the conclusions derived from the small group pieces, but the Henderson piece is unique in its developmental use of the riff. The pieces were selected with a view to showing various approaches, not only in style, but also in size ("small" big band; standard size; and expanded instrumentation) and to viewing three outstanding big band jazz composers of three different eras.

All of the compositions mentioned in this article—small group or big band (with the exception of the Henderson example)—illustrate "blurring" of a familiar form. Students of jazz composition can explore creative avenues by investigating this technique as used by master jazz composers.

Notes

1. For an outstanding analysis of "Versailles," with notations, see Thomas Owens, "The Fugal Pieces of the Modern Jazz Quartet," *Journal of Jazz Studies* 4, no. 1 (Fall 1976): 27-31.
2. The writer chose to analyze this piece in *larger* terms than the foregoing ones (again the military analogy of strategy and tactics) because it was easier to make sense with this type of breadth. Over the years, experience has shown that whenever one is pushed into an analytical corner, looking for *larger* units almost always solves the problem. It is worth going over the other pieces in the small group analysis to illustrate the procedure for those interested readers.

    The "Original Jelly Roll Blues" would be large binary, with all of the first section (ABA) becoming large A and all of the repeats of the trio (C) becoming large B. In other words the beginning material never returns in the form as a whole. "From A*b* to C" would have the song form (AABA) becoming large A and *all* the improvised material becoming large B; the return (partial) of large A makes it a large ternary form. The Lewis piece, however, is a rondo and can best be analyzed in relatively small terms:

    AB AC AD AE coda A (stretto)

    The theme presentations are the A designations and all other are improvised episodes.
    "Israel" perhaps best illustrates how the "large form" procedure can be applied to an apparent single-form piece:

```
a   -- melody ─────────────────┐
a'  -- melody plus countermelody │ A
a'  -- improvised (variation)    │
a   -- improvised (variation) ───┘

b   -- Key change - improvisation ─┐ B
b'  -- improvisation - major mode ─┘

aa' -- elements of both ───────────── A
```

    Note that this analysis procedure can be subjective at times. In "Israel," for instance, one could designate all the improvised material as the large B section. The writer based the analyses above on harmonic and tonal elements as well as melodic.

Book Reviews

Louis Armstrong: An American Genius
By James Lincoln Collier. 1983. 383 pp.
New York: Oxford University Press. $19.95.

In spite of its promising title, this critical biography is a deliberate attempt to overthrow the established view of Armstrong. In his preface, the author states that ''much of what (has) been published about Armstrong was simply a rehash of the old myths,'' and some of it ''sheer fiction. . . . The body of reliable writing about [him] was surprisingly small.''

It is true that book-length studies of the most influential (and arguably the greatest) of all jazz musicians are few in number and less than scholarly in approach. The earliest, Armstrong's own *Swing That Music* (1936; the first biography of a black jazz figure), was heavily ghosted. Next came *Satchmo: My Life in New Orleans* (1947; the first installment of a full autobiography on which Armstrong continued work throughout his remaining years; the fate of the manuscript is unknown). This was definitely by Armstrong himself, if somewhat pedantically edited, and Collier's attitude toward it is revealing. He states that Armstrong ''probably'' wrote it ''in the main,'' though no one acquainted with Armstrong's writing can doubt that the voice is authentic, and also claims that the book is ''unreliable.'' He quotes much more extensively from Richard Meryman's *Louis Armstrong: A Self-Portrait*, published in 1971 and based on an extensive interview in *Life*. While often revealing, this little book contains frequent mishearings and garblings of Armstrong's transcribed spoken words. Hugues Panassié's *Louis Armstrong*, published in France in 1969 and in English translation two years later, contains much valuable information about the recorded works but can be regarded as idolatrous. Max Jones and John Chilton's *Louis*, published in 1971, is journalistic and not well organized, but contains many interesting facts, prodigious quotes from its subject, and an excellent essay on Armstrong the musician by Chilton, a professional trumpeter. One must agree with Collier that Robert Goffin's *Horn of Plenty* (1947) is fiction rather than biography. There are several Armstrong biographies for the juvenile market (a field in which Collier has been active), but these are of little significance.

Some of the best writing on Armstrong's music, however, is contained in more general works, notably Gunther Schuller's *Early Jazz*, Martin Williams's *The Jazz Tradition*, André Hodeir's *Jazz: Its Evolution and Essence*, and Humphrey Lyttleton's *The Best of Jazz*. While Collier analyzes Armstrong's playing at some length, it can fairly be said that he adds nothing to what can be learned from these sources.

But then, musical analysis is not the focal point of Collier's book, which is biography first and foremost. As such, does it tell us anything new? Collier has organized and presented his considerable research well and gives a detailed account of Armstrong's life and career, bringing together many facts and minutiae hitherto scattered among numerous sources. In this he has performed a valuable service. Unfortunately, he also insists on psychoanalyzing Armstrong at every turn.

In that respect his ideas are decidely novel. Early on, he tells us that Armstrong was "clearly afflicted with deep and well-entrenched insecurity, a sense of his own worthlessness so thoroughly fixed that he was never to shake it off." Further, Armstrong was driven by an "insatiable, visceral lust [sic]" for applause, and eventually applause became the only balm that could "quench that relentless, sickening interior assault on his self-respect," and, if only for the moment, push "away the feeling that nobody liked him, that he was basically no good."

Strong stuff, more from Adler than from Freud, and a view of one of the most beloved men of our age that is, to say the least, bewildering. If accurate, it would make Armstrong one of the most successful dissemblers in history—a man who craftily managed to hide his true, stunted self not just from the world at large but also from those closest to him. (As if to guard against any nagging doubts, Collier insists that Armstrong had no "truly" close friends.)

To this reader, who knew Armstrong personally and professionally for some 24 years, this interpretation of his personality (Collier trots out every cliché regarding absent fathers and neglectful mothers a fan of *Psychology Today* could ask for) seems absurd. But like any writer possessed by a preconception, Collier selects his "facts" to fit the model. Thus he gives us liberal doses of "insights" from Marshall Brown, who for a few days occupied a dressing room adjacent to Armstrong's and only worked with him for a few hours, but fails to consult such close associates as Trummy Young, Armstrong's right arm for 12 years, or bassist Arvell Shaw, whose long tenure with Armstrong, starting with the last big band and stretching over two decades, he totally ignores. And, convinced that Armstrong had no real friends, he didn't bother to look for putative ones.

On the other hand, he presents the negative comments of such New Orleans contemporaries as Pops Foster (whose reliability may be gauged from his straight-faced claim that Jelly Roll Morton employed a second pianist on his solo recordings because he had a weak left hand) and Zutty Singleton, with whom Armstrong had a lifelong, complex relationship. Collier makes much of the conflicts between these proud, stubborn men as seen from Singleton's and his wife's points of view. Clearly, Collier has no understanding of the peculiar ways of elder New Orleans musicians.

Collier's relentless pursuit of his slanted view of Armstrong frequently overwhelms his sense of reality. A revealing example on which I must dwell at some length is his surreal interpretation of the recording sessions made by Armstrong and his band for Victor in January and April of 1933. Twelve sides were cut over a three-day period in January; a further 11 on April 24 and 26. To Collier, this level of output is evidence that Armstrong was "held in contempt" by "the white men who were overseeing his career," in particular manager Johnny Collins. "It is doubtful," Collier claims, "that any important show-business figure, much less a major artist, has ever been so driven like a pack mule as Armstrong was at this time." Characteristically, he adds that Armstrong "of course should have stood up to Collins."

Collins was indeed an unsavory man, as has been well documented by others, including Armstrong himself, who eventually fired him. But it is nonsense to present these recording sessions as paradigmatic of Collins and others being "callous to [Armstrong's] needs to the point of cruelty." There was nothing unusual about marathon recording sessions, which were scheduled when performers were available in cities with studio facilities; since prolonged touring was part and parcel of any band's working life, the most was made of such opportunities. The all-time record for a single day's jazz output in a studio is held by Benny Goodman, whose band, on June 6, 1935, cut 51 tunes—for which the sidemen were paid the munificent sum of one dollar per song!

Having set the stage with such misleading melodramatics, Collier must now find supporting evidence in the records themselves. Of "Dusky Stevedore" he hallucinates that Armstrong "barely gets through" the performance "at all," though that record is filled with trumpet pyrotechnics. Here and elsewhere, a problem seems to be that Collier mishears Armstrong's imaginative use of space and his stretching or contracting of the time-values of notes—stylistic traits especially in evidence at this period—for pauses caused by the need to rest sore lips. Thus he says about "Son of the South" that "Armstrong leaves gaps after each high note . . . to steal a couple of seconds rest," and elsewhere in his comments on these records points to "thin" tone and "faltering upper register." Trumpeter-critic John Chilton, however, has this to say about "Son of the South": "A master of the unexpected, [Armstrong] unites stamina and skill . . . again takes the first trumpet part [Collier fails to state, or cannot hear, that Armstrong plays lead in addition to solo on most of these discs] and tops a fine performance with a spine-tingling coda." Listening to these sessions, Collier works himself up to the point of tears as he fancies how Armstrong "was jamming the sharp circle of steel of the mouthpiece deep into the flesh of his lips to give them enough support to reach the high notes." Collier, a trombonist, at least ought to know that mouthpieces are made of brass.

Collier further imagines that for these sessions, "Victor supplied Armstrong with commercial rubbish: mediocre pop tunes, nonsensical jive songs, and worse," the "worse" being one of Collier's pet peeves—what he choses to call "coon songs." (In this instance, one such is Hoagy Carmichael's "Snow Ball," also recorded by that notorious Uncle Tom, Paul Robeson). The "mediocre pop songs" include two brand-new Harold Arlen pieces, which these recordings helped make jazz standards ("I've Got a Right to Sing the Blues" and "World on a String") and a couple of more-than-decent tunes of the day. Almost all the other material is the work of black songwriters and composers, such as "St. Louis Blues," "Mahogany Hall Stomp," and "Basin Street Blues" (the latter an Armstrong masterpiece which Collier inexplicably fails to mention); two songs written especially for Armstrong by the noted West Indian composer-arranger Reginald Forsythe ("Son of the South" and "Mississippi Basin"), and other special Armstrong material, including "Laughing Louis," to Collier no doubt a "nonsensical jive song," to others, like Stanley Crouch and this reviewer, a magical performance that must have mystified the Victor executives as much as it does Collier, who evades it. (In any case, humor is not Collier's strong suit, a handicap when it comes to Armstrong). He does pounce on "Don't You Play Me Cheap," but this was written by the drummer in the band, Harry Dial, and recorded by Armstrong as a favor to him. And does Collier really assume that the "viper's chorus" on "Sweet Sue" was mandated by white exploiters?

The incontrovertible fact is that Victor, Collins, et al. had little or nothing to do with chosing this repertory, which was intrinsic to Armstrong and his band, and that the flaws Collier hears in the trumpet playing on these records simply do not exist—esthetic judgments aside.

Collier's incessant harping on Armstrong's presumed failings as a man result in tainting even the praise he frequently (and sometimes fulsomely) heaps on Armstrong's music. He is at home with the Hot Five and Hot Seven series and other works from the 1920s, but finds the mature Armstrong solo style less to his liking. *De gustibus non est disputandum,* but it is peculiar that Collier fails to see that Armstrong's solo architecture and sense of the dramatic stem straight from nineteenth century vocal traditions, notably Italian grand opera—which also influenced Sidney Bechet. Approval is not required; understanding is.

By the time Collier arrives at Armstrong's post-1946 music, he is as exhausted as he perceives Armstrong to have been on those 1933 sessions. He identifies a few highlights, such as the superb 1957-58 *Autobiography* dates, but omits mention of the significant collaborations with Duke Ellington, Ella Fitzgerald, and the Dukes of Dixieland, among others. His avoidance of the Fitzgerald albums might well be deliberate, since the superior quality of the repertory (the cream of American popular song) and the excellent production values (notably the luxurious original edition of *Porgy and Bess*) contradict his claim that unworthy and/or redundant material and shoddy production marred Armstrong's later recorded work. Since Collier quite clearly comes to the later Armstrong as an outsider, he can't be blamed for merely having skimmed through the enormous recorded output of the All Stars, which he nevertheless dismisses rather cavalierly. He is also puzzled by the great success of the All Star format in live performance, and one cannot avoid the suspicion that he never witnessed one himself—or never encountered Armstrong in the flesh.

Among the many gaffes in the text is the resurrection of the old canard that Don Redman composed the verse to Carmichael's "Stardust." To add spice to the opening of his Chicago chapter, Collier would have us believe that the white clarinetist Don Murray was beaten to death in that city for having associated with a gangster's moll. Murray of course died in Los Angeles, after a fall from the running board of a friend's car. Minor errors often are caused by lack of proper background knowledge: Armstrong did not switch from the Okeh label to Victor due to a dispute with Tommy Rockwell, but because Okeh was going bankrupt; the band that made the *Medley of Armstrong Hits* was not "a pickup group, hastily put together," but the pit band of the Philadelphia theater where Armstrong was appearing when making the record; and he recorded with Chick Webb's band in 1932 during a joint tour with *Hot Chocolates.* For dramatic effect, Collier states that Armstrong and Zutty Singleton never worked together again after their 1930 parting, but they recorded in 1946, the year they also appeared in the film *New Orleans* (which Collier inexplicably claims starred Bing Crosby).

Technically, Collier seems no more secure. Reams of conjecture concerning embouchure problems rests in the main on wisdom gleaned from the aforementioned Marshall Brown. It is astonishing that, as a brass player, Collier mislabels Armstrong's frequent use of the glissando as "half-valving," which he condemns. Armstrong hardly ever used the half-valve device, yet Collier claims that Rex Stewart picked it up from Armstrong. But then, he is rather weak on Armstrong's influence on specific trumpeters, lumping Bobby Hackett in among "dixieland" players. The statement that Armstrong's direct influence as a trumpeter had ceased by the early 1930s is astonishing, but par for Collier's idiosyncratic course.

Collier makes much of his suspicion that Armstrong was born several years before 1900 and not on the Fourth of July, mainly to set up his subject's "unreliability" as a witness to his own life. But mere suspicion it remains as only circumstantial evidence is offered. (Collier of course ignores Armstrong's remark that his mother called him her "firecracker baby" due to the events surrounding his birthday.) He also intimates that shooting off a pistol loaded with blanks was not the true reason for Armstrong's commitment to the Colored Waifs' Home. Throughout the section on the early life, Collier paints a doleful picture of physical and spiritual deprivation that runs counter to Armstrong's own sunny view of his upbringing.

In doing so, and in (for one telling example) defining the Harlem of 1930 as a "virulent slum," Collier reveals the cultural preconceptions that permeate his book, culminating in the astounding observation that "we cannot perceive Louis Armstrong as we might Ralph Ellison, James Baldwin. He was, by the standards of middle-class America, rough, uncivilized, naive, and ignorant." Clearly, these are also Collier's standards. (Neither Baldwin nor Ellison appear in the index; the reader is referred to p. 74.)

Whose perception of Baldwin, born in Collier's "virulent slum," the son of a storefront preacher and one himself before his teens? And *whose* of Ellison, a jazz trumpeter in the image of Oran "Hot Lips" Page (who idolized Armstrong) long before he became the writer who made Armstrong emblematic of his masterpiece, *Invisible Man?* In Ellison's terms, Collier's book proves Armstrong's invisibility. I recall no references to Armstrong in Baldwin's work. But at the 1958 Newport Jazz Festival, as Armstrong concluded a long set with the National Anthem, Baldwin turned to me and said: "You know, that's the first time I've liked that song."

Perceptions may differ, but Collier's are consistent. He believes that as late as 1929, "many blacks, perhaps the majority, however much they might deny it, truly felt they *were* inferior" (Collier's emphasis). And he goes on: "Even when blacks were beginning to be successful, in show business especially, it was hard to prove that they were 'better' at it than whites." (Note the quotes around "better.")

Prove it to whom? To themselves, as Collier clearly implies? The presumption that black artists and entertainers, at that late a stage of the game, could be unaware of their superiority to the white stars who came in droves to learn and "borrow" from them goes beyond disingenuousness. But it does help us understand Collier's peculiar perception of Armstrong.

Always at pains to place events in their proper context, Collier neatly explains away every forceful act performed by Armstrong on behalf of himself or others by dint of psycho-social rationalization. Even Armstrong's legendary generosity becomes a guilty reflex conditioned by childhood deprivation. Facts that can't be neutered in this fashion are simply ignored. Nowhere does Collier mention that this "ignorant" and "uncivilized" man, who had barely finished fourth grade, was a virtuoso letterwriter. In 1924, he acquired a typewriter, fell in love with it, and from then on produced a ceaseless stream of correspondence with friends and associates, old and new, close and distant, expressing himself in a unique style remarkable for its playful approach to the rhythms, rhymes, and patterns of speech and prose. Conveniently, this omission enables Collier to ignore what the content of the many published (and unpublished but accessible) Armstrong letters might reveal about their author.

But I do Collier an injustice. He does mention that Armstrong wrote letters, if only to dwell on that he signed them "red beans and ricely yours," proof to Collier that he was "obsessive" about food. Armstrong's favorite dish is dismissed by Collier, who has already demolished gumbo and fish-head stew, with "and red beans and rice are—well, beans and rice." Quite so. And wine is fermented grape juice.

In the course of his summation, Collier grapples with larger issues, such as changing perceptions of art and artists. Ultimately, he has to confess that he "cannot think of another American artist who so failed his own talent. What went wrong?"

It is easier to guess what went wrong with Collier. The first thing required of a good biographer is empathy with his subject. In taking what he doubtless considers a hard-headed, unsentimental approach to the legend of Armstrong, Collier succeeds only in creating a phantom. Armstrong, the man, eludes Collier because he is unable, from his white, middle-class, and essentially puritanical perspective, to identify with the culture and environment in which Armstrong's psyche is rooted. Armstrong, the creative artist, remains a puzzle to Collier, whose sober, serious, rational, and essentially classicist esthetic is in constant conflict with Armstrong's passionate, playful, intuitive, and essentially romantic gift for transformation—indeed alchemy—which transcends (or simply bypasses) the bourgeois conventions of Western European "high" culture.

So deep is this gulf that Collier the listener, having arrived at 1947—Armstrong's 25th year of recording—can't tell Armstrong's playing from that of Irving "Mouse" Randolph, though he is surprised that the solo he thus misattributes is played, uncharacteristically, with a cup mute.

Alas, given our undue respect for appearances, what seems to be the first scholarly book about Louis Armstrong has predictably been hailed as authoritative. Armstrong's music, of course, is the best answer to this attempt to reduce a great artist's humanity to the scale of rat psychology and "explain" his art in terms of socio-cultural stereotypes. In lieu of a vintage Armstrong cadenza, I offer the words—not to be found in Collier—of two great musicians.

First, Teddy Wilson: "Every musician, no matter how good, usually has something out of balance. But in Armstrong, everything was in balance. He had no weak point. I don't think there's been a musician since Armstrong who has had all the factors in balance, all the factors equally developed."

Next, Jaki Byard, on his first meeting with Armstrong: "As I watched him and talked with him, I felt he was the most *natural* man. Playing, talking, singing, he was so perfectly natural the tears came to my eyes."

To Collier, of course, it was all an act.

—**Dan Morgenstern**

Black Music in the United States: An Annotated Bibliography
of Selected Reference and Research Materials
By Samuel A. Floyd, Jr. and Marsha J. Reisser.
1983. 234pp. Milwood, New York: Kraus. $30.

International Bibliography of Jazz Books
By Carl Gregor Herzog zu Mecklenburg. 1983.
Baden-Baden, Germany: Verlag Valentin Koerner
(Collection D'Etudes Musicologiques Sammlang
Musikwissenschaftlicher Abhandlungen, 67)
Vol. I: 1921-1949. 108 pp. DM 40.

Black Music in America: A Bibliography
By JoAnn Skowronski. 1981. 723 pp.
Metuchen, New Jersey: Scarecrow Press. $37.50.

These three entries in the bibliographic arena occupy somewhat different niches than works previously reviewed in *ARJS*. Floyd and Reisser's *Black Music in the United States* is largely successful as "an organized survey of research materials and archives related to black American music . . . designed for research at the undergraduate level." As noted in the introduction, this work complements the exhaustive *Bibliography of Black Music* by Dominique-René De Lerma (see *ARJS 2*), condensing some of the latter's copious listings into more accessible form.

Like De Lerma, *Black Music in the United States* transcends jazz, citing sources on spirituals, concert music, minstrelsy, musical theater, etc. As in our assessment of De Lerma's wide-ranging work, our comments will concentrate on the jazz component of Floyd and Reisser's bibliography.

On the whole, the book is well-organized, and accessibility is enhanced by complete title, author, and subject indexes. Furthermore, every entry is annotated—many rather extensively—and review citations for each work are included. In general, the annotations are accurate, but occasionally can be misleading. For example, Jepsen's *Jazz Records, 1942—* (#67) does not really cover "jazz to 1969." Its termination date varies from 1962 to 1969, depending upon the volume. The authors might also have pointed out that Rust's *Jazz Records, 1897-1942* (#72) does not, as a rule, list LPs. In both annotations, the word "instrumentation" is used when "personnel" would be more precise. One general annotation serves all six volumes of the MacMillan Jazz Masters series. The unique perspective of Rex Stewart's *Jazz Masters of the 30s* might have merited a separate description. One also wishes that some of the annotations were more critical. To call Len Lyon's *The 101 Best Jazz Albums* (#68) "an excellent handbook for the beginning jazz researcher" is certainly overly kind, if not erroneous. Collier's *The Making of Jazz* (#195) is "recommended as an analytical model for inexperienced researchers in jazz music." Whatever their merits, Collier's often opinionated and idosyncratic pseudopsychological interpretations are *least* suited to the uninitiated reader.

The work is intelligently divided into seventeen sections, with most citations appearing under logical headings. Exceptions include the confusing section VII, Indexes and Catalogues of Printed and Recorded Music. There seem to be no "recorded music" entries here and, if there were, they would probably belong with the discographies in section V, Discographies and Catalogues of Sound Recordings. The latter section includes buying guides such as the Tudors' *Jazz* and critical anthologies such as *Jazz on Record* by McCarthy et al. among the various general discographies, of which the authors have listed "only the primary and necessary ones." These do not include specialized works, which is a pity since one can learn more about sources of information on black music from such works as Walter C. Allen's *Hendersonia* than from many bibliographies. Section VIII, Pedagogy, contains a few technical works such as George Wiskirchen's *Developmental Techniques for the School Dance Band Musician* (#281), although the introduction specifically excludes "how to" books. More useful would have been Martin Williams's *Where's the Melody,* a general introduction to listening.

More significant oversights include: Delaunay's seminal *Hot Discography* (Schleman's *Rhythm on Record* and Blackstone's *Index to Jazz* are included); Smith and Ramsey's pioneering *Jazzmen;* Brask and Morgenstern's *Jazz People;* and, most incredibly, *The Story of Jazz* by Marshall Stearns. The authors exclude individual biographies, citing instead "collective sources" covering three or more individuals. One would think Whitney Balliett's collected "profiles" would qualify, but none of his anthologies appear.

Since section XIV, Periodicals, contains only five items, the authors might have broadened their criteria of "currently published scholarly journals and newsletters that devote all or significant portions of their space to black music" to include some of the major jazz publications such as *Cadence, Coda,* and *Down Beat.* Arbitrary rules have also been applied to section XVI, Record Collections. Under jazz, only five anthologies appear, three of which have been out of print for many years. Novices would have been better served by a brief overview of some of the major reissue projects (e.g. Prestige/Milestone "two-fers" and Original Jazz Classics, MCA Jazz Heritage, Columbia Special Products, RCA Bluebird, Savoy, Verve/Polygram, Time-Life), which are far more readily available and contain a significant portion of the essential jazz recordings. Section XVII, a valuable guide to repositories and archives by state, inexplicably omits one of the two major jazz research collections—the Hogan Jazz Archive at Tulane. Finally, there are some annoying misspellings, including Sarah Vaughan, Ahmad Jamal, Bix Beiderbecke, Thelonious Monk, Manuel Perez, and Billy Eckstine.

Notwithstanding these flaws, which are relatively minor considering the broad scope of sources covered, this is a well-conceived reference work.

A new edition of Mecklenburg's *International Jazz Bibliography* has been underway for some time. Volume One of the *International Bibliography of Jazz Books* is the first product of that revision, covering the period through 1949. Three more volumes are planned, each devoted to a decade, to extend the work to 1979. In the preface, the author states his welcome intention to continue to document jazz books into the 1980s, either at five- or ten-year intervals.

As pure bibliography, Mecklenburg's work is impeccable. Whenever possible, he examined originals of every edition of every book listed. When this was not feasible, he sought photocopies of the title pages and tables of contents. Mecklenburg not only provides a full bibliographic description for each title, he also indicates whether his source was an original or a copy, and which informant from his worldwide network provided that source!

The scope is narrowly focused, excluding works not directly and exclusively pertaining to jazz. Among the tangential areas omitted are African folklore, influence of jazz on classical music, and rhythm and blues. Also excluded are record catalogs, instructional material, poetry and fiction, and articles in periodicals.

Arrangement is alphabetical by author and chronological for multiple works by one author. Each entry is numbered, with editions of each work listed under the original and lettered a,b,c, etc. Although entries are not critically annotated, tables of contents are reproduced in their entirety.

The indexes have been changed slightly from the original *International Jazz Bibliography* and are more manageable. Six separate indexes of co-authors, editors, compilers, etc., have been consolidated into a single index of collaborators. The former subject index has been divided into an index of key-words and persons named in the titles and an index of subjects. Repeated from the *IJB* are the index of collections and series, and the index of countries.

New to *IBJB* is a chronological index, a particularly fascinating feature for this volume covering the earliest period of jazz criticism. One can easily locate the earliest entries, such as the German *Jazz und Shimmy* (#203) by F. W. Koebner, published in Berlin in 1921, and other interesting citations such as *Le Jazz* (#55) by André Coeuroy and André Schaeffner, published in Paris in 1926.

The index of countries is equally intriguing, yielding such gems as a 1934 Polish master's thesis dealing with "Problems of propagation of the musical culture concerning Jazz" (#204), as well as a 192-page monograph called *Jazz* and published in Prague in 1927. These indexes are not flawless, however. We note that the Russian language entry #81 (translated title: *Sketches on the History of Dance Music,* Leningrad, 1936) does not appear under the Soviet Union in the country index, while entry #90, a German translation of a 1947 English treatise on bebop is listed for some reason under the Soviet Union.

Mecklenburg's new format, streamlined indexes, and elimination of items of peripheral interest have made this work less cumbersome than its predecessor. By its very comprehensiveness, however, this is not a "finding guide" for the beginning researcher. One distinct disadvantage of the strict chronological division is that reprints are assigned to a particular volume by date of reprint, not by the date of original publication. Thus, the many classics in jazz literature reprinted by Da Capo Press do not appear with their original editions in volume one of *IBJB,* but presumably they will be listed in volumes four or five when they are published.

Nevertheless, this is an exemplary reference work which, when completed, will certainly constitute the definitive, comprehensive jazz bibliography.

Skowronski's *Black Music in America* is a very strange compendium. The wide range of musical genres covered is admirable in theory, but the melange that has resulted has little to recommend it beyond catholicity.

The work is divided into three parts: Selected Musicians and Singers; General References; and Reference Works. The first, and by far the largest, section consists of individual bibliographies of some 90 artists, of which approximately a third are primarily jazz-oriented, a third from the "pop" world, and the rest classical, blues, and country. The introduction states, "Several musicians were selected from each musical style to provide a balanced treatment." Thus we find Ivie and Marian Anderson residing peacefully side-by-side, as do Sidney Bechet and Harry Belafonte, Ornette Coleman and Samuel Coleridge-Taylor, Leontyne Price and Charley Pride, Fats Waller and Dionne Warwick. This may constitute a "balanced treatment" of styles, but within each style the selections are often baffling. "Fame," we are told, "was not used as a decisive criterion [for inclusion]," but we are given no further clues as to what was. Among the jazz figures, we find most of the important creators (i.e. Armstrong, Ellington, Gillespie, Parker, Davis, Monk, Coltrane, Coleman). Curiously, Arnett Cobb is included, but not Coleman Hawkins or Lester Young; Oliver Nelson, but not Johnny Hodges or Benny Carter; Anthony Braxton, but not Sun Ra; George Benson, but not Charlie Christian.

We are warned, however, that artists unfortunate enough to share the same name, such as the Billy Taylors (pianist and bassist) and Joe Turners (pianist and singer), have been "eliminated to prevent confusion," since "it could not always be determined which reference referred to which individual." Even this nifty bibliographic legerdemain is not wholly successful: the listings for pianist Willie "The Lion" Smith include an article entitled "Willie 'the Alto' Smith Rides Again" (#10850). The author also confuses two Smiths who do not share the same first name: Mamie and Trixie. She lists the latter as a nickname for the former.

The criterion for inclusion of articles is no more explicit than that for artists. The author has obviously relied heavily on the secondary sources cited in the introduction, particularly the *Music Index*. Almost without exception, among the jazz artists listed, coverage begins in 1949, the first year of the *Music Index*. This holds true even for artists whose careers predated the *Music Index* by some three decades. The only pre-1949 references cited are a few monographs and an occasional article in *Time* or *Newsweek*. This is not to say that what appears is of no use; obviously, 899 references about Louis Armstrong or 1242 about Duke Ellington are valuable. But are these the most important pieces written about Armstrong and Ellington, or simply a random listing gleaned from other indexes? And what about the wealth of material in pre-1949 *Down Beat* and *Metronome* (not to mention a host of smaller periodicals)? Skowronski would have rendered researchers a true service had she cited references from these largely uncharted (bibliographically speaking) waters.

Section Two—General References—is divided by decades (except for the earliest period, 1840-1899), with items listed chronologically within each decade. Lumped together are books, periodicals, and dissertations, with no attempt at subject access. Again, there is much useful material here, but all is hit and miss. And again, we find nothing from *Down Beat* or *Metronome* before 1949. We are given no indication as to what periodicals (if any) the author has systematically examined, and why particular articles are singled out for inclusion. This becomes painfully clear when isolated examples of ongoing magazine features appear, such as a "Lightly and Politely" column by Stanley Dance in the March 1974 *Jazz Journal* (#13809) and "New Books," "New Music," and "New Recordings" (nos. 13661-3), all from the *Black Perspective in Music,* no. 1, 1973.

Section Three—Reference Works—is another chronological hodgepodge, this time of discographies, record guides, encyclopedias, bibliographies, catalogs, and the like. But the paucity of entries suggests that Skowronski may have been running out of steam by this time.

The book concludes with an author index that, while reasonably accurate, manages to split Martin Williams's contributions between M. Williams and Martin T. Williams. It also credits Bessie Smith with authorship of ''The Anthony Braxton Interview'' (#2258), showing that the singer was even further ahead of her time than previously assumed.

—Edward Berger

The Otis Ferguson Reader
Edited by Dorothy Chamberlain and Robert Wilson. 1982. 307 pp.
Highland Park, Illinois: December Press. $10.*

Otis Ferguson (1907-1943) is a rarity in the jazz field—a writer with a literary reputation. Until the welcome appearance of this volume, which collects all his published pieces on jazz as well as several previously unpublished ones, that reputation in jazz circles rested on ''Piano in the Band,'' his affectionate portrait of Jess Stacy reprinted in *Frontiers of Jazz,* and his chapter on New York Jazz in the imperishable *Jazzmen.*

Both are here, but there are others every bit as good. He writes about his hero, Bix Beiderbecke (Ferguson was first to call him ''young man with a horn''); about Benny Goodman and Teddy Wilson and Ziggy Elman and the band (with which he spent time on the road as a self-described ''all-around stooge''); about Armstrong, Ellington, Henderson, Teagarden, Red Norvo and Mildred Bailey, the Spirits of Rhythm, John Hammond, jive talk, critics, and some records and books—35 pieces in all, ranging from sketches to substantial articles and adding up to 130 pages.

In some ways, Ferguson was very much of his time. An intellectual who'd rather be considered a plainspoken man of the people—not, thankfully, a self-styled ''proletarian,'' but legitimately from a working-class background—he enlisted in the Navy at 17, finished high school at 21, and then in three years earned his B.A. at Clark University, where he was on the staff of the literary quarterly and won a poetry award and first prize in *The New Republic's* college writing contest. But in other ways he was not. He despised cant, toed no party line, and had a rare and genuine affection for, and understanding of, what is now called popular culture.

The bulk of his writing was done for *The New Republic,* where he served as assistant editor and reviewed books, plays, and movies (there is a smattering here of his first-rate film reviews, most of which were collected in *The Film Criticism of Otis Ferguson,* published by Temple University Press in 1971) and became the first American writer to regularly turn his attention to jazz in the pages of a prestigious generalist publication. After Pearl Harbor, he joined the Merchant Marine. He was killed in Italy in 1943, exactly one month after his thirty-sixth birthday.

The *Reader* contains much that is not about jazz (all of it well worth reading) but enough about that subject to substantiate the legend. Ferguson had style; he was a real writer. He also had insight, an excellent ear, and enough basic knowledge of music (apparently he played an instrument, though he doesn't let on which it was) to appreciate what was involved in the making of jazz. The scholarly documentation of this music was still in its infancy when he wrote, and there are occasional errors of fact, but these are more than compensated for by his sympathy (we might even call it love, and why not?) for what he perceived to be "a native true spirit of music" that "came from the American ground."

There is much in Ferguson's approach that is unfashionable today. He was at times unashamedly romantic. He had no use for classification and categorization in terms of style, geography, or race. (It has been recently suggested that Ferguson overestimated white jazz players, but any close reading of him would seem to show that he simply appreciated talent wherever it manifested itself within his hearing, and that he was eminently fair.) His critical method was often impressionistic rather than analytic, and he also concerned himself with the social settings within which the music grew and expressed itself. And sometimes, as he notes, he got himself "bound up in coils of metaphor."

But fashions change while style and substance survive, and Ferguson had plenty of both. When he was on target, he hit home. Here are some bull's eyes:

About Bix: "It was as though jazz was a house that had been built for him. And he moved in."

About Ellington: ". . . of all in his field, [he] has had to shift around least because he grew so naturally in music and built so well. It is not simply that out of all the good bands, his holds the long-distance record for staying power and high average of hit tunes; the band is unique because of a collective integrity and feeling within."

About the Goodman Quartet (but also good jazz as such): ". . . and it is a collective thing, the most beautiful example of men working together to be seen in public today."

About a big band when things go right: "And music is such a close mutual thing that the feeling that the whole band is effortless and right will give individual power to each man as he stands out to play alone, and in turn each man who plays his few individual bars with inspiration will inspire the rest as a unit, until they come as near to forgetting selfish pride and ego as any artist has come. . . ."

About what the jazz language (or an aspect of it) is: ". . . there is the major fact that the composer-performer tradition of American jazz has spread the single possibilities of brass and reeds out like a fan, for these men no longer read aloud but speak, and speech develops many voices."

About Robert Johnson (I said Ferguson had ears): "If you want to know what true regional blues singing is like, complete with falsetto, you can forget Mr. Lomax's Leadbetter, who has three chords and four notes but a long, fascinating knife. If you can still get hold of the Johnson record, it's all there."

And he is certainly right on target when, in passing, he describes jazz as "an American mode of playing and singing and lifting the whole place in defiance of all known laws of gravity," or when (using a metaphor that works) he speaks of "music as unforced and fluent as a column of smoke in the air."

Jazz was still new and fresh when Ferguson shared his ongoing discovery of it with his readers from 1936 to 1941. He was a fine writer with a fine ear, true to himself and what he wrote about. To read him today serves as a welcome and timely reminder of just what it was about jazz that so moved those who could truly hear it, and should make us think about just how much of that spark remains today—within the music and within ourselves.

—**Dan Morgenstern**

(*Please note: *The Otis Ferguson Reader* is not available in bookstores, but only from the publisher at 3093 Dato, Highland Park, Illinois 60035. The price includes postage and handling.)

Addenda:
More Current English-Language
Jazz Periodicals

Thomas G. Everett

Thomas G. Everett, Director of the Harvard University Band, contributed an article, "An Annotated List of English-Language Jazz Periodicals" to *The Journal of Jazz Studies*, vol. 3, no. 2, pp. 47-57. As a continuing service to jazz scholars, he has updated his original list five times, including the listings below and those which appeared in *ARJS I* (1982), pp. 167-169. Three earlier addenda were published in *JJS*, as follows: vol. 4, no. 1, pp. 110-111; vol. 4, no. 2, pp. 94-97; and vol. 5, no. 2, pp. 99-103. *The Annual Review of Jazz Studies* will continue to publish addenda to his listings in future volumes. Readers interested in obtaining back copies of *ARJS* and *JJS* containing Mr. Everett's listings should write the editors of *ARJS,* c/o Transaction Books, Rutgers University, New Brunswick, New Jersey 08903.

—The Editors

Be-Bop and Beyond (bimonthly, $12 per year, $14 outside USA)
   Gerald Mack, Editor
   Creative Music Collective, Publisher
   P.O. Box 54337
   Los Angeles, California 90054
Started in January, 1983, *Be-Bop and Beyond* is an attractive, 30-page glossy magazine. Features include worthwhile interviews of major artists as well as less well known but deserving artists, jazz quizzes, news, obituaries, reviews of live concerts, record reviews, and selected discographies on featured artists. The magazine includes many photographs.

Big Bands, The (monthly, $15 per year) *(new address and format)*
   Sandy Beck, Editor
   4914 Lankershim Blvd.
   Suite 1
   North Hollywood, California 91601
The Big Bands is a nostalgic view of the swing era and its personalities. Several columns center on big bands in England, an East Coast report, itineraries of some swing bands, and a few feature articles on major personalities.

Disc'ribe (published irregularly but at least annually; $6.75 for 4 issues)
David Wild, Editor
P.O Box 2138
Ann Arbor, Michigan 48106
Disc'ribe is subtitled *A Journal of Discography Information*. Each issue includes an interview, fascinating discussion, answers to discography questions, and a specialized discography of a particular artist (e.g., Miles Davis's Miles Smiles Quintet, 1964-68). Each issue focuses on updates and continued dialogue on discographies of Ornette Coleman and John Coltrane.

Hot House (monthly, $12 per year, $18 foreign; available free in participating New York City clubs and record stores)
Gene Kalbacher, Editor
29 Rawson Street
Bloomfield, New Jersey 07003
Hot House is a 5½ by 8½ glossy and attractive guide to jazz clubs in the New York City area. Started in March 1982, *Hot House* is devoted to promotion and preservation of jazz nightlife, with comprehensive club listings, addresses, phone numbers, show times, as well as a few interviews, record reviews, and a short feature article.

Impetus (by subscription, six issues for approximately $9, surface mail)
Kenneth Ansell, Editor
587 Wandsworth Road
London SWB 3JD, England
Impetus investigates, reviews, and reports on new music activities and artists in Europe. This includes music that might come under such categories as avant garde, rock, improvised, contemporary classical, jazz, and free. Articles include discussion of musical politics, numerous pictures of artists, and concert and record reviews. Much of this music is not discussed in English elsewhere.

International Records News (monthly, U.S. and Canada, $25 per year)
Francesco Fini, Editor
The Fini Editions
P.O. Box 31
Imola, Italy 40026
International Records News is a monthly magazine of discographical information for jazz collectors and experts. Vol. 1, no. 1 included information on new listings, the complete Artist House Catalog (dates, personnel, matrix numbers, place of recordings, titles, timings), the Muse label, an Art Pepper discography (including reissues and collections), and similar discographical items.

Jazz Heritage Foundation Newsletter (bimonthly, $3 per year; free with $20 membership)
Paul Bullock and Shirley Christy, Co-Editors
P.O. Box 19080
Los Angeles, California 90019

The *Newsletter* of the Jazz Heritage Foundation consists of printed announcements, recording information, reviews, editorials, and usually one feature article and/or interview related to West Coast musicians and jazz activities.

Jazz Letter (monthly, $25 per year)
    Gene Lees, Editor
    P.O. Box 205
    Ojai, California 93023
Vol. 1, no. 1 of the *Jazz Letter* was a four-page newsletter with chatty but fascinating reminiscences about an old New York City musicians' hangout, Jim and Andy's Bar. Articles will be written by editor Gene Lees and will deal with jazz and the recording field.

Jazz Line (monthly, $18 per year)
    Annette Williams, Editor
    185 Willis Avenue
    Mineola, New York 11501
Jazz Line is a glossy, 7 by 10 periodical of special interest to those in the radio and media fields. Besides short feature articles, interviews with current artists, label profiles, news items, and book, concert, and record reviews, *Jazz Line* has regular columns listing record sales activity, airplay listings from participating jazz stations, and record chart ratings. Record reviews are chatty in tone, usually by the jazz radio programmer.

Jazz New England Journal, The (four issues for $15)
    Peter Landsdowne, Editor
    143 Main Street
    Box 337
    West Upton, Massachusetts 01587
The first issue of *The Jazz New England Journal* (fall 1983) consisted of fifty typed pages of interviews, profiles of New England musicians, a roundup of jazz news in New England (by state), a jazz theory article, and record reviews. It is reported as out-of-print as of 1984.

Jazz Scene (monthly, $20 per year)
    Lynn Darrock, Editor
    Box 968
    Portland, Oregon 97207
Jazz Scene is the publication of the Jazz Society of Oregon, available for the above annual membership fee. The newsletter includes several short articles, detailed listings of local jazz clubs, concerts, radio activities, society news, and a few record reviews.

Jazz String Newsletter (quarterly, $8 per year)
    Randy Sabien, Editor
    P.O. Box 1513
    Milwaukee, Wisconsin 53201
Founded in 1982, *Jazz String Newsletter* consists of articles, interviews, pictures, and

transcriptions of jazz string performances. The entire March 1983 issue (vol. 2, no. 1) was a tribute to the late violinist Joe Venuti.

Jazz World (bi-monthly, $25 including membership in JWS)
    Jan Byrczek, Editor
    Jazz World Society
    Box 777, Times Square Station
    New York, New York 10108
Earlier called *Swinging Newsletter, Jazz Echo,* and *Jazz World Index,* this periodical now appears in a glossy 5¹/₂ by 8¹/₂ format. A typical issue of approximately 15 pages contains short interviews with musicians, announcements of activities, a few short record reviews, and items about jazz on radio. It is a publication of the Jazz World Society, an "offspring of the International Jazz Federation, initiated in 1965 in Warsaw, Poland." JWS also publishes an annual *Jazz Festival International Directory.*

Jazziz (bimonthly, $4 yearly, $7 outside USA)
    Michael Fagien, Editor
    P.O. Box 8309
    Gainesville, Florida 32605-8309
Jazziz, founded in January, 1984, includes approximately 30 pages of record reviews, short feature articles about current jazz, news items, and a historic perspective on a particular artist/style/period in jazz. The articles focus on recorded material of popular artists.

Joslin's Jazz Journal (quarterly, $15 per year; $8 additional for overseas air mail)
    Gene Joslin, Publisher and Editor
    c/o Phonograph Records
    Box 213
    Parsons, Kansas 67357
Joslin's Jazz Journal (vol. 1, no. 1, February 1982) appears in newspaper format and is "Dedicated to the Glory of Record Collecting." The paper includes articles on early jazz band artists and recordings, 78 rpm auction lists, and advertisements aimed at record collectors.

Meritt Rag (published regularly as part of the Duke Ellington Treasury Series and for members of the Meritt Record Society)
    Jerry Valburn, Editor
    P.O. Box 156
    Hicksville, New York 11807
The *Meritt Rag* includes listings of records available from the Duke Ellington Treasury Series and other early historical records of the Meritt Record Society. Other discography, label data, and reissue information are included.

Not Just Jazz (quarterly, 9 per year)
    Randy Fordyce, Editor
    314 West 52nd Street, Suite C
    New York, New York 10019

In addition to its new address, *Not Just Jazz* now has an entirely new format and has designated the spring 1983, issue as its "premiere" number. Although the content remains similar (regular columns, aesthetics, interviews, self-help), the periodical now appears in an 8½ by 11 size.

Off Beat Jazz (bimonthly, $5 per year)
    Wilma Dobie, Editor
    15 Autenrieth Road
    Scarsdale, New York 10583
Off Beat Jazz is a four-page publication of the Overseas Jazz Club. Each issue is made up of announcements of jazz activities, plus short features and reviews.

Texas Jazz Magazine (Monthly, $15 per year)
    Dale McFarland, Publisher/Editor
    P.O. Box 64855
    Dallas, Texas 75206
In newspaper format *Texas Jazz Magazine* includes advertisements, reviews, and articles on musicians appearing in the state of Texas.

Wire, The (Jazz, Improvised Music and . . .) (quarterly, but expecting to become a monthly, £1 per issue, £1.50 overseas)
    Anthony Wood, Editor
    51 Beak Street
    London W 1, England
The name of the magazine is taken from the title of a Steve Lacy composition. *The Wire* intends to cover the field of contemporary jazz and free/improvised music, with emphasis of new and recent directions. The magazine includes several feature articles on performing artists, jazz festivals, record reviews, and some discographical information. The first issue also includes a brief but articulate history of bebop singers.

The Institute of Jazz Studies, in collaboration with Scarecrow Press, Inc., has initiated *Studies in Jazz*, a series of books dedicated to the highest standards of jazz research and scholarship, which will include works in the areas of biography, discography, musicology, historiography, and documentation, by both academicians and independent scholars, covering the full range of the music.

The first volumes in the series, published in the fall of 1982, are *Benny Carter: A Life in American Music*, by Morroe Berger, Edward Berger, and James Patrick (2 vols., 877 pp., $45), and *Art Tatum: A Guide to His Recorded Music*, by Arnold Laubich and Ray Spencer (359 pp., $17.50). The Carter work presents the career of one of the most important and versatile figures in jazz, and treats a number of social and musicological aspects of jazz and popular music through an interdisciplinary approach combining biography, social history, musicology, and discography. The Tatum work includes all known details of the pianist's issued and unissued performances, fully indexed and cross-referenced, as well as information concerning Tatum's appearances on film, published music taken from his recorded performances, and piano rolls and recordings made in the style of Tatum.

The third book in the *Studies in Jazz* series is *Erroll Garner: The Most Happy Piano* by James M. Doran (500 pp., $29.50), which includes one of the most exhaustive discographies of any jazz artist. This volume documents more than 1,200 discs issued in 18 countries, almost 2,000 Garner performances, and 30 film and television appearances. Also included are a career chronology; more than 40 interviews with Garner's family, friends, and colleagues; and many previously unpublished photographs.

Coeditors of *Studies in Jazz* are Dan Morgenstern, director of IJS, and Dr. William M. Weinberg, Chairman of the IJS Advisory Council. Future books in the series will include volumes on James P. Johnson and George (Pee Wee) Erwin. Submission of manuscripts is invited by the editors; they should be addressed to Mr. Morgenstern at the Institute of Jazz Studies, Bradley Hall, Newark, New Jersey 07102.

The address of Scarecrow Press is P.O. Box 656, Metuchen, New Jersey 08840.